The Renaissance Cartoons of the Accademia Albertina

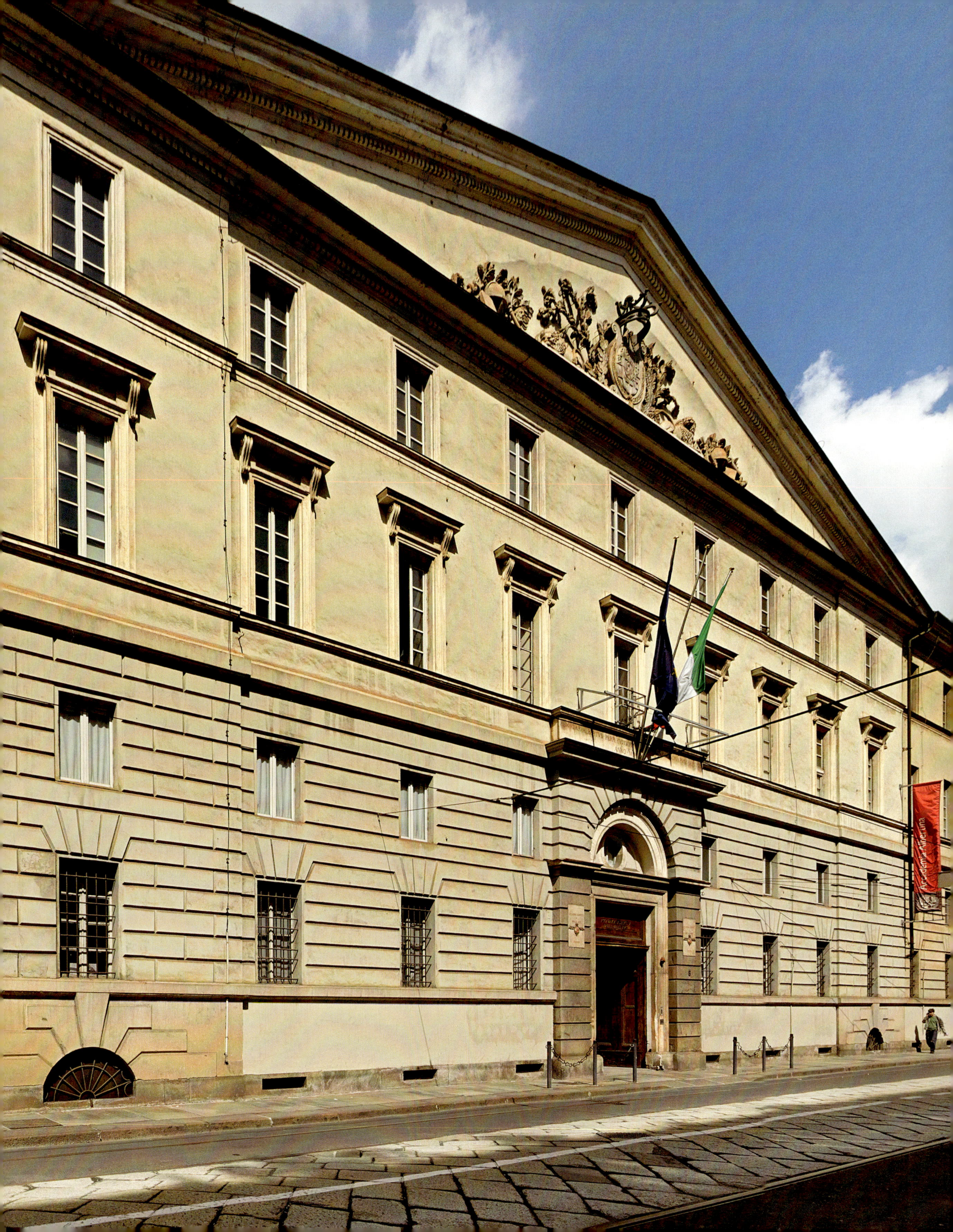

Accademia
Albertina
di Belle Arti
di Torino

CONSULTA
VALORIZZAZIONE
BENI ARTISTICI E
CULTURALI DI
TORINO

THE RENAISSANCE CARTOONS OF THE ACCADEMIA ALBERTINA

edited by Paola Gribaudo

SKIRA | ALBERTINA PRESS

Cover
Gaudenzio Ferrari
Saint Agabius and Saint Paul
1514–16, detail
inv. 302
(cat. I)

Pages 2, 6, 8 and 10–11
Views of the Accademia Albertina:
the facade, the entrance hall, the Room
of the Gaudentian Cartoons,
and the Pinacoteca

Page 12
Vittorio Nesti, *Portrait of the King Charles Albert of Savoy*, 1834

Design
Marcello Francone

Editorial Coordination
Vincenza Russo

Copy Editing
Doriana Comerlati

Layout
Sara Salvi

Translations
Gordon Fisher, Traduzioni Liquide

We thank for the images courtesy:
Associazione Abbonamento Musei
Arcidiocesi di Vercelli
Diocesi di Novara
Szépművészeti Múzeum, Budapest
Pinacoteca di Brera, Milano
Musei Reali, Torino
Museo Borgogna, Vercelli
Banca Patrimoni Sella & C.

First published in Italy in 2020 by
Skira Editore S.p.A.
Palazzo Casati Stampa
via Torino 61
20123 Milano
Italy
www.skira.net

Printed and bound in Italy. First edition

ISBN: 978-88-572-4475-4

Distributed in the world by Thames and Hudson Ltd., 181A High Holborn, London WC1V 7QX, United Kingdom.

Special thanks to
L'Artistica Savigliano
for its support to the project

Accademia Albertina di Belle Arti di Torino

President
Paola Gribaudo

Director
Edoardo Di Mauro

Vice Director
Laura Valle

Academic Board

Edoardo Di Mauro
President

Elisabetta Ajani
Salvo Bitonti
Roberta Fanti
Maria Claudia Farina
Antonio Musiari
Monica Saccomandi

Chiara Cosentino
Camilla Intini
Student Representatives

Interim Administrative Director
Paola Spezzaferri

Accounting Director
Daniela Coluccio

Pinacoteca Albertina

External Relations
Enrico Zanellati

Services for the Public
Sara Vigliocco

Educational Services
Stefania Davico

COOP CULTURE

CONSULTA VALORIZZAZIONE BENI ARTISTICI E CULTURALI DI TORINO

Members of the Consulta
2 A
Armando Testa
Banca del Piemonte
Banca Fideuram
Banca Passadore & C.
Buffetti
Building
Buzzi Unicem
CLN
Chiusano & C.
Costruzioni Generali Gilardi
Deloitte & Touche
Deltatre
Ersel
FCA Fiat Chrysler Automobiles
Fenera Holding
Ferrero
Fondazione Compagnia di San Paolo
Fondazione Crt
Garosci
GMT Holding Co.
Gruppo Ferrero-Sied Energia
Intesa Sanpaolo
Italgas
Lavazza
Martini & Rossi
Mattioli
M. Marsiaj & C.
Reale Mutua Assicurazioni
Reply
Skf
Unione Industriale di Torino
Vittoria Assicurazioni

Essays by
Andreina Griseri
Giovanni Testori
Simone Baiocco
Diego Giachello and Michele Cirone
Enrico Zanellati

Catalogue of Works by
Beatrice Zanelli and Erika Cristina

Bibliography by
Angela Griseri

Photographic Reproductions by
Fabio Amerio – School of Photography of the Accademia Albertina di Belle Arti

In partnership with

ALBERTINA PRESS

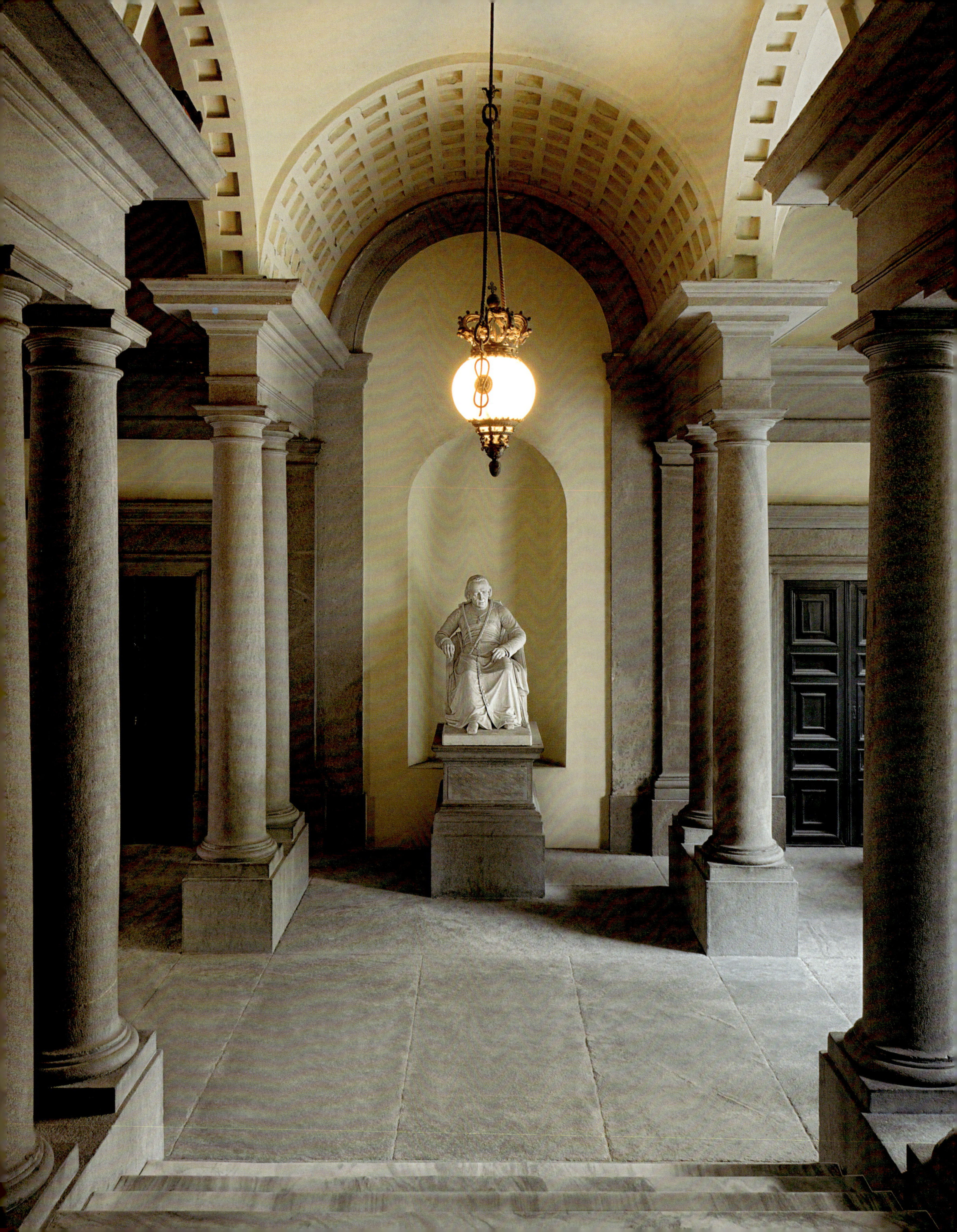

"An intelligent Duchess, Marie Jeanne Baptiste of Savoy-Nemours, who ruled the state in the name of the future first Savoy king, founded on 29 August 1678 the Academy of Painters, Sculptors and Architects, as if to signify that one could only approach Italy, cradle of the Renaissance, by paying homage to the Arts" (Luigi Bollea, 1930).

The extraordinary collection of 16th-century cartoons that this book describes was donated in 1832 by Charles Albert of Savoy to the Royal Academy of Painting and Sculpture in Turin. This is a unique collection – unlike any other, anywhere – in terms of the number and importance of the drawings attributed to Gaudenzio Ferrari and his school. The fifty-nine cartoons, housed in the Pinacoteca of the Accademia Albertina in line with the most modern methods of conservation, are rare and relatively unknown works that allow us to enter the workshops of the 16th-century artists and to discover how an artistic education was gained during the Renaissance, prior to the establishment of academies of fine arts. The cartoons of Gaudenzio Ferrari, Bernardino Lanino, Gerolamo Giovenone and Giuseppe Giovenone the Younger are testament to the fact that their studios, active in Vercelli and Valsesia, worked side-by-side, with ongoing exchanges that the essays and entries in this volume help to clarify.

The updated content of this publication goes hand-in-hand with the new light that the December 2019 overhaul casts on the Gaudentian cartoons, thanks to the support of the Consulta per la Valorizzazione dei Beni Artistici e Culturali di Torino and of Reale Mutua. My first thought, when faced with the coup de théâtre *created by the surprising illumination of the room, was that I wanted to transmit the great excitement it engendered in me to the largest possible audience, both nationally and internationally. And so what better vehicle could there be than a book, which survives forever – an instrument of seduction and knowledge? The book is being published in Italian and English by Skira in partnership with the Albertina Press, complete with time-honoured essays by Andreina Griseri and Giovanni Testori and a new reading by Simone Baiocco.*

The collaboration with the Consulta has always been valuable for the Accademia Albertina, since as far back as 1996, and I offer my gratitude first and foremost to Adriana Acutis, who believed in the project, and to the current president Giorgio Marsiaj, who engaged with it in the shared conviction that the development of Turin must also involve a process of internationalisation that sees the city's rich historic and artistic legacy taking centre stage.

I would like to thank Professor Fabio Amerio for his breathtaking photographs that, for the first time, enables us to see the entirety of the cartoons in colour, with reproductions that are exceptionally faithful to the originals. I am also grateful to all those who have worked to bring this book to fruition.

My hope is that this publication will contribute to raising the profile of one of the most luminous chapters in the artistic journey taken by Gaudenzio and his pupils, and will give people the low-down on our gallery's hidden treasure, with a view to triggering a new Renaissance and a new Humanism.

Paola Gribaudo
President
Accademia Albertina di Belle Arti, Turin

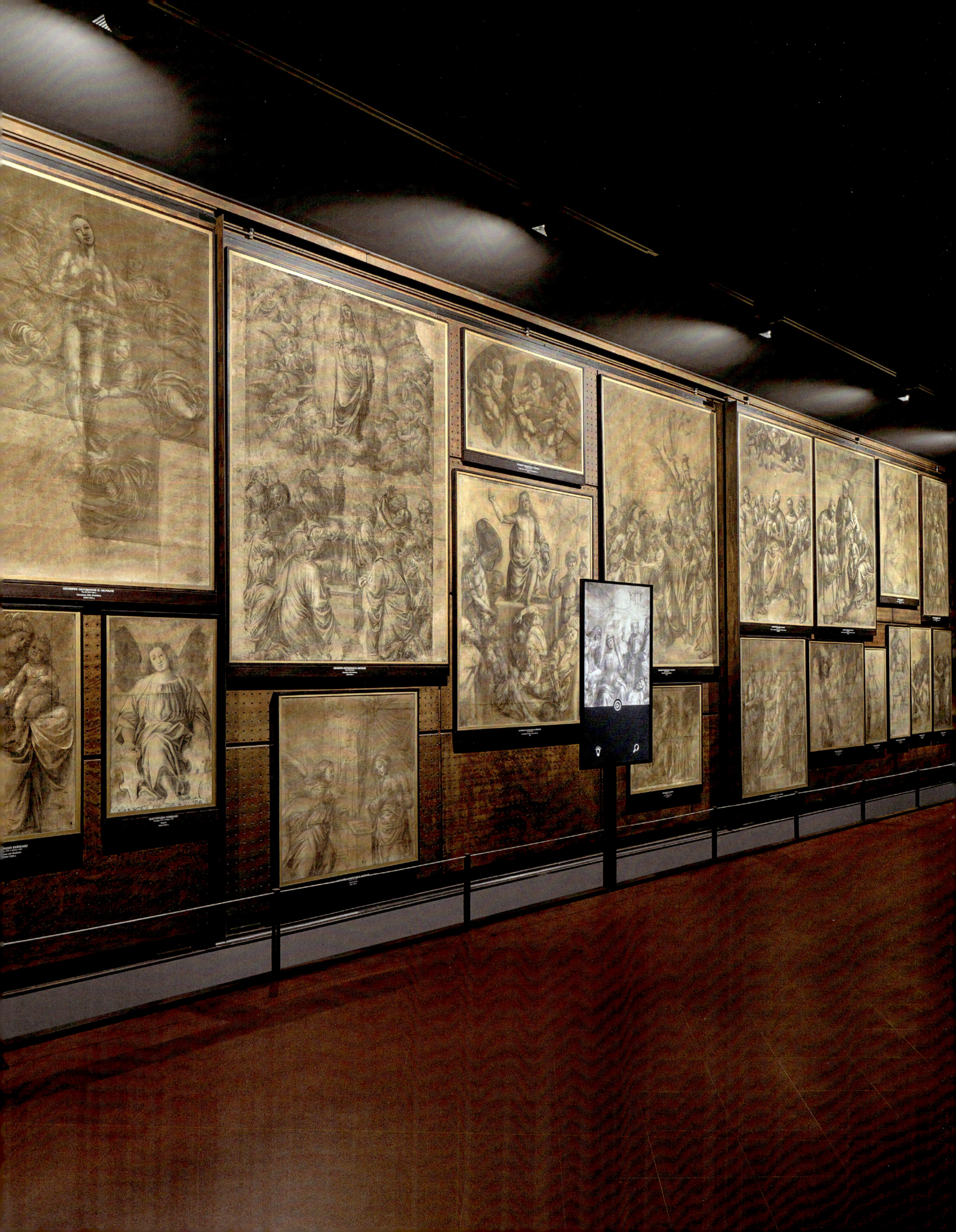

The Consulta was established in 1987 on the initiative of a number of friends working within leading companies in Turin; the shared intent was to take on – and contribute to resolving – the problem of degradation affecting the city's historic and artistic assets. The sense of civic responsibility driving the Consulta's ethical patronage was highly innovative for the time. It was a journey that began, not by chance, in Turin – a city rich in history and creativity, the one-time capital of Italy, the city of the "Social Saints", of innovation and manufacturing.

The Consulta's commitment towards the Pinacoteca of the Accademia Albertina began in 1995, with the renovation and reopening to the public of the current twelve exhibition rooms, with a particular focus on displaying the priceless group of fifty-nine 16th-century cartoons drawn by Gaudenzio Ferrari and his school, donated to the academy by King Charles Albert of Savoy in 1832.

The aim of tapping the potential of the Pinacoteca as fully as possible continued with a series of exhibitions: in 2005, "Bartolomeo Cavarozzi. Sacre famiglie a confronto"; in 2011, "Incontrare Bagetti"; in 2013, "Gaudenzio Ferrari e Bernardino Lanino. Cartoni e dipinti a confronto"; and in 2014, "Dipinti e disegni della Grande Officina di Gaudenzio Ferrari".

In 2019, the Cartoon Room was equipped with a new lighting system, and a latest-generation multimedia monitor was installed to guide visitors on the discovery of the entire body of work, thus affording an opportunity for comparison with the associated paintings, currently held in some of the most important museums in the world.

To enhance and raise the international profile of the Renaissance cartoons, the management of the academy commissioned the Consulta to put together this bilingual publication featuring a new, in-depth set of photographs. Despite the very challenging economic circumstances, the Consulta's efforts remain geared towards the cultural sector, in which it has been active from the outset. With the same passion, dedication and professionalism that have always been its watchwords over these first thirty-three years, the association intends to continue working for the benefit of everyone. This part of the world has suffered more than others, and our commitment to the common good remains unwavering.

Giorgio Marsiaj
President
Consulta per la Valorizzazione dei Beni Artistici e Culturali di Torino

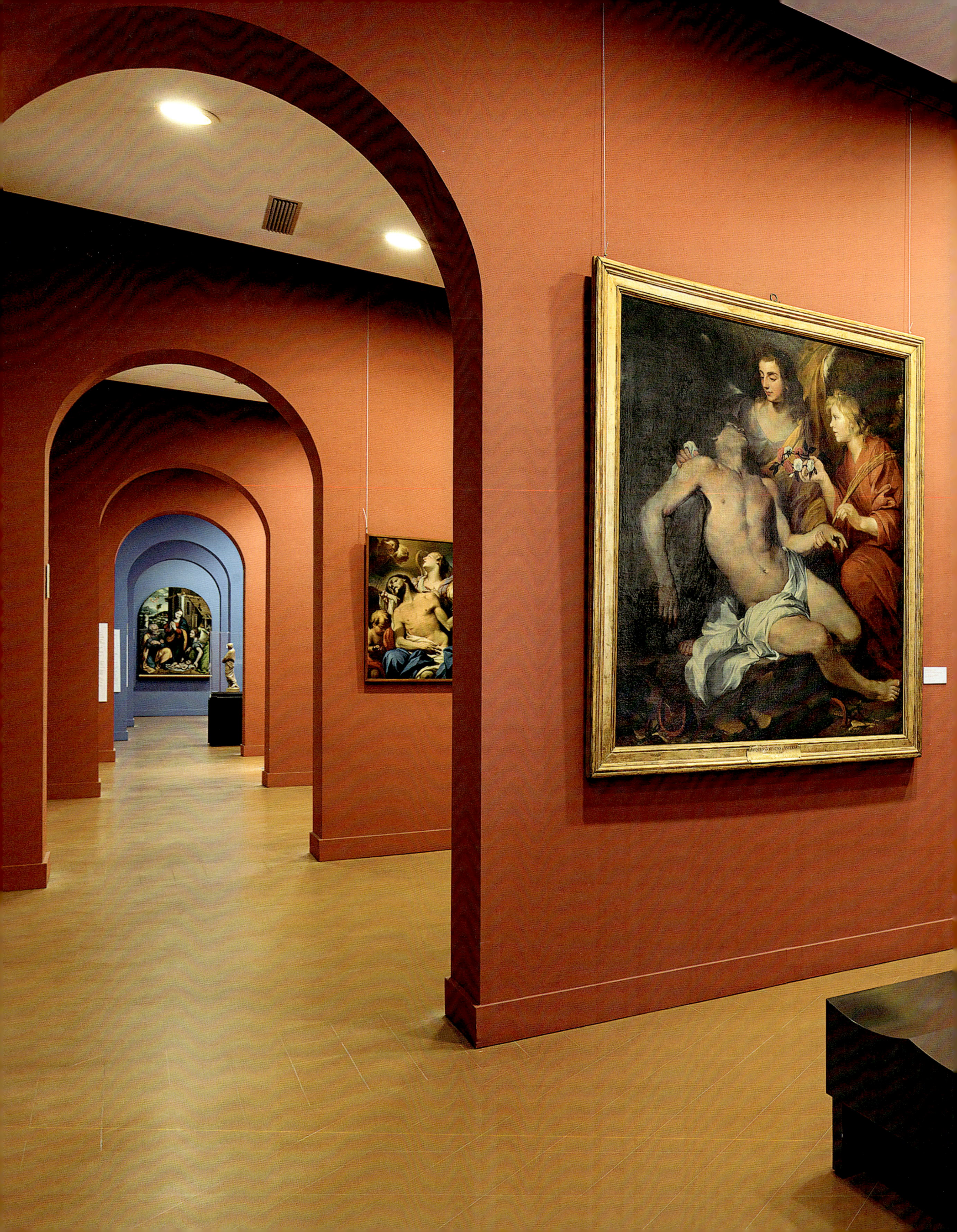

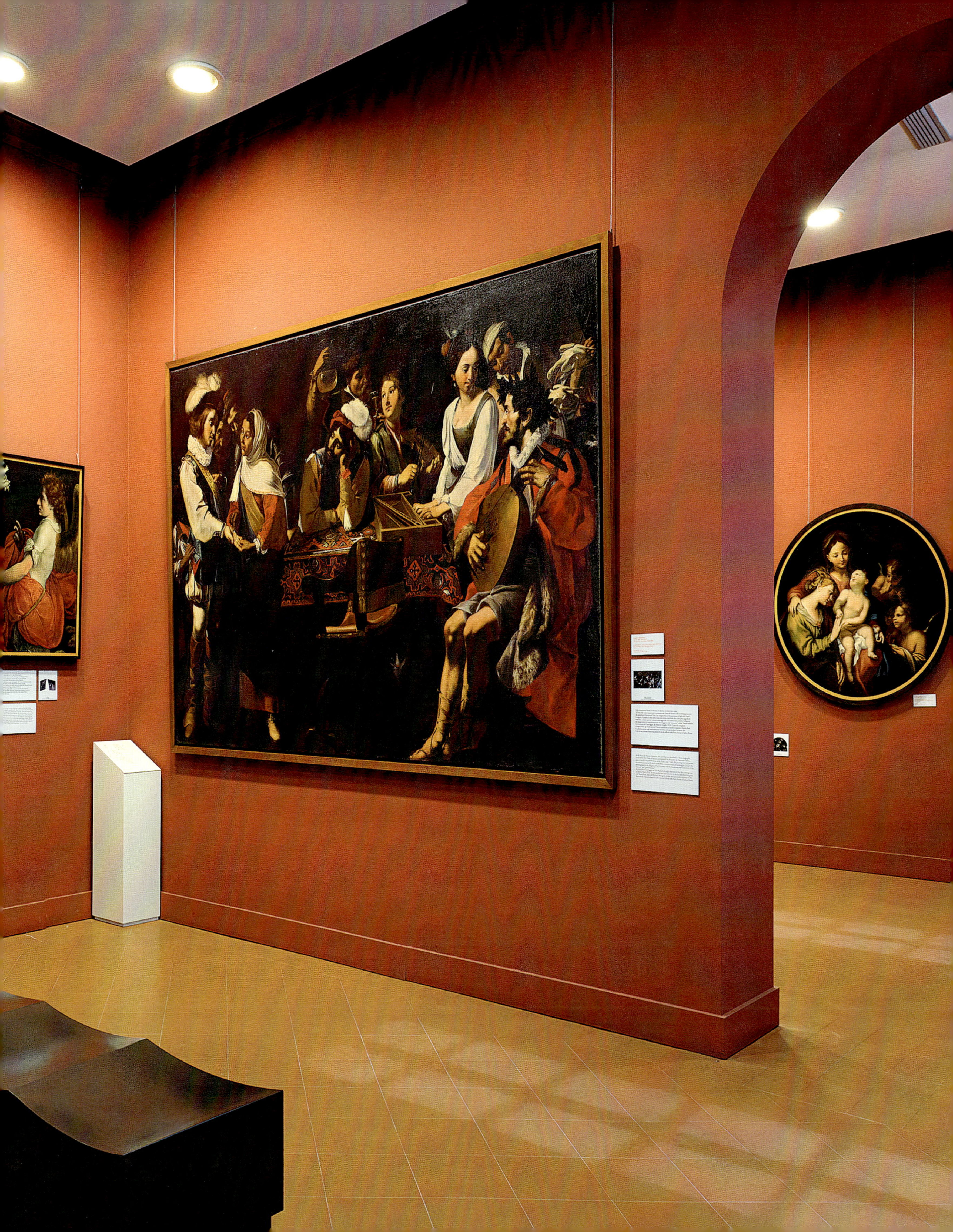

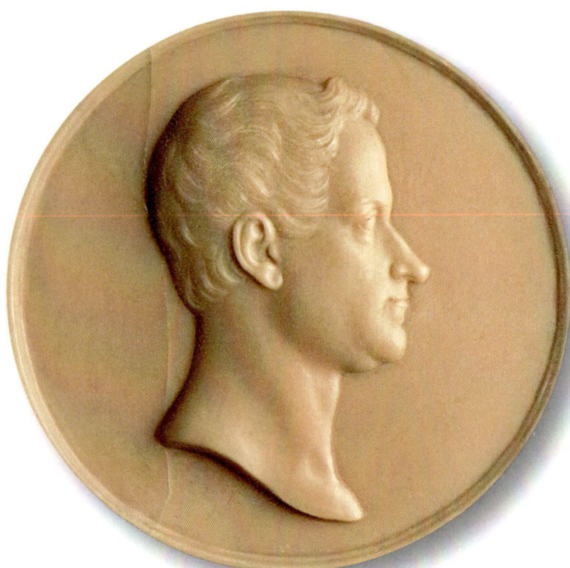

Contents

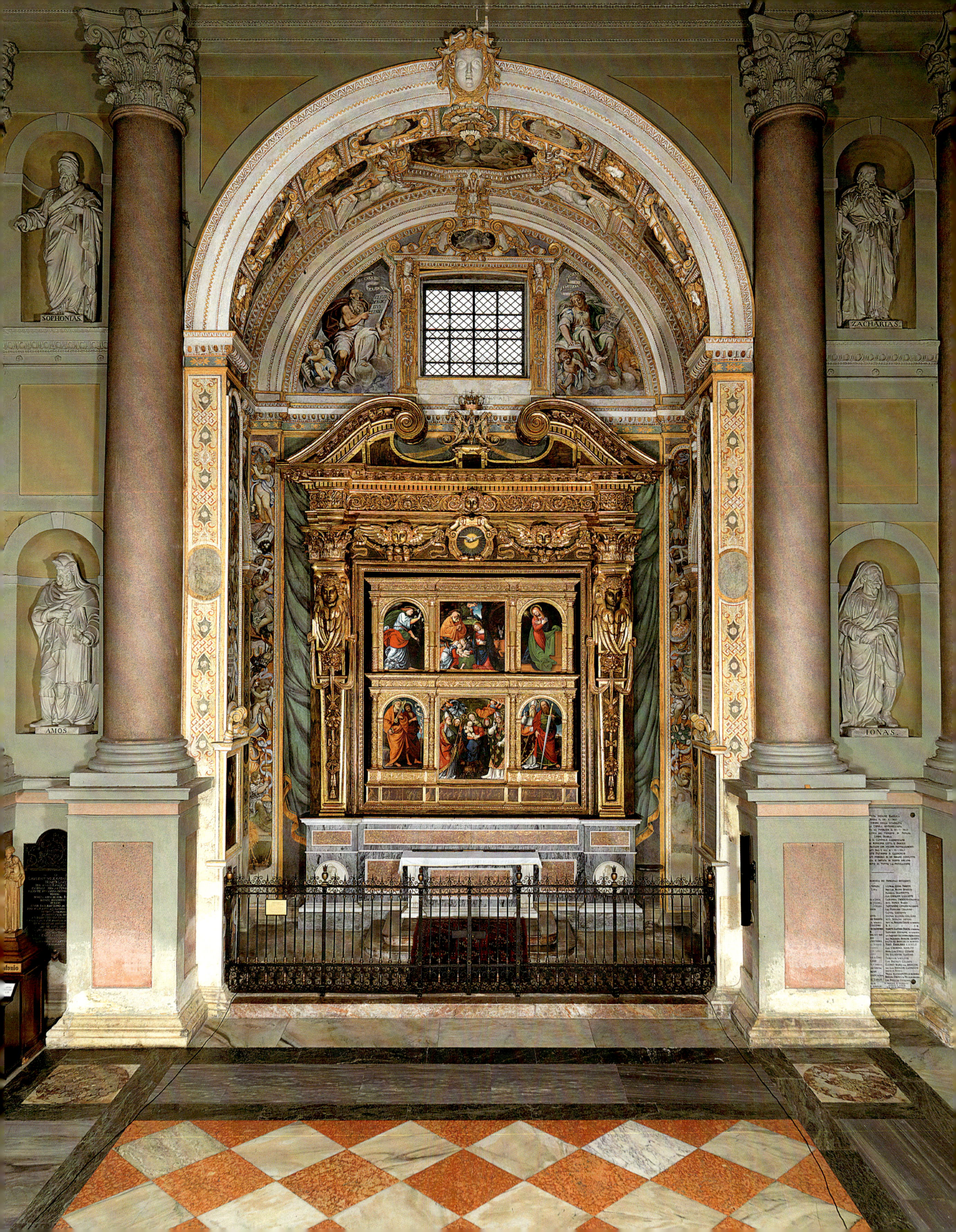
SOPHONIAS
ZACHARIAS
AMOS
IONAS

Gaudenzio Ferrari and the Vibrating Reality of the Cartoons

Andreina Griseri

Gaudenzio Ferrari and his workshop, emotional core embedded in the Varallo woodlands: a wondrous sensibility, spectacular landscape of chapels, frescoes, sculptures, the Sacro Monte, the "great mountaintop theatre" – a tangible, eloquent image, originated by Giovanni Testori.

In those roots, a catalyst dominated by the intransigent rhythm welded with the cartoons; a pleasurable reality, a warm, light-bathed deviation from the late-Gothic taste, an authentic accent of the Po valley, captured in the act of becoming.

The decisive autonomy of that mimetic project, layered through the dialogues exchanged in the workshop – a dynamic, creative hub, on the cutting edge, blazing a trail towards sharp social delineations.

Having avoided the whimsical ramifications, the anxiety-riven thread of Mannerism, having eliminated the serial skirmishes and rapid drawings, there had been a bolstering of the culture of tradition, cornerstone of the devotees' journeys, a comment recited in the spoken idiom of the popular drama of the Holy Performances, guide plot outline "the stage"; intrepid nerve for the growth of the itineraries guided to live out through prayer the stages of the life of Christ leading to Calvary, climatic message of salvation; and the answer was clear, the target achieved together with vigour by the faithful, custodians of the procession and of the praises – the song transmitted and shouted in the ethnocentric rhythm, the reference to folklore, authentic and modern link, very much alive.

The great theme of Calvary had entered the collective memory with learned parameters, ready to be of-the-moment, perceived in their concrete reality of felicitous permeation: on this expanded line, experienced through devotion, a reappearance was made by the giant manifesto of the *Life of Christ*, frescoed by Martino Spanzotti in the church of San Bernardino, Ivrea, poetry writ large, a unique voice. Another step towards redemption in the abbey of Sant'Antonio di Ranverso with the *Ascent to Calvary*, bedrock, tones filtered in the tumult of lived experience, all set to enter into the verities of the oral style; on another side, the vehicle of Nordic culture was strong, imbued with ecclesiastical erudition, focused on the rays of light sensitive to the *Life of Christ* with sublime, high-profile works from Jan van Eyck to Hans Memling.

Over it all, with enthralling results, the climate of the Sacro Monte discerned a myriad of elements designed to bring the Padanian hinterland to life, with ratings proffered by the Milanese scene. The growth of the texture pervaded by the signature of Vincenzo Foppa would lead then to the area reigned over by Bramante. From here, in his workshop Gaudenzio engaged profoundly with the values of the original heritage of the valley, and, by making the most of this independent thinking, expressed his message in figures with decisive openings based on the primary choice of the fresco: the "new thread" of a clear figuration

Gaudenzio Ferrari
San Gaudenzio Polyptych
1514–21
San Gaudenzio, Novara

Gaudenzio Ferrari
Saint Agabius and Saint Paul
1514–16
inv. 302
(cat. I)

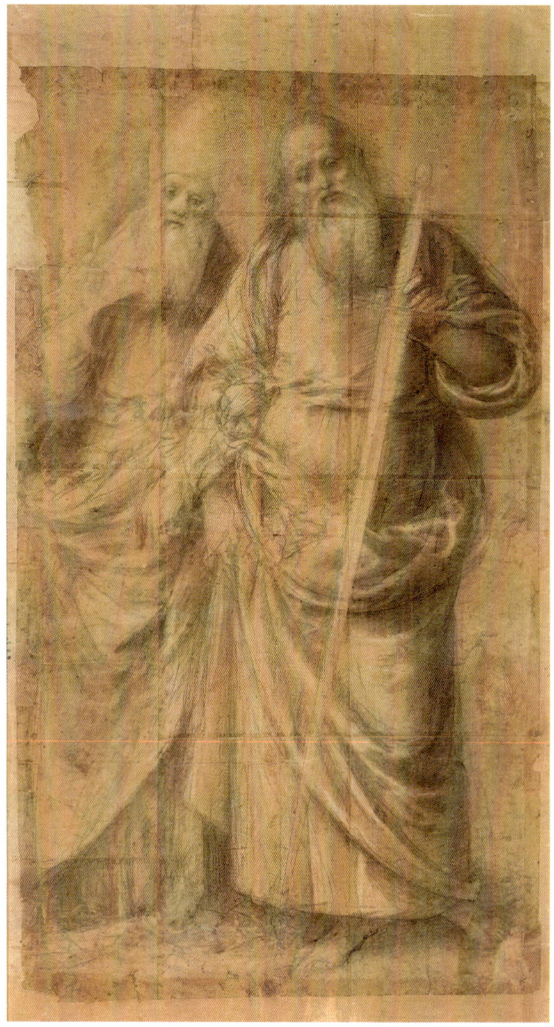

was reinforced, geared towards the new world in the expressive tones, vibrating in the act of telling. In this way, in the frescoes of the early chapels of the *cinquecento*'s first decade, commentary was made by means of figures: time was measured with filtered encounters, leaving the sign to simplify the religious culture, recorded in recent years on various occasions, indicating analogies and convergences, marked by the valuable comparisons with Pinturicchio, Luca Signorelli and Perugino.

While the invitation to fix multiple models for the stages of the Holy Journey broke through in the valley, the paradigm of the journey to Jerusalem remained mythical and difficult, and at the end of the *quattrocento* other sensations triggered the desire to experiment with alternative lifestyles, other ways of engraving the joints of worship, and a new sense of a simple, clear response, shot through with secrecy and profundity, was felt. Gaudenzio faced up to aspects of the identity of his Sacro Monte, and thought of a line that could impact and change the infinite practice – cement, he decided, for devotion: the time was right, urgent questions prevailed, and visible responses awaited. Hence the assertive language that speaks from the chapels with the frescoes that are dedicated to the *Life of Christ* and that succeed in endowing the conversation with profound affection. It is the new world, essential yeast for an intense dialogue that flows like never before with the narrative; having overcome trapped time, everything is clearly bound up, targeted towards feeling the present time, this very moment, here and now, audible guiding voice, stretched out in the great themes for which what matters is the compelling sense of iconic beauty, discovered by the faithful with precious moments experienced by perception, and it is not an acted form of seeing,

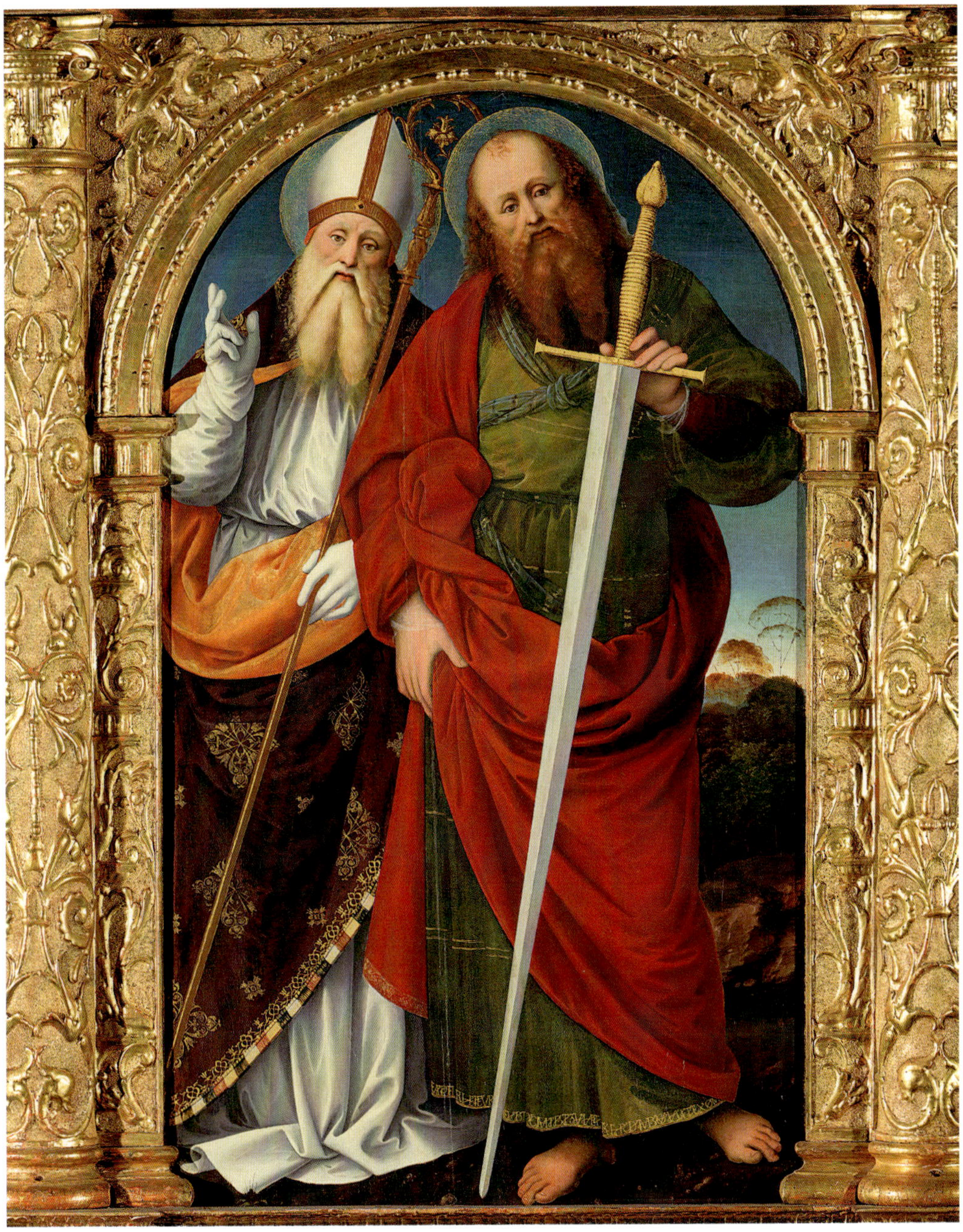

Gaudenzio Ferrari
Saint Agabius and Saint Paul
1514–16
San Gaudenzio, Novara

it is generated with the wide-ranging rhythm of dialogue. What emerges clearly is the autography of the details, the supreme truthfulness of tactile perception, which we recognise to this day. Particular types are set: the little Jesus, the young boy that everyone discovers as their child, human presence of the sacred, a theme experienced next door, identifying nature and passion, lynchpins of life.

What emerges with clarity in these results is the nucleus of the new mode filtered by the fresco: the colour choices are sensed, purified by the Alpine air, immersed in the fixing of infinite variations, *sfumato* and sketched, always associated with the culminating truth.

Gaudenzio saw fertile ground opening up before him: time was reflected upon through journeys, to test out other perspectives. Accordingly, he planned his visits to Florence and Rome. Gaudenzio comes across as an astute connoisseur of the surprising, sublime space lived through by Raphael – mirror archetype of classical beauty on the frescoed walls.

And it is the nucleus that leads us to re-read Lomazzo's discourse, in his *Idea of the Temple of Painting*, 1590, with the "men of gold", ideal poetic crown; Gaudenzio is one of the governors

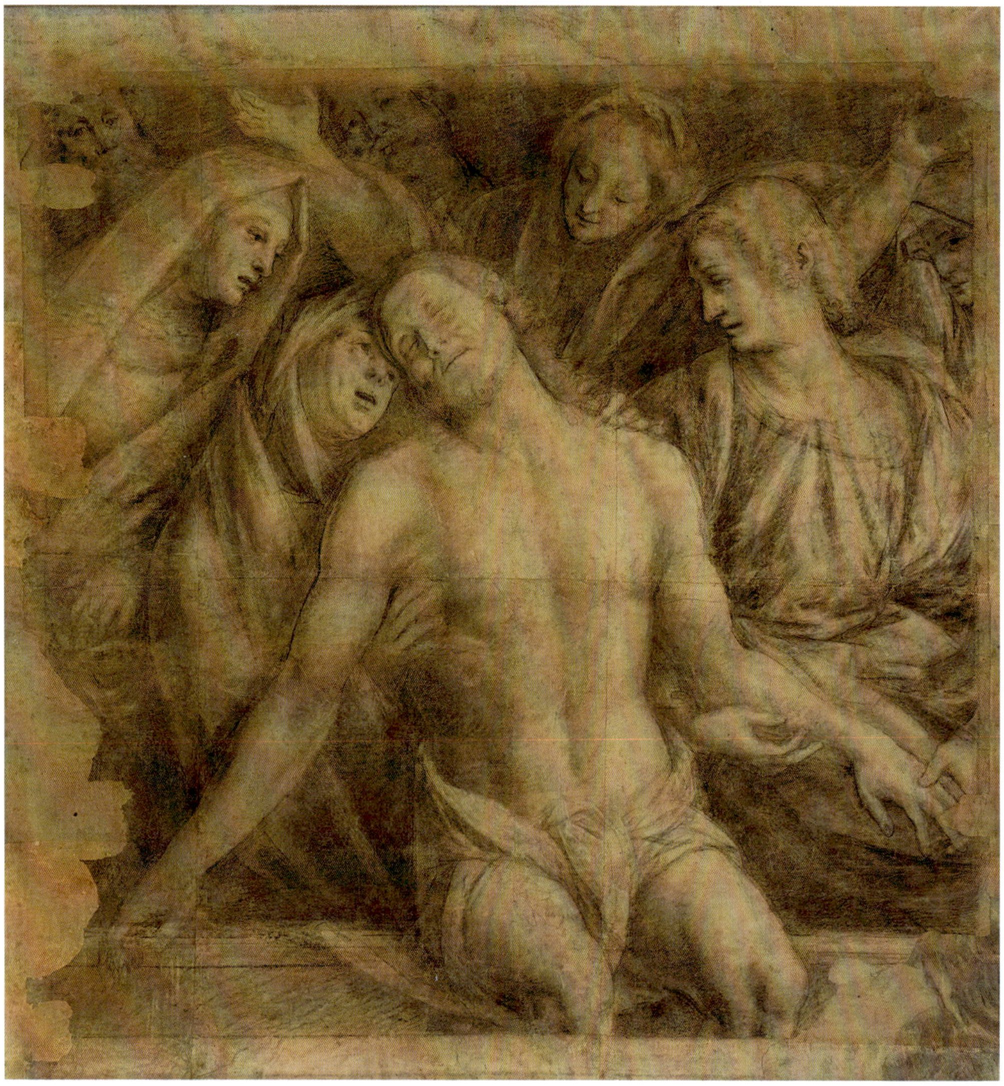

Gaudenzio Ferrari
Pietà
c. 1535
inv. 323
(cat. III)

of art, together with Michelangelo, Raphael, Polidoro, Leonardo, Andrea Mantegna and Titian, and is associated with the planet Jupiter. A decisive chapter in Varallo came with the early frescoes, which provide new indications and refer to works done by original framings, ready to underline the subtle perception of a change of image, crucial pursuit of the surprising message with the modes of recounting, the open, clear dialogue. The horizon grows, and touches on themes and critical thinking nourished by the rites of passage between sin and grace; variants of cult, religion, custom are transposed in space, carved signs appear, coming form the Swiss and German prints, and they will be clear in the frescoes.

That horizon charts the time of a turning point, and the winning strategy in Gaudenzio's workshop is evident: with the sense of a planned opening, the cartoon project is developed, the original sign orienting and co-ordinating with synergy the key accent, the vivid tone of the pilaster line of the incisive frescoes of the *super parietem*, with the character that differentiates the religious message clearly emerging – modern mirror of a recognisable human reality that aims to make its way onto the stage in order to define an open, liveable devotion, link-point of encounters and messages. Increasingly abuzz with work was the area opposite the church of Santa Maria delle Grazie, active centre of the community.

The push towards a channel that would open up other forms of worship and prayer was conclusive, giving rise to the strategic value of the cartoons, filter of the fevered perceptions that impacts the authentic, expressive method to pare down religious culture. There

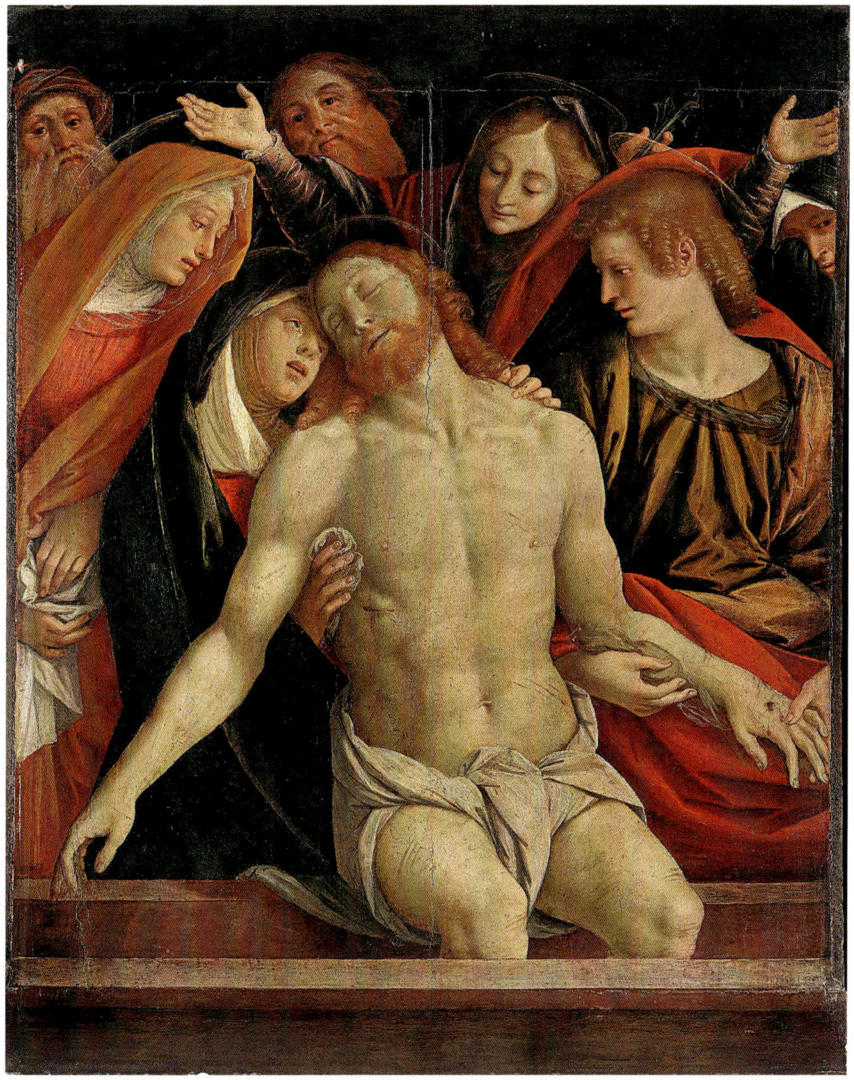

Gaudenzio Ferrari
Lamentation over the Dead Christ
c. 1535
Szépművészeti Múzeum, Budapest

surfaced the Padanian sign, acquiring the fascination of a new language, tried out in a radical fashion, which would go on to signal a sure critical expansion, returning to well-defined templates for the frescoes, with pre-set analogies and convergences, for life-size figures. The first choice was to use thick paper, resistant to the challenging weather of the Alpine valley: the cartoons would have to remain protected while the frameworks were being taken down for transport, and such paper would also be suited for potential installation in parishes and confraternities, as requested by the new religious areas.

They were carriers of an existential message, refined on the canvas of Gaudenzio's art. To achieve the overall result, the task was entrusted in the workshop to the synergic technical expertise of artisans, artists, engravers, carpenters, master framers, with borders finished to the highest standard. At the apogee, the leading light is the transparent sign, luminous in its entirety, expressed with joyful rhythm, an exceptional result maintained over time in its richness, right up to the present. Exhibited since 1996 in one of the rooms of the picture gallery at the Accademia Albertina, created by the Consulta per la Valorizzazione dei Beni Artistici e Culturali (Council for the Enhancement of the Artistic and Cultural Assets) of Turin, the cartoons can once again be seen in direct light, following the development of the research and the results of the critical studies, including the 1982 exhibition at the Accademia, the catalogue for which can no longer be found, sold out from the start and renowned for its layering of archival news and carefully delineated comments – curator Giovanni Romano.

Gaudenzio had by this time garnered an international reputation, though in truth even back in the 19th century many British aristocrats on the Grand Tour had endeavoured to make a stop-off at the woodlands of Varallo, and in the 20th century studies had been carried out into his frescoes and his chapel architecture, focusing for instance on his sculptures – prime examples of the creative output of this master modeller, which would influence 17th-century artists from Tanzio to Morazzone. In the 1970s and 1980s the tireless research of the Culture Departments operating in Vercelli, Arona and the valleys was greatly increased, producing precious inventories, with documents on the difficult years of the Counter-Reformation, setting the chronology for the origins of the Sacro Monte at 1486, year zero for this method of worship, bound up with the processions and the language spoken by the Holy Performances, the ever-increasing rhythm that drove the popular theatre, with models to re-live through prayer the Stations of the Cross, the primary stage being the performance honed along the lines of an open ritual, with the invitation to the faithful for the unitary performance, with multiple, insistent speeches, invoking the "Christian soul", reappearing in the pages of the guides that have come down to us now as archival models.

Another spirit, and we measure it with the turning points marked by the cartoons, a highly figurative chapter. They did not come about in a sophisticated studio, Gaudenzio had surely preferred a large room glimpsed from the courtyard of a farmhouse, and the square in front of the church of Santa Maria delle Grazie, still today the site of his frescoes, dating from 1513, continued to remain open to the works. As a paradigm of the output of the workshop, the cartoons mirror the multiple decisive result developed with great richness, now legible in the current arrangement, to better understand the truth of the subjects: coming through clearly is the initial plan, which had envisaged true-to-life dimensions, embodied by the gentle, warm colour, typical of a cartoon selected to capture the soul of the details, highlighting just a few strokes, for the intertwined threads of the beards, for the wavy hair on the clothes, modern tunics, and there were only a few profiled strokes for the breadth of the modelling with white *gesso*, excluding even today the urge to apply make-up.

A reflective conversation had been established, which would then detach itself from the obsessive modes of the popular theatre, handled through the Holy Performances. With the cartoons, an articulate message was selected, ready to deviate the progress of a story endowed with close-ups of a new type, a surprising choice, signalled with natural, vigorous dimensions, document of clear autography, associated with the Sacro Monte. The format targeted space viewed as an interactive stage, leaving aside the tones beaten out by the sermons, thus giving rise to a prestigious result, intended to filter and simplify the religious culture, safeguarding the level of dissemination.

We confirm them today, underlining that figurative language in its luminous, interactive maturity, captivating like a musical theme of the area dominated by Gaudenzio, mainstay of the new mode of experiencing the feelings developed in the perspectives of the sacred theatre.

The expressive calm of the cartoons responded exhaustively to the compelling new psychological sense, encapsulated through tactical modern choices that would control the references to ecclesiastical figures, and were in this regard a vehicle for culture, designed to transmit the identity of the engaging figures of the sacred theme, strengthened by the sense of responsibility accumulated while the myriad invites from the enterprising Protestant areas kept on growing. A wide-ranging transplant, the cartoons were an eloquent element, geared with an open-ended idiom towards painters, sculptors and modellers working to meet the demands of the new parishes attracted by the expressive mode – a new filter of the religious canons, awaiting unambiguous, up-to-date answers.

Gaudenzio Ferrari's Cartoons, Five Lustra Later

Giovanni Testori

When my Turinese friends, first and foremost Sergio Saroni, were so kind as to ask me to come up with a few words as an introduction for what will undoubtedly be a memorable exhibition, they were certainly aware that they were leading me towards, or better still, ushering me into, the realm of – or as I prefer to put it, the rooms filled with – those memories that are held most dear and, for that very reason, are the clearest and at the same time the most painful. By submitting this request to me, they were the ones who were providing the introduction to what would be, were I to accept the commission, the only words possible for me, the only ones I could reach.

Not entirely joking, I replied that an afterword would be both more respectful and more pertinent; by which I meant an essay that would consider the "totality" of the works that this catalogue compiles; and which could thus express my "open-mouthed" reaction to such an extensive, nuanced and fearless capacity to pursue a theme of which I was very much enamoured and which, in the ways afforded to me, I had had the opportunity to explore when I was more or less the same age as them, those tenacious, undaunted scholars who – under the equally unperturbed but also paternal guidance of Giovanni Romano – wrestled once more with and, for the most part, resolved the exquisitely Gaudentian matter of the "legacy" of the "cartoons". Vis-à-vis the explanation for the use of that word, "legacy", I would request that you, dear reader, be patient; perhaps, in the end, you will work out for yourself the true reason and the true meaning. Indeed, getting you to work it out may be the only real purpose of the contribution that – having accepted the invitation and, as you can see, now floundering around in space and time – I am preparing to make.

In short, I would have liked to acknowledge and chart the vicissitudes of the critical standing of the great, domestic father (and master) of Piedmontese art, in the quarter-century

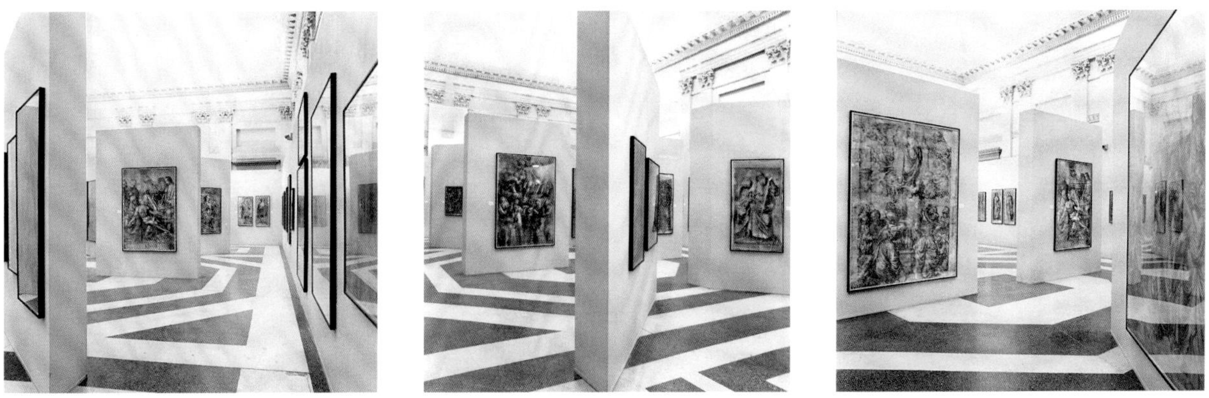

Installation of the exhibition
Gaudenzio Ferrari e la sua scuola
1982
Salone of the Accademia
Albertina di Belle Arti, Turin

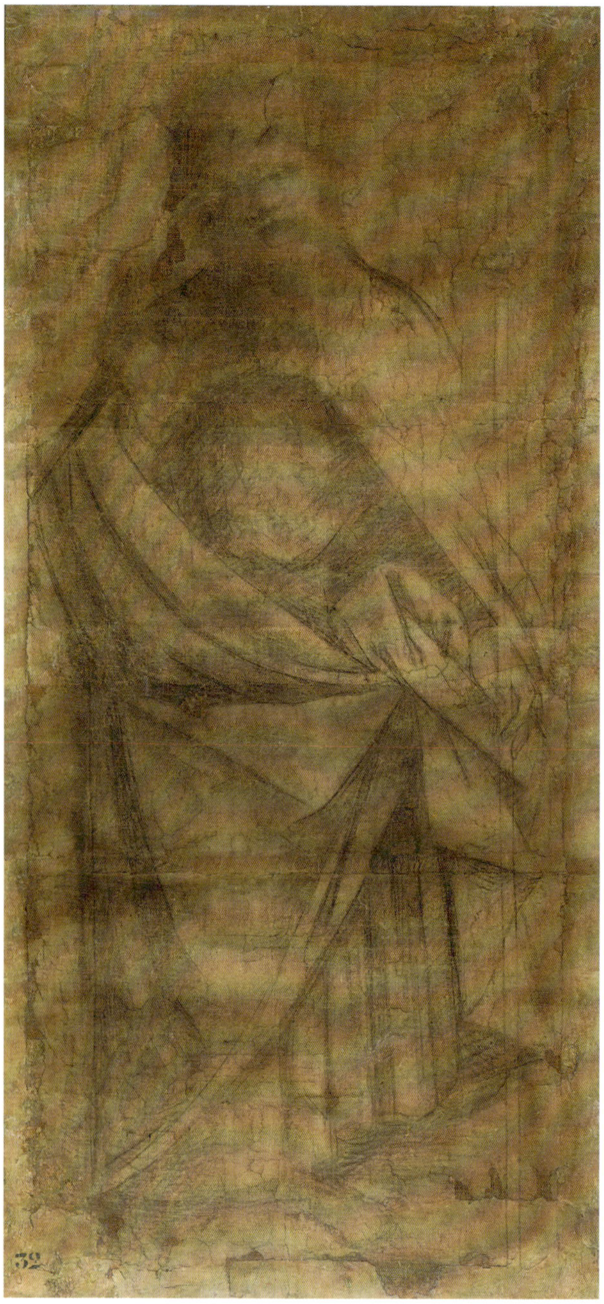

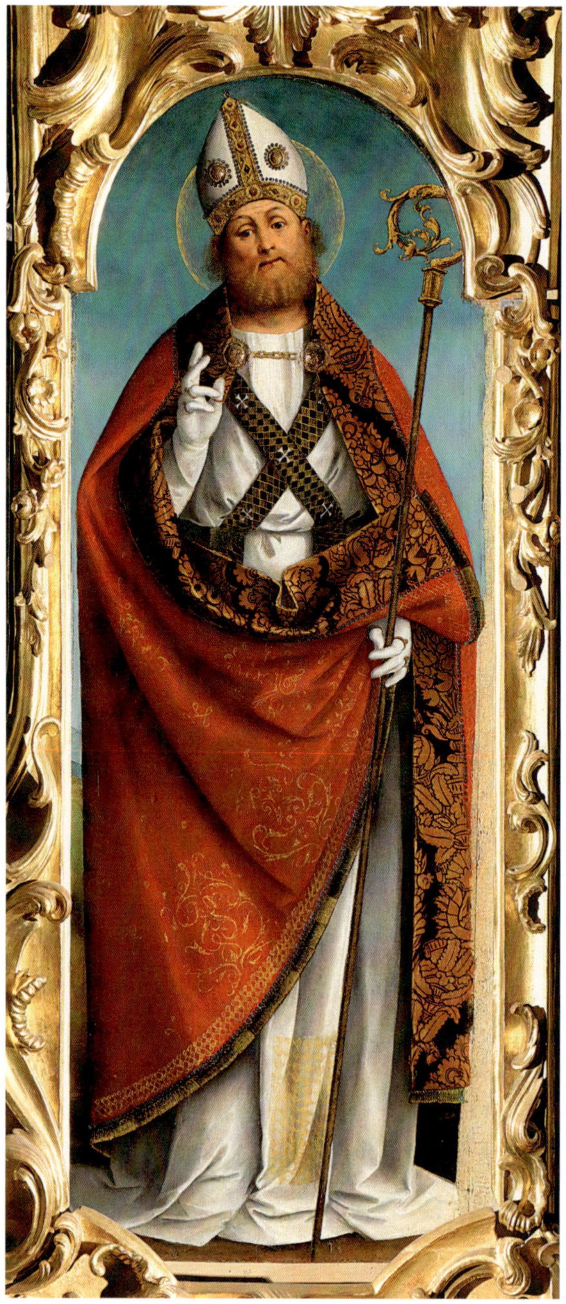

Gaudenzio Ferrari
Saint Gaudentius
1519–20
inv. 32bis
(cat. II)

Gaudenzio Ferrari
Saint Gaudentius
c. 1516–20
San Gaudenzio, Varallo

(or slightly longer period) that separates this exhibition from that of 1956. "Seven years is no brevity", says Thomas Becket in *Murder in the Cathedral*; "I shall not get those seven years back again", continues the immortal protagonist of Eliot's sacred tragedy. There can be no doubt that the Archbishop of Canterbury had endured those years in the hopeless oppression of imprisonment; for me and the rest of those who, having staged the exhibition in 1956, are still alive, those years were spent in freedom (at least in that modicum of freedom that life actually grants); but, in our case, we were dealing – or rather, we *are* dealing – with a full five lustra. "Twenty-five years is no brevity" is, then, what I should say to my Turinese friends, especially to the younger ones.

That said, having made this chronological leap, what else could I offer them aside from an astonished eye and an admiring ear?

The afterword would have required a capacity for encapsulation that – since those behind this showcase and the associated catalogue had deliberately denied themselves the opportunity to do so – I simply cannot see how I could have had the nerve to take on or, even worse, to propose directly, off my own bat.

Not that in the meantime I had fallen out of love with all things Gaudentian – he remained a beloved ancestor or household god. Perhaps it was that, for me, he was no longer (and this was inevitable) at the forefront, undergoing destruction and re-creation, of events, actions, studies and writings, given that my life – and this may well still be the case – had not been easy or straightforward: tremors, abysses, flashes, misery, cursing, falls, shouts and prayers were part-and-parcel of my existence, and remain so to this day. And a specific thread keeps me going, or rather, marks me out (since, perhaps, there is no longer anything at all that keeps me afloat). That thread has the sacred – but also staining and trivial – colour of his, blood, and of hers, passion. . . I say this because in my disordered drawers there is still something left to be revealed about him, the sweet, steadfast and certainly unforgettable Gaudenzio. But this is surely not the moment to extract some unknown albeit important relic.

If, then, my friends were encouraging the memories and comparisons that, with respect to the present, would emerge from it, let us remain within her, within memory; not to regret anything, nor to evoke anything other than the testament to a human and moral climate that, after numerous and (in many different ways) necessary breaks, seems now to be getting put back together; naturally, this climate is not the same as before, since the times – and their associated necessities – are forever changing. It is not, moreover, the first time that I have happened to recognise (and to write about) how, in the studios of the artists who are based here, in Turin – and who branch off in their research throughout the whole of Piedmont – that climate, constantly renewing itself, appeared so radical as to withstand all of the aforementioned lacerations and to stitch them back up, not to extinguish reasons, but to recognise them in the most essential truth; that truth that, elsewhere, abuses of mere political instrumentation have rapidly suffocated or blinded. That commitment to "being on the sidelines", of which Piedmontese morality is so enamoured, if experienced – not as a folkloric temperamentality but as a profound, faithful constancy – leads, not to preserve, but to set aside, which is something else entirely. And what on earth has it got to do with this exhibition?

An extraordinary heritage has been "set aside", so to speak: it has been restored; and it has once again been studied (even ending up with hairs being split over it). But all of this happened "on the sidelines"; without trumpet blasts; without melodramatic warnings. Therefore, as happens in a multitude of noble comedies, the actors came from the "wings" onto the stage and now here they are exposing the moral of their actions and the fruit that they have drawn from them; both of which are, to say the least, wonderful, for those like me who already knew and who had already had a chance to engage with comedy, and so with inheritance, legacy, treasure.

The text is the same as before, nor could it be any other way; but the words, or rather the signs, have become clearer and more acute; with a certain amount of lucidity, philology put its sharpest tools back into it; and the production, in continuing the tradition, is of an entirely different certainty and, therefore, of an entirely different confirmation.

To what extent was what is described here able to take place because, along with my friends from the exhibition of 1956 (most of whom, alas, have already passed through to the other, calm, eternal shore), I too, in some way, devoted time and soul to the previous phase of conservation and study?

As far as the "cartoons" are concerned, which came down from Gaudenzio, in the branching out and multiplying of his great, ever-present family, the answer to that question could be given, rather better than we can, by none other than Andreina Griseri who, in the exhibition of 1956, was responsible for dealing with the complicated machinations of the

Gaudentian "reunion", encompassing his direct and indirect relations. It is, indeed, from her that the response comes in the beautifully rendered, dense and comprehensive study that follows this prefatory trifle. Griseri assures us that the past twenty-five years have not been about overturning but about further exploration and development; according to her, the terms of the problem had been set out very clearly from the outset. We do not have time to pat ourselves on the back; in truth, we do not even want to. Memory stings us; or rather, the sweet, grey, vanishing memories do, with their cloaks that, often, have the character and colour of the many teachers and friends who have left us. Should we now mix those teachers and those friends with those who have in the intervening years gone from being youngsters – or better still, young bucks champing at the bit – to being teachers themselves; a prime example being our very own Saroni?

"A Milanese in Turin": this was to be the title for a long tract of my life, on the proviso that it would never be worth narrating. But my Turinese friends tried to get me to do just that; and so, I let the fragments of that period tell their tale – by which I mean, actions and dates, because I must be the first to recognise just how much – and forever – I owe to Turin and to those who supported the art world in those days.

It began in 1954 in Ivrea, "Ivrea the beautiful" – supported by the Olivetti Cultural Centre, led at that time by Luciano Codignola – with the Guala exhibition. At the behest of Costantino Baroni, the exhibition moved from the Canavese capital to Sforza Castle in Milan; and then from Milan, before coming to an end, it made its way, at the behest of Vittorio Viale and Noemi Gabrielli, to Palazzo Carignano in Turin. Once again propped up by Olivetti (clearly ahead of the curve in terms of the present-day fashion for sponsorship), in 1955 came the turn of the exhibition that, albeit restricted, I have good reason to consider as having been the origin of the renewed interest in the great 17th-century Lombard and Piedmontese artists on the part of the generation to which I belong. I am referring here to the exhibition entitled *Manieristi piemontesi e lombardi del Seicento*. It was first staged at Palazzo Madama, in the Acaia Hall. To see it, no less than Roberto Longhi came up from Florence. Imagine this: for an indirect student, at least to the extent to which he was undeservedly favoured, as I was, there could be no greater joy! It was on that occasion that I met Saroni. He was training at that time with Piero Ruggeri, the up-and-coming young duo busy disrupting Turinese painting; and it would have been extremely difficult to predict that the restless colt in question would slowly but surely arrive at the conscious, neo-Defendentian miniaturist obsession that everyone, from Piedmont and beyond, now knows him for; and for which he is rightly celebrated, as we ourselves did relatively recently.

No longer with Olivetti, with which in 1958 I had brought out the essay-tale or essay-dialogue on *Martino Spanzotti a Ivrea*, once more with the faithful Viale in 1959 there came the turn of the great and until then unknown Tanzio. Longhi again came up from Florence. More encounters, endless, in the late afternoons and evenings; along the streets and boulevards; under the colonnades; in the rooms of the museums; in the galleries; within studios. . . An air, once more, of great hope: as if hope were right there, within reach, just waiting to be picked, like a shining, ripe fruit. The future was, in other words, yet to come; or so at least it seemed to us. "Consumption" was yet to be formulated as an atrocious divinity, like Moloch the assassin. Perhaps we should already have predicted, already understood. . . And in any case, who can be sure that, here and there, some shadows were not stirring in the essays on those exhibitions? Would it be too much to request, in this regard, the effort of a re-reading? These days we forget about things so rapidly!

Indeed, just before the Tanzio exhibition, Arialda, I remember well, let loose her invectives and curses on our humble pages, and ended up invoking the dead. For my part,

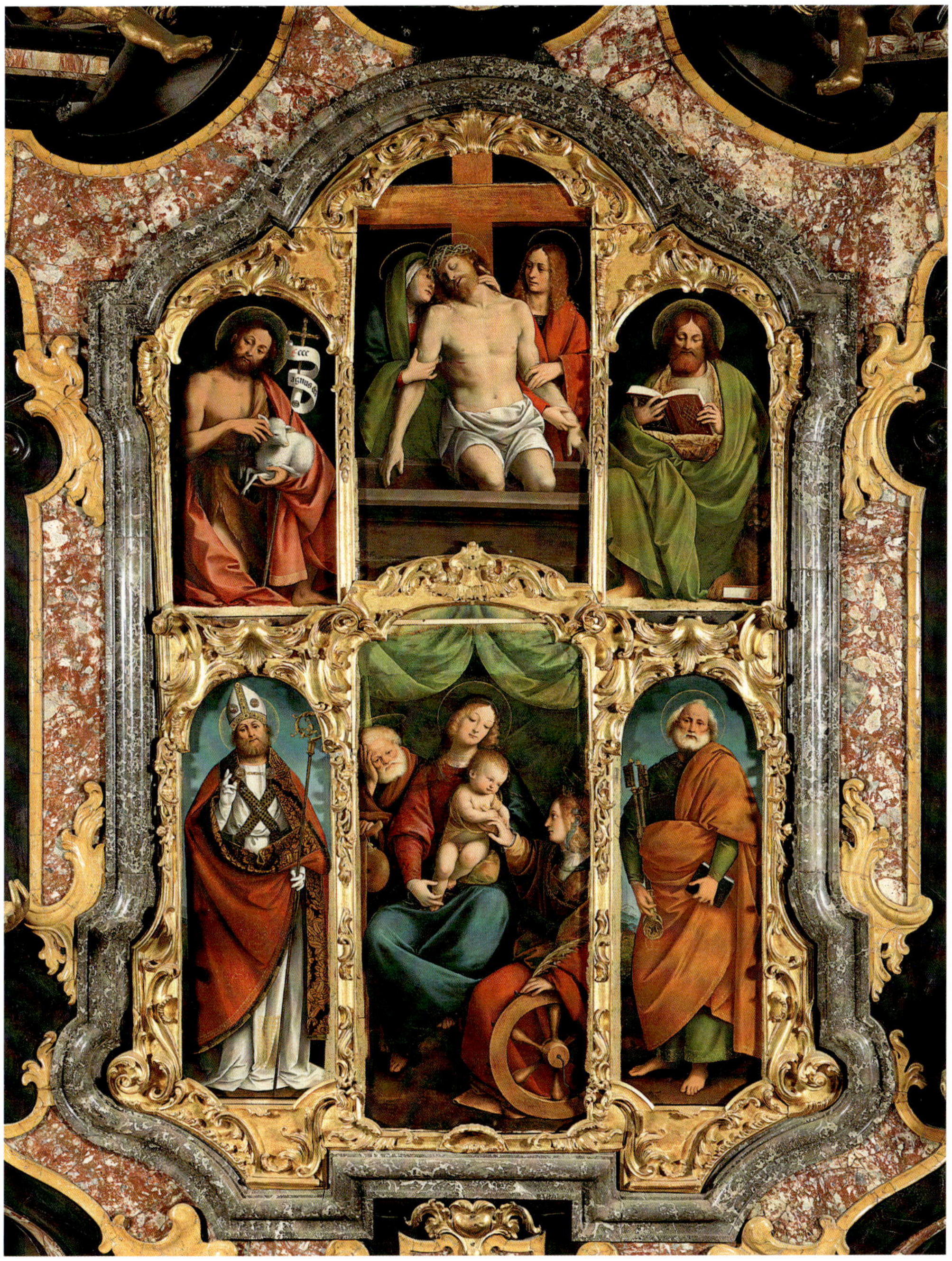

Gaudenzio Ferrari
San Gaudenzio Polyptych
(Mystical Wedding of Saint Catherine of Alexandria)
c. 1516–20
San Gaudenzio, Varallo

with that cry *I segreti di Milano* (The Secrets of Milan) came to a close, those "secrets" that certain people would like to reopen (and who knows, perhaps that may soon come to pass, but in what different, horrendous ways!). Were the "secrets of Turin" perhaps also being closed? How should one answer that?

After that, the Milanese returned; or went touring around Europe. And, at this point, the story could better be told by the person who, in *L'Ambleto* (1972), takes Horatio's place. But I would not want to lapse into excessively private matters – as things stand, one no longer knows if it is fashionable to do so or not. It will be worth re-entering that period, in the centre of which we find the great Gaudentian exhibition of Vercelli.

The wave of memories, here, has many names other than those already recalled; again, and as always at the forefront, was Viale; then Gabrielli, Brizio, Bertini, Mallé. . . I have already spoken of Griseri and her presence here, in this context, her consummate ability to provide a precis being a guarantee of the oft-referenced continuation of the spirits, and of the studies.

What then can I say about me, in 1956, in front of or inside the "cartoons"? What can I, here and now, write or report: at once sign, wound, kiss and unction? It seemed to me – or perhaps, rather than seemed, I had the certainty that it was the case – that they really were like sheets, pillow cases and tablecloths on which the embroidery and the "figures" were the work of the mother, but with the mark being that of the entire family, with the father at the head of the table; that they *were*, subjunctively – or rather, that they were, indicatively – like the "dowry" that used to be saved up for the daughters of the family; it would remain there, ready, awaiting the day the girls went off to be married.

In times of destruction, objecting against everything, and *above all* against the family, this image, I know only too well, may seem to go against the grain; for that matter, going against the grain is something I have been getting accused of for quite some time; since the time when, in the same instant, others, from other shores, accused me of the contrary and put me on trial. . . What is one supposed to do?

Revisiting this complex – unique, if I am not mistaken, in the entire history of graphic art – the image that comes to mind is the same. Feeling guilty for having failed to move forward? And what if, by chance, not me, not us, but him, Gaudenzio, precisely with that offering of his to his infinite lineage, not just the stylistic elements, but the heart of his own heart, were to find himself, in this day and age, way ahead of many so-called advances? If, in the abyss of indifferent desperation (and of indifferent destruction), specifically because one does not want either to withdraw or to turn one's gaze elsewhere, but rather to make one's way through it and participate in it fully, would Gaudenzio's "familiar" proposition be the most revolutionary? Few poets have known how to wait like him, trusting in mankind and in the design of its Creator. He had already been waiting for a great many years, when the exhibition of 1956 re-cast him in his primarily human truth; that truth that reduces to Man every problem of form and style. Because, in effect, what was the polemic with "the men of gold" on which the exhibition back then was based? And, to say it all, and with more provocative clarity, did the Moloch of "consumption" have like his eventual generators the flesh and bone of the protagonists (of the shepherds) of the Sacred Mountain of Varallo instead of that of the kings of that "gold"?

Focus more on philology? Others, here, have already done so; and as was the case for us, it never was and never will be granted. It is down to us. Perhaps, as both a right and a duty, we should pull on the heart strings, which become a mark, a drawing or, better, a skein which is deposited on the large sheets of paper and then, like an inheritance, passes from family to family, from country to country, from generation to generation; and so it mutates; it changes; it fades; perhaps, here and there, it is emptied out. Certainly it shall never again reach the fullness of those "cartoons" produced by Gaudenzio, of which there is one that seems to me to be among the greatest drawings in the history of humanity (that of the Budapest *Pietà*) but something of that centre remains forever. . .

And why should we be amazed if, corresponding to the centrality and familiarity of the artistic event under consideration there is the centrality and familiarity of the group that, once again, has returned to study and engage with this event? What better eulogy could be written for Giovanni Romano and his community of scholars than to recognise him as the "critical correlative" of the poetry that is there, or rather here, in these "cartoons"?

So, neither preface nor afterword; only some shading; a story, one hopes, of moving tenderness, for the past and for the present; and the light and hope that always come from those who have worked hard and worked well, with probity and justice of intelligence and of heart.

At this point, all that is left for me to do is to put myself on the sidelines. And that is what, having thanked those who called upon me to open this "summa", I shall silently do.

The Italian version of this text has been published on the catalogue of the 1982 exhibition *Gaudenzio Ferrari e la sua scuola. I cartoni cinquecenteschi dell'Accademia Albertina*, edited by Giovanni Romano.

On Gaudenzio's Cartoons, Since 1982

Simone Baiocco

On the occasion of the recent presentation, at the Pinacoteca Albertina, of a new Giovenone painting, the entire group that had been working together at that time shared an awareness that the catalogue for the 1982 exhibition was irreplaceable, its very existence shoring up the new initiative.[1] At the time when they had before them the new photographs – specifically shot by those involved in the academy's photography course – thought was given to a possible (or perhaps impossible) reissuing; a plan fostered with a view to making available to the new generations of scholars the immense wealth of philology contained within it. Borrowing a felicitous expression attributed to an illustrious scholar of Gaudenzio, it can be said that we find ourselves in the presence of a "monument to philology and passion",[2] the quality of which is confirmed even now by the continued relevance of that research.

The exhibition at the Accademia Albertina constituted one of the first and most highly accomplished results of that methodological training ground that was the Turin Superintendence during those years in which the unanimously acknowledged expert guidance of Giovanni Romano had achieved its deserved institutional recognition; years, moreover, in which the generally favourable historical and political circumstances were complemented by another strong element – the running of the Albertina by Sergio Saroni.[3] The fact that it was a *bona fide* test bed is clear from the collaboration of all the functionaries of the office, together with a number of up-and-coming academics, based on an arrangement destined to endure through a long series of episodes, whereby Romano – who, a few years later, would move once and for all into university lecturing – succeeded in implementing and developing a teaching methodology that was to prove very important in raising the profile of the region's cultural heritage. Within the 1982 team, it fell to Pierluigi Gaglia to deal with the news on the formation of the group of cartoons that reached the academy with the 1832 donation; his essay was the first to attempt to associate those drawings with the documentary reports on graphical material within the Vercelli workshops in the 16th and 17th centuries.[4]

The conservation of these cartoons in a coherent group is a distinctive trait, never sufficiently underlined, of the "Vercelli school", which constitutes a relatively unique case study precisely because it saw the transmission of cartoons within the tradition of the workshop.[5] The school was analysed by a series of 19th- and 20th-century scholars who were able to make the most of a wealth of documentary information on those ateliers. As if to compensate for the absence of an older historiographic tradition, for the workshops of Vercelli there is an extensive set of archival documents that make it possible to discern the commissioning practices and the social dynamics, as well as the interpersonal relationships (almost penetrating the private sphere) and the operations of the workshops across several generations. Alongside these archival documents, the graphical material was fundamentally important and, read in parallel with the finished works, served as a different but complementary source of information. As was opportunely stressed in 1982:

> The theme of exchange between workshops is the most evident: the cartoons were not a secret treasure, and this was even more the case when the release of a finished work ended up rendering them no longer unpublished. The fact that the cartoons were in any event conserved – indeed they enjoyed many decades of renown – gives rise to numerous questions on the matters of competition or stylistic solidarity between masters who were contemporaries of each other and often blood relatives, as it does on the parallel theme of the artistic professionalism of the Vercelli painters in the 15th and 16th centuries.[6]

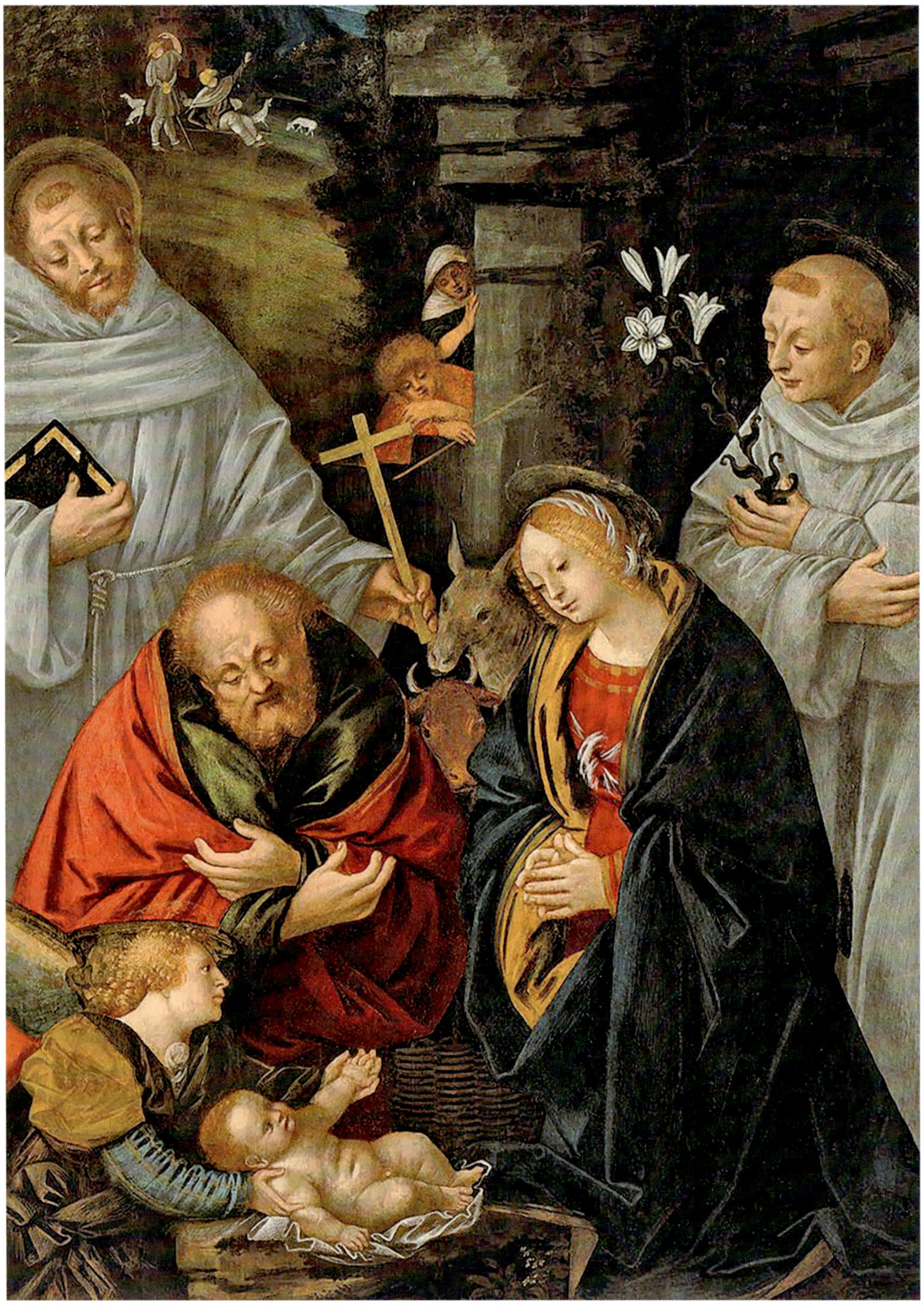

Gerolamo Giovenone
(and Bernardino Lanino)
Adoration of the Child with Saints Francis of Assisi and Anthony of Padua
Collection of Banca Patrimoni
Sella & C.

Gaudenzio Ferrari
Adoration of the Child
1514–16
San Gaudenzio, Novara

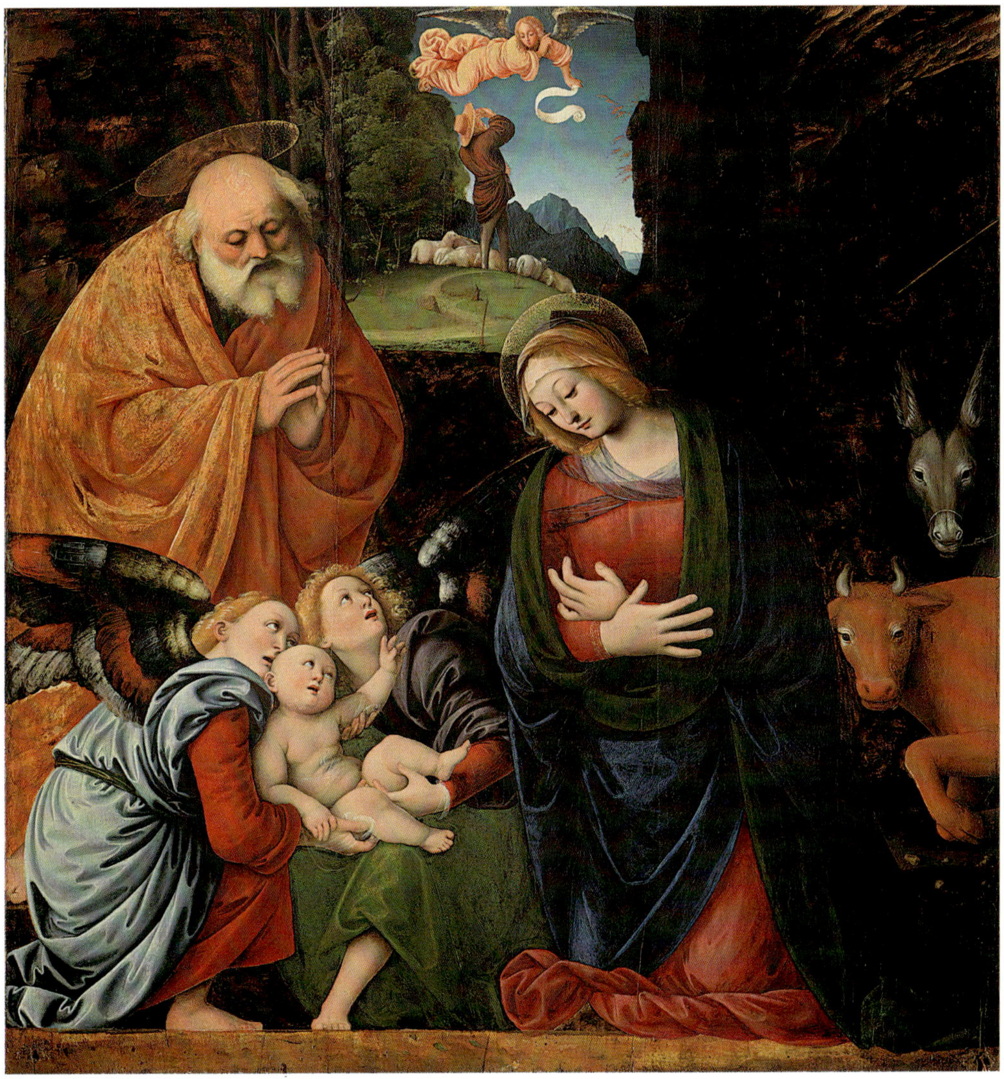

Also in terms of the relationship between archival and figurative sources, the 1982 catalogue is a methodological *sine qua non*. At the beginning of each section on the various artists, there is an up-to-date documentary summary, which in more than one case states that it is dependent on the documents compiled and indexed by Alessandro Baudi di Vesme, owned by the Società Piemontese di Archeologia e Belle Arti but held at the Musei Civici. The opportunity to consult those materials had only arisen recently, and at the same time their publication in Volume IV of the *Schede Vesme* was being defined – a publication which appeared, however, only at the end of that year.[7]

After 1982, the research endeavoured to reconstruct the shift from drawings and cartoons (these, specifically, but also others cited in, or inferred from, the documents) on the part of the workshops of Vercelli in the late 16th and early 17th century towards an approach more focused on collecting. It was a change that led to a number of reflections on the altered status of these materials.

These attempts were clearly based on the aforementioned archival documents, as was the case of an agreement stipulated on 27 January 1583 between the painter brothers Giuseppe, Amedeo and Paolo Giovenone to define the destiny of the estate inherited from their father Gerolamo, who had died several years previously. Within this agreement there is a special focus on the graphical material, on the so-called "drawings of their art":

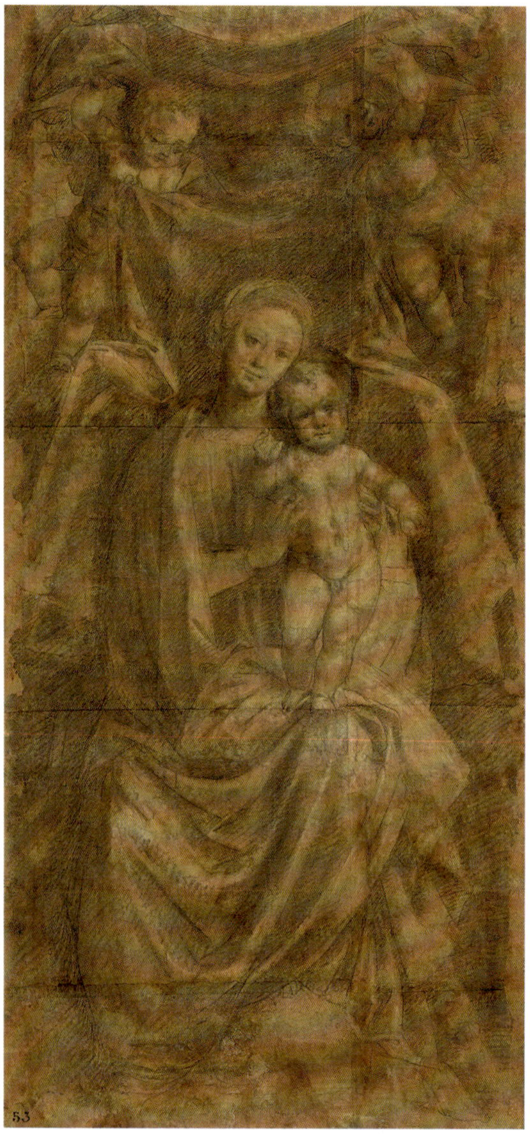

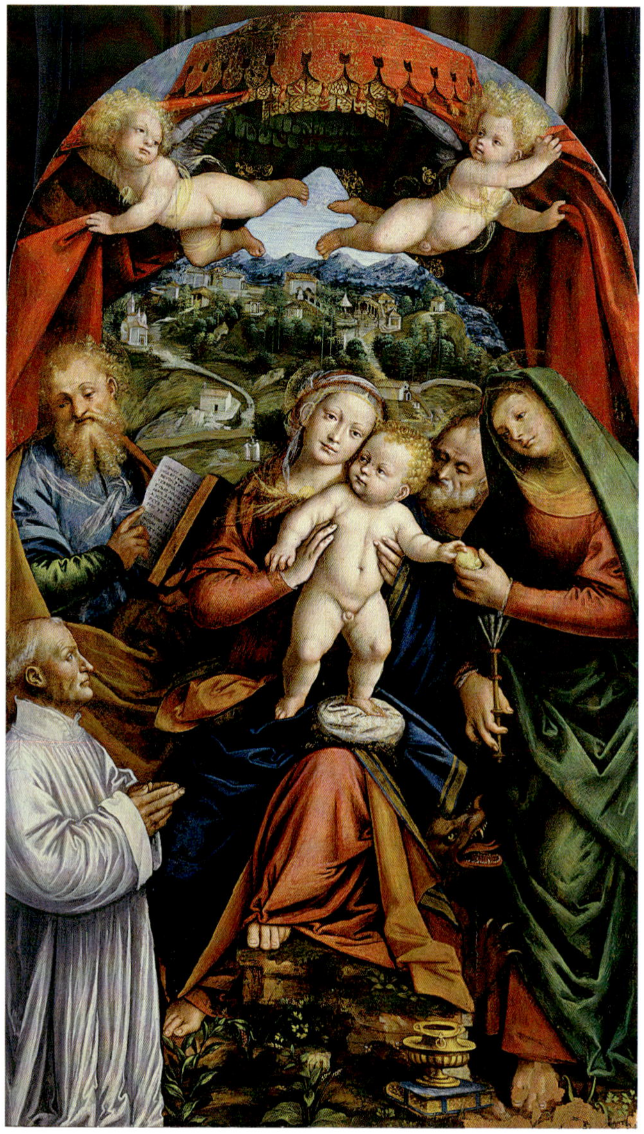

Giuseppe Giovenone the Younger
Virgin and Child Enthroned with Two Angels
c. 1560
inv. 353
(cat. XXXIV)

Gerolamo Giovenone and workshop
Virgin and Child with Saints
c. 1543
Pinacoteca di Brera, Milan

> It has been agreed that during the lifetime of Giuseppe, the eldest of the aforementioned brothers, the drawings of their art shall remain with him, and that he shall provide however the necessary description of them and inventory, and of which nonetheless each of these brothers also during the life of *messer* Giuseppe may at every request make use and rectify, just as *messer* Giuseppe here present promised and promises . . ., and after the death of *messer* Giuseppe . . . said drawings shall be divided between *messer* Amadeo and *messer* Paulo if they are still alive, otherwise between their heirs, each receiving a half, and their descendants.[8]

Certainly, the document does not state as much as we may be tempted to read into it – i.e. that among those drawings there was material dating back to the previous generation, constituted by those who had supped directly from the Gaudentian wellspring; rather, it concerned once again the sons of Gerolamo Giovenone and the brothers-in-law of Bernardino Lanino. It does, however, refer openly to a precious patrimony, which is to remain in the possession of Giuseppe Giovenone the Younger – an artist to whom we can now attribute an independent, verified profile[9] – but which was still to be considered as being at the disposal of his brothers, too. What also emerges is how the fate of these materials was already laid out also for the subsequent hereditary handovers, even though, a few years later, the eldest brother wrote a will of which the only beneficiary was Amedeo, with whom he had always lived – a factor that indicates a close, ongoing collaboration between the two, more so than with their brother Paolo.[10] The agreements between the three brothers were concluded, without further reference to the graphical material, in two successive documents of 21 February 1584 and 31 October 1585; everything seems to have been smoothed over between them, even if in the second document mention is made of the money that Paolo was to have contributed to the project of a polyptych intended for the town of Trino, on which his brothers were working.[11]

This reference, albeit vague, appears once again to indicate the presence of a separation between Giuseppe (the eldest brother and the one with the most authority, who as such was in charge of the workshop's drawings) and Amedeo on the one side, and Paolo, who was much younger than his two brothers, on the other. It was, however, one of Paolo's children, Gerolamo, who after his father's death (which probably occurred in 1608) came into possession of a series of inherited items, with specific reference being made to "the drawings discovered in the home of the late Giuseppe Giovenone", which at this point should correspond to those already being talked about in 1583.[12]

Gerolamo di Paolo Giovenone, who is named after his painter grandfather, had been baptised in 1590 and therefore here we encounter him when he is still very young; later on he will be referred to as a doctor, particularly in his will drafted in 1650, the probable year of his death.[13] Another doctor, a cousin of Gerolamo, is implicated in matters relating to the drawings of the Vercelli workshops: Pietro Antonio Lanino, son of Bernardino and Dorotea Giovenone – i.e. the sister of Giuseppe, Amedeo and Paolo. Pietro Antonio, whom Vesme's notes describe as the Court Physician to Victor Amadeus I, Duke of Savoy,[14] drafted an initial will in 1632 in which he named his cousin Gerolamo, to whom he left certain books, but also referred in particular to his father's drawings, or rather to the "study of drawings for paintings" (a description that almost seems to hint at a cohesive set of artworks); for these he identifies a specific heir in the form of his nephew Don Carlo Soleri.[15] Revising in part this first will, in 1636 Pietro Antonio wrote another in which he clarified that the drawings, at that time in Carlo's hands, should upon his death pass to his heirs "since they are of great value and judged by experts to exceed the sum of four hundred gold *scudi*".[16]

On the basis of the known, still-extant documents, it would seem that there are two main groups of drawings, the Giovenone and Lanino groups: that which in 1608 was in the possession of Gerolamo di Paolo Giovenone, and that which in 1636 was still in the hands of the canon Carlo Soleri but which, as per his uncle's second will, was not destined to remain with him.

There is, however, no dearth of other evidence concerning drawings in the family context. It is far from certain, for example, that the "Lanino group" ended up including a number of drawings that contributed to great tension between Bernardino Lanino and his illegitimate son Cesare, in late 1568, when the latter responded to the summons filed against him by the former: "In relation to the batch of drawings described he states that his father made those drawings for him and gave them to him for him to learn. And then they are not of the value he has stated, nor even half of it."[17] But the references to drawings are frequent and continue for some considerable time: by selecting an example of two successive generations we arrive at 1676, when the widow of Giovanni Battista Lanino (grandson of Cesare) bequeathed to her brother-in-law "one of the two drawings made by the forebears of the house of Lanino":[18] a reference that evokes a certain authority, almost allowing us to step back in time.

The canon Carlo Soleri is worthy of further investigation, in part because at present it is still not clear what his role was nor why his uncle prioritised him vis-à-vis the inheritance

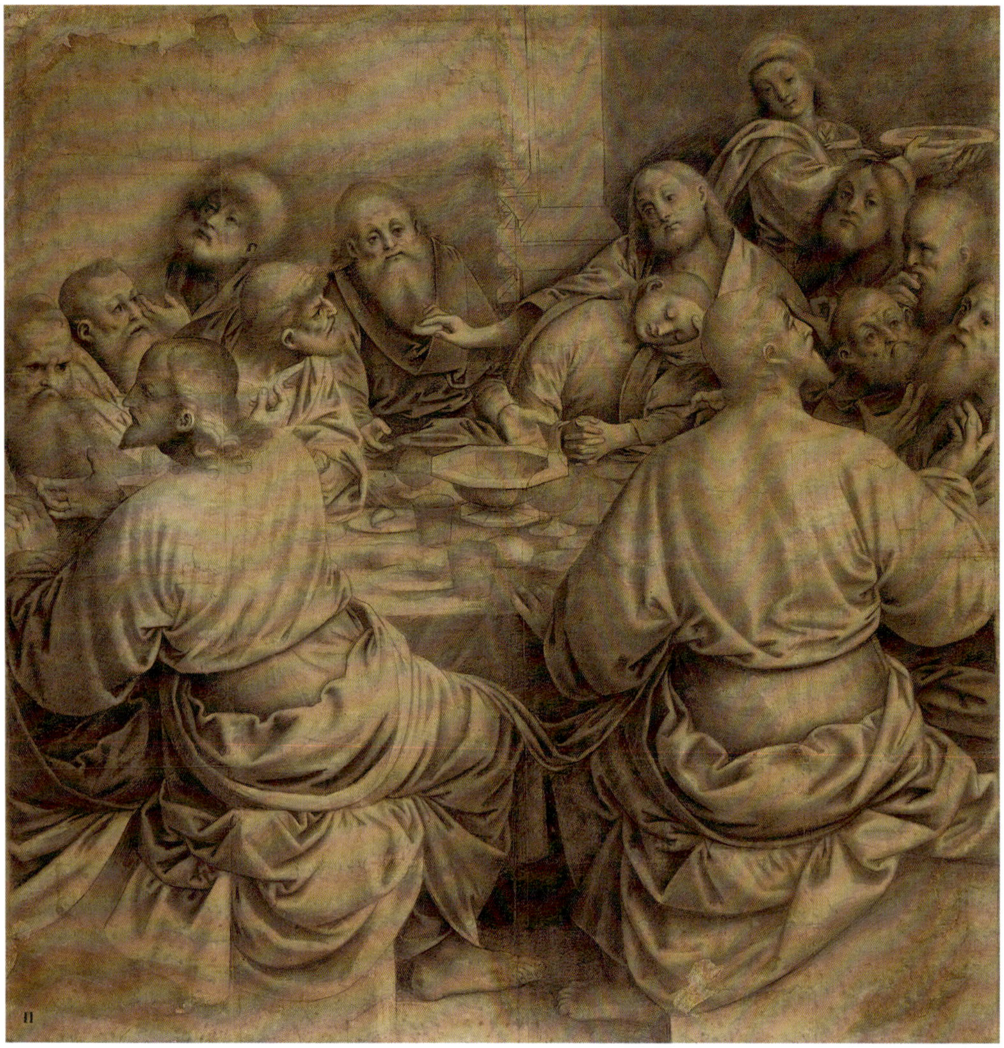

Workshop of Gerolamo Giovenone (?)
Last Supper
c. 1540
inv. 311
(cat. XVI)

of the family drawings, going so far as to draw a distinction (at least in the second will) between the interest in the drawings and their commercial value, now defined by "experts". His link with the local figurative art scene, which encompassed Vercelli and the court, is however confirmed by the fact that he was the son of the painter Giorgio Soleri and his second wife, Laura Lanino, who in turn was the daughter of Bernardino and Dorotea Giovenone, sister of Pietro Antonio, the testator and custodian of the drawings.[19]

It is at this point possible to venture a step forward and, connecting the dots between the figurative and documentary sources, to offer up a different reading that brings the current group of cartoons at the Pinacoteca into contact with this milieu. I am referring here to the proposal, put forward by Carlenrica Spantigati and then revamped by Clelia Arnaldi, to recognise the hand of Giorgio Soleri in cartoon inv. 340, portraying the *Virgin and Child with Angels Worshipped by a Devotee Presented by Saint George*, thus going rather further than the entry in which Romano had set aside the traditional attribution to Bernardino Lanino, indicating that the drawing is "more akin to the Lombard Mannerism of Lomazzo and Aurelio Luini".[20] It is clearly the case that the physical presence of a drawing by Giorgio Soleri amongst those that eventually, across the years, reached the Pinacoteca Albertina may substantiate the input of his son Carlo into this whole matter.

Baudi di Vesme did not conceal his doubts in relation to the subsequent transfers of this group and persisted in annotating the documents on the generations of the Lanino family up to the end of the 17th century and beyond, in an endeavour to reconstruct the

Gaudenzio Ferrari
(and Sperindio Cagnoli)
Last Supper
c. 1515–20
Cathedral, Novara

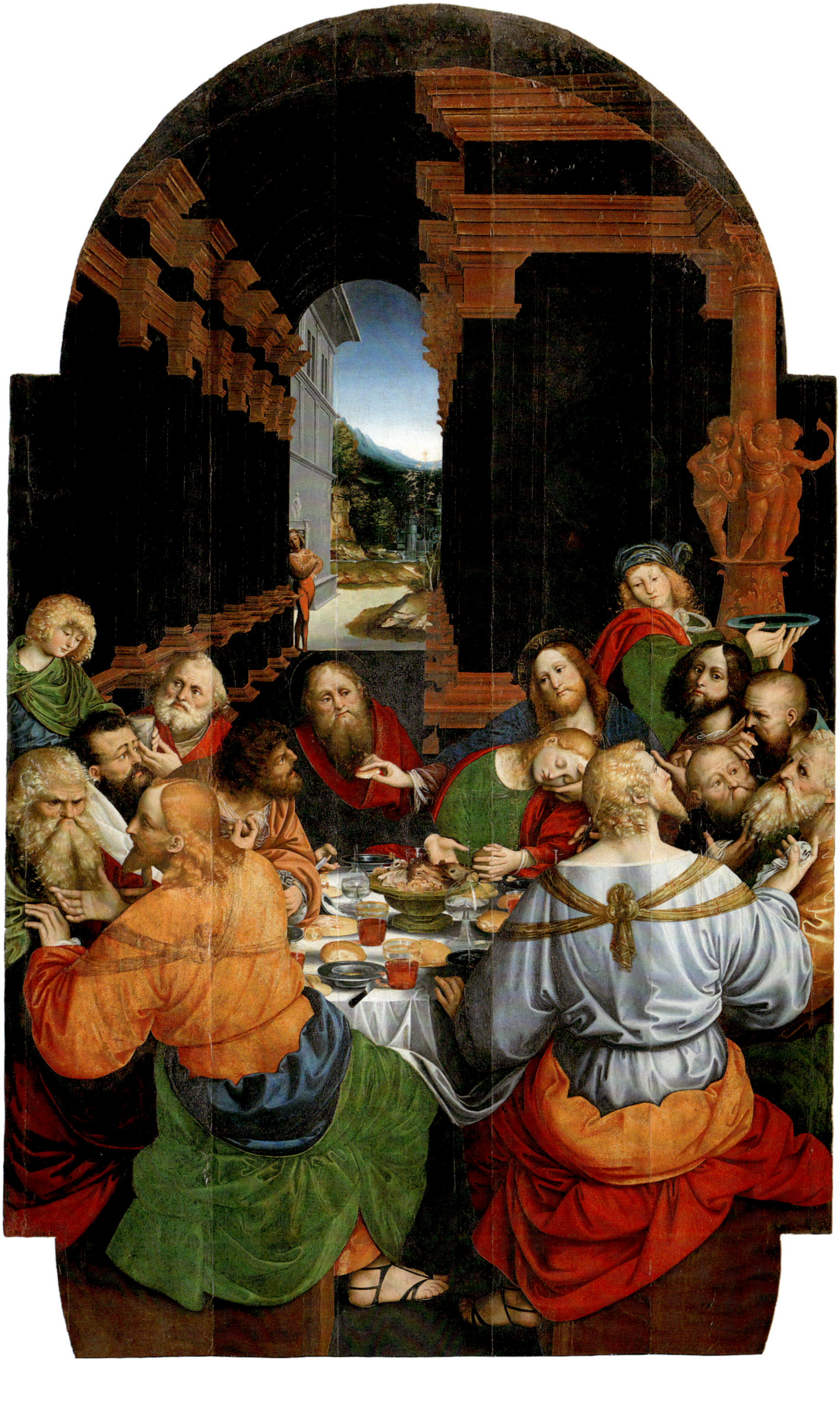

later vicissitudes of that family's cartoons. This remains the area most affected by a lack of in-depth knowledge and – the attempts made thus far notwithstanding – the matter is worthy of some further research.

For example, the information on the sale, to Marquis Giovanni Francesco Serra, of the drawings that belonged to Carlo Soleri comes up time and again, but the details are yet to be scrutinised and at present are surrounded by an air of uncertainty. On the one hand, Giuseppe Colombo cites a 17th-century manuscript by Carlo Amedeo Bellini and refers to a transfer from Soleri to Serra for 800 *scudi*,[21] whereas Giuseppe Roberti's essay, from which even Vesme takes an annotation, contains in an almost incidental manner, in a footnote, a letter from Giovanni Antonio Ranza to Giuseppe Vernazza (dated 1 August 1775) in which there is no reference whatsoever to drawings:

> Out of curiosity I transcribe this other piece of artistic news: "Up for sale are two small plaquettes around as long as a hand's width, cast in bronze, one of which represents the sacrifice of Isaac, the other (the more attractive) the deposition of the cross containing seven figures, they are works of some [?] centuries and I believe that they were in the famous gallery of our Lanino, the deposition by his heirs was sold for 800 golden *scudi* to the Marquis Serra of Genoa in the last century, but was then lost: and perhaps the deposition served as the model for Lanino himself for his similar picture existing in the gallery of the royal chapel."[22]

Reference is then made to a plaquette, which is involved in a sort of game of mirrors, recalling other drawings and paintings: in this case the *Deposition* in the Galleria Sabauda signed and dated by Lanino in 1558, cartoon inv. 327 and the variants that it proposes, taking its cue from the model of Gaudenzio himself.[23]

Over and above the consequence of rendering slightly more vague the often accepted reference to the collection of graphical works, the allusion here to a plaquette recalls an important early episode in Gaudenzio's fortunes, concerning the fascinating goldsmith, art collector and merchant Gasparo Mola, who in 1608 supplied works to the Duke of Savoy.[24] In this instance, works by Gaudenzio were not included in the provision, but Mola certainly studied the Budapest *Lamentation of Christ*, which he sold to the Duke of Mantua in 1606, and of which he made at least one replica, in a plaquette at the base of a *Crucifix* today in the Museo della Città of Rimini (identified by Giovanni Agosti).[25] It is also true that a bronze plaquette derived in turn from the Gaudentian *Lamentation* had already been produced by an anonymous Lombard artist around the mid 16th century.[26] A further notice involves Mola, with more specific reference to the drawings that are of interest to us, and it concerns the fact of having supplied, again in 1608, a frame for the "Cartoon of the Virgin and Child with Saint Anne by Leonardo Da Vinci"[27] – i.e. the cartoon that would seem to coincide with no. 348.[28]

With the presence of Mola we have now addressed the events relating to the ducal collections. Even though we are yet to clarify the timescales and methods with which this transfer occurred, we are getting closer to the moment in which the drawings destined to pass from the ownership of the sovereigns to that of the Accademia Albertina can be effectively identified. Also datable to the early 17th century – during which time, even outside Piedmont and Lombardy, the renown of Gaudenzio in historiographic terms was gaining ground[29] – is the output of another Vercelli native, the painter Pompeo Secondiano. Having in all likelihood been trained within the Vercelli milieu in which we are interested, Secondiano collaborated with the court-based artistic initiatives in Turin from at least 1607, taking on the role of "conservator of paintings and drawings", with responsibilities also in the

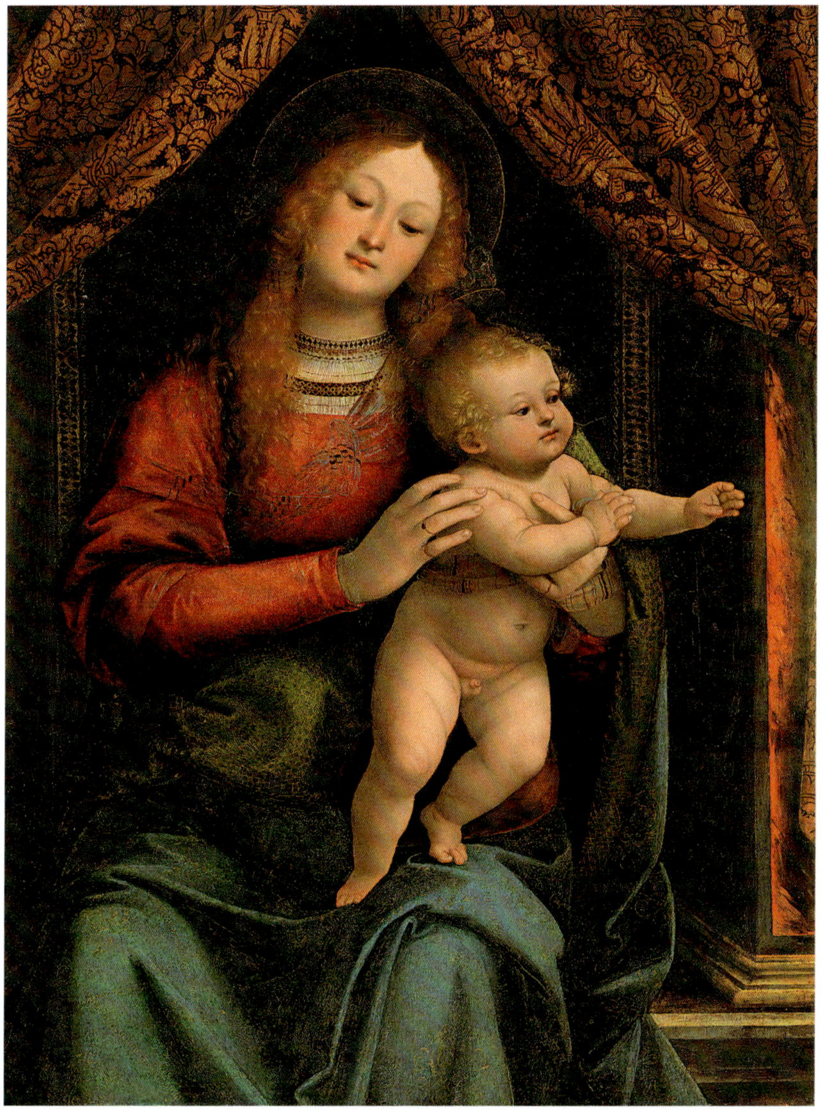

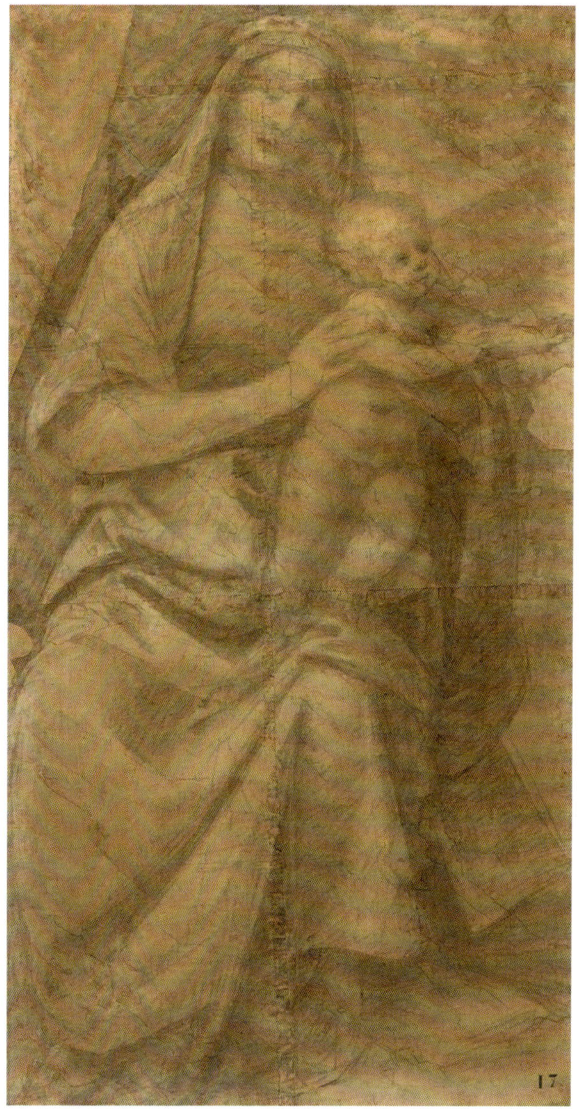

Gaudenzio Ferrari
Virgin and Child
c. 1517–18
Pinacoteca di Brera, Milan

Gaudenzio Ferrari
Virgin Enthroned and Child
1539–46
inv. 317
(cat. V)

field of restoration. As Gelsomina Spione has stated, behind the documentary information on him, we can discern his skills as a "connoisseur", a role that was taking on new, modern characteristics.[30] After his death, the recruiting of his successor specified that the "post of conservator of our paintings and drawings, for which is sought a man as appropriate, practical and intelligent in one and the other profession, as he is faithful, vigilant and diligent".[31]

One of the operations conducted in this guise of his as a "consultant" was concerned specifically with the field of drawings, and it is for this reason that his name is often mentioned: on 23 June 1611, a registration in the chamber archive makes reference to a transfer of 6 ducatoons to Secondiano "in payment of what he must have from His Highness for going to Vercelli to collect the drawings to show them to His Highness"; once again the next year, on 12 October 1612, there is an explicit reference to the "money that we owe to him for the cost of so many paintings and drawings sold to us and priced between him and us verbally only".[32] With a view to being precise, the information is not definitive: while there are drawings that came from Vercelli and were put up for sale for the ducal collections, the payment the following year does not specify whether those drawings were the ones in question; in truth, we cannot discount that there were amongst these some of the works today at the Albertina.[33]

Secondiano's heirs would gradually refine their role and would find themselves at the forefront of efforts to compile the inventories in which we can begin to recognise the works

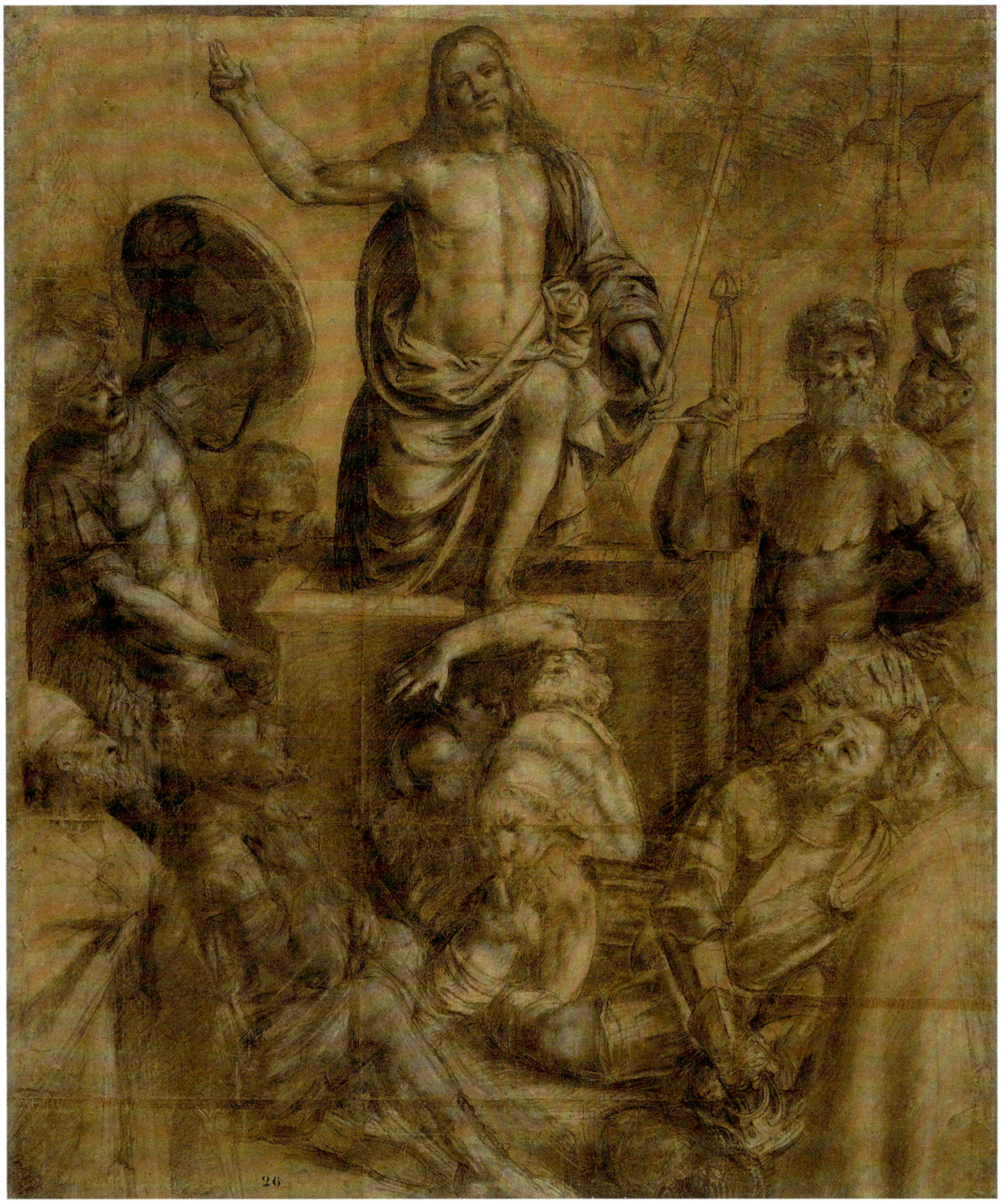

Giuseppe Giovenone the Younger
Resurrection of Christ and Two Bishop Saints
c. 1550
inv. 326
(cat. XXIX)

familiar to us. In the inventory of the collections drafted in 1631, shortly after the death of Charles Emmanuel I, we can identify here and there a number of drawings, referred to as *disegni*, *disegnetti*, *cartoni* or *cartonetti*, together with all of the others which, in the absence of further information, must be deemed paintings: in the third room after the Great Gallery, we can identify the Leonardo cartoon ("Cartoon of the Virgin and Child with Saint Anne by Leonardo Da Vinci") along with "another cartoon of the nativity of Christ, by a skilled hand", which is followed by another, stated as being by Gaudenzio, portraying a Circumcision, whereas slightly later on we find listed "two little cartoons of angels lying down, in chiaroscuro".[34]

The reference to the drawing based on Leonardo's *Saint Anne* constitutes a valuable clue in that it is the work most often cited and most identifiable. This was certainly the case in the episode that saw the provision of a frame by Mola, but additional checks would be required since the same type of reference was made when, in 1671, the painter Giovan Battista Natali flagged up to Cardinal Leopoldo de' Medici the possibility of acquiring "illustrious drawings by Gaudenzio", indicated at that time as still being in Vercelli.[35]

At least in one case, there are good reasons to identify one of the Albertina cartoons in the Della Cornia inventory, dating from 1635, which is sufficiently precise in describing

Giuseppe Giovenone the Younger
Resurrection of Christ
c. 1555–60
Galleria Sabauda, Musei Reali, Turin

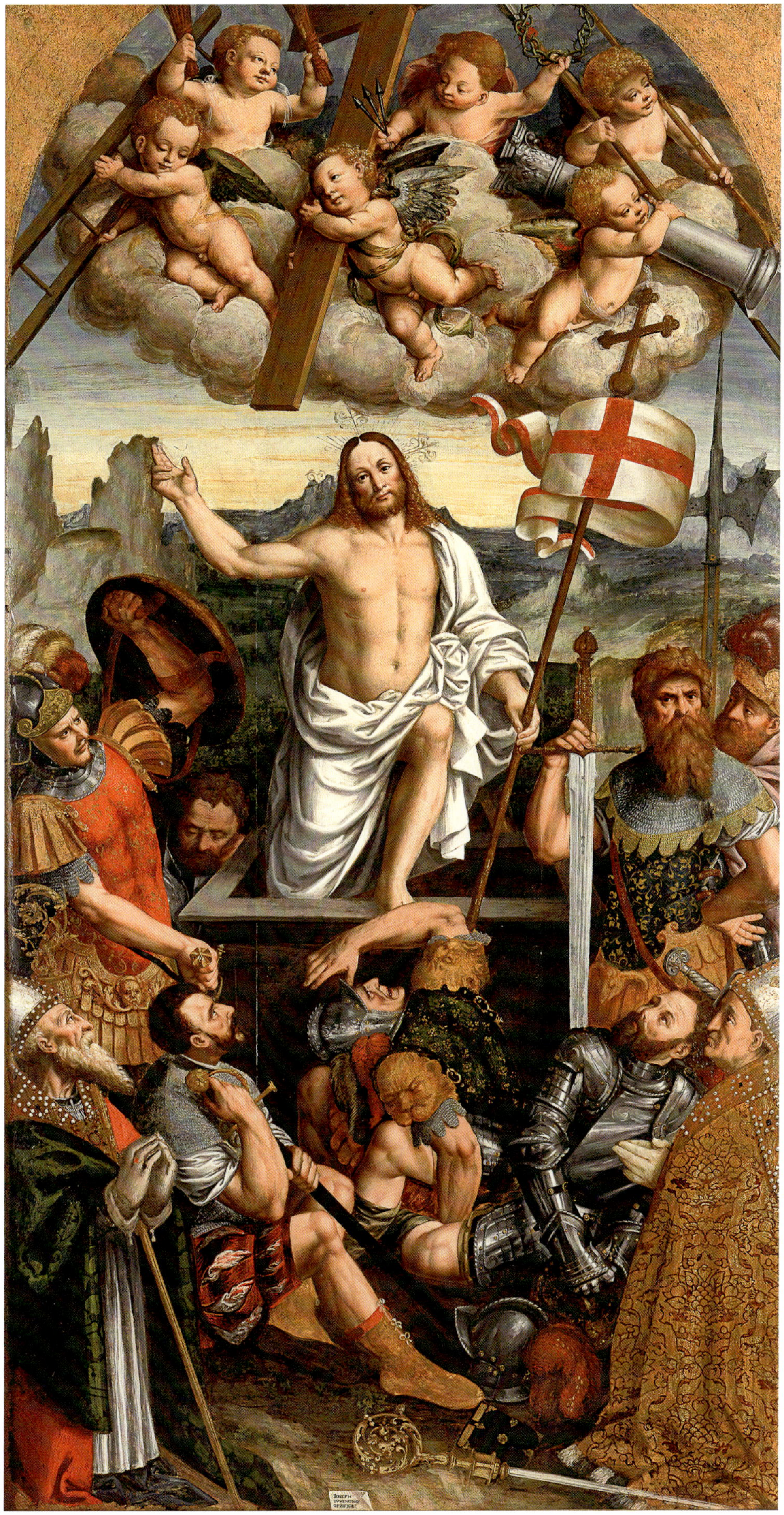

"The Virgin with Child who has a crown in his hands, full figures. By Gaudenzio. Beautiful", and it is above all the reference to the crown of the rosary that permitted Michela di Macco to confirm its identity as cartoon inv. 304, also used as a starting point by Gerolamo Giovenone in a drawing held at the Uffizi.[36] With respect to the early years of the century, his expertise and his value for collectors had increased, as evinced also by the inventory compiled in 1634 for what is undoubtedly the most important Piedmontese collection of the period, belonging to Amedeo dal Pozzo, Marquis of Voghera, in which there is an entire section expressly given over to "Cartoons and drawings" within which the Guadentian and Laninian context is very well-documented.[37]

In contrast, the group of cartoons currently at the Albertina is, finally, identifiable in the inventory of the chattels of the Royal Palaces, drafted in 1682: at the end of the Great Gallery there is an actual "Cabinet of drawings", in which the by now very numerous drawings were organised and arranged ("compartmentalised with gilded frame featuring arabesques") in a way fully coherent with the rest of the collection and specifically with the paintings in the Great Gallery. It then becomes important to underline that the payments for this arrangement of the works date from 1665 and as such, according to Michela di Macco's reconstruction, this is the date by which we should consider the Gaudentian cartoons currently held at the Pinacoteca Albertina as having entered the Savoy collections.[38]

Certainly, in terms of the mixed fortunes of this group of works, there are many aspects yet to be clarified. Amongst these, additional checks should be conducted, for example, on the parallel Vercelli provenance of a group of drawings that then arrived at the Royal Library. It was Giuseppe Colombo who highlighted that certain drawings by Gaudenzio had been sold by the Vercelli painter and merchant Vincenzo Ballocco (1772–1828), who had probably intervened also to rectify a number of conservation problems, with some interpretative input.[39] The matter is curious also in terms of the transfers that we charted earlier, given that Gaspare De Gregory states that he was able to observe thanks to Ballocco some of the drawings passed from Pietro Antonio Lanino to Carlo Soleri: if this statement were to be confirmed, then at least some of the drawings whose traces we have sought in the early 17th century would still have been in private hands two centuries later, and perhaps some of these may then have been transferred to the Royal Library.[40]

Looking back over the information on the compilation of the group of works at the Pinacoteca Albertina, the hope was that the new, highly valuable photographic material would encourage new investigations not only in terms of the history of the works but above all with a view to exploring them in more detail. Monographic research and new evaluations of the context could be carried out, focusing on the Vercelli workshops between the late 16th and early 17th centuries, taking in the output of Giorgio Soleri and Pompeo Secondiano, alongside that of Giuseppe Giovenone and the children of Bernardino Lanino, amid the old Gaudentian models and the new impetus that came from Moncalvo. While inching ever closer to the Turinese court, at the same time Vercelli also looked to Milan, adhering to the lines of ecclesiastical and liturgical reform laid down by Carlo Borromeo from the 1570s onwards, with the appointment of Bishop Bonomi.[41]

[1] *Gaudenzio Ferrari e la sua scuola. I cartoni cinquecenteschi dell'Accademia Albertina*, ed. Giovanni Romano, exhibition catalogue, Accademia Albertina, Turin, March–May 1982 (Turin, 1982); the reference to the recent exhibition is to *Gerolamo Giovenone. Un capolavoro ritrovato*, ed. Daniela Magnetti, exhibition catalogue, Pinacoteca Albertina, Turin, 7–25 February 2018; Museo Borgogna, Vercelli, 10 March – 1 July 2018 (Milan, 2018).

[2] Rossana Sacchi, "Prospettive sulla fortuna di Gaudenzio", in *Per Giovanni Romano. Scritti di amici*, eds. Giovanni Agosti, Giuseppe Dardanello, Giovanna Galante Garrone and Ada Quazza (Savigliano, 2009), pp. 164–65; later republished in Rossana Sacchi, *Gaudenzio a Milano* (Milan, 2015), pp. 67–69 (I quote from p. 67).

[3] See *Accademia Albertina. Opere scelte della Pinacoteca*, eds. Franca Dalmasso, Giovanna Galante Garrone and Giovanni Romano, exhibition catalogue, Accademia Albertina, Turin, 11 February – 14 March 1993 (Turin, 1993). The whole 1993 exhibition is based

on the selections and on the work of Saroni, who died in 1991, but to understand his significance fully it is important above all to refer to the texts by G. Romano, "Un dono di Sergio Saroni" (ibid., p. 13) and G. Galante Garrone, "Saroni direttore e la Soprintendenza: una storia anomala", ibid., pp. 19–24.

[4] Pierluigi Gaglia, "Notizie e ipotesi sui cartoni gaudenziani dell'Accademia Albertina", in *Gaudenzio Ferrari*, 1982, pp. 26–33.

[5] Sacchi 2015, p. 168.To comprehend the specificity and exceptional nature of the case of Vercelli, see Giovanni Romano, "Pittori in bottega: Gaudenzio Ferrari tra avanguardia e tradizione", in *Fermo Stella e Sperindio Cagnoli seguaci di Gaudenzio Ferrari. Una bottega d'arte nel Cinquecento padano*, ed. Giovanni Romano, exhibition catalogue, Museo Adriano Bernareggi, Bergamo, 29 September – 17 December 2006 (Milan, 2006), pp. 11–21; republished with notes under the title "Modelli di bottega: Gaudenzio Ferrari tra avanguardia e tradizione", in *Pratiche del disegno in Piemonte Liguria e Provenza (secoli XV e XVI)* (Turin, 2008), pp. 79–108.

[6] I quote from the "Premessa" to the entries by Giovanni Romano: *Gaudenzio Ferrari*, 1982, p. 58.

[7] Alessandro Baudi di Vesme, *Schede Vesme. L'arte in Piemonte*, vol. IV (Turin, 1982). On the events relating to the sources compiled by Vesme and the publication of the *Schede*, of crucial importance is the chapter on it in Alessandra Giovannini Luca, *Alessandro Baudi di Vesme e la scoperta dell'arte in Piemonte. Erudizione, musei e tutela in Italia tra Otto e Novecento* (Milan, 2015), pp. 199–223. Returning to the events in Vercelli during the Lanino exhibition of 1985, Romano stressed in relation to Volume IV that "unfortunately, the documents that Vesme had carefully kept together in a Vercelli file were separated and scattered in the *mare magnum* of a generic alphabetical order": Giovanni Romano, "Bernardino Lanino e il Cinquecento a Vercelli", in *Bernardino Lanino*, eds. Paola Astrua and Giovanni Romano, exhibition catalogue, Museo Borgogna, Vercelli, April–July 1985 (Milan, 1985), pp. 13–26 (note 1 on p. 25). The Vesme material had already been reprinted, in the case of the Giovenone brothers, by Luigi Mallé in *Spanzotti Defendente Giovenone. Nuovi studi* (Turin, 1971), pp. 209–28.

[8] The document is cited and partially transcribed by Giuseppe Colombo, *Documenti e notizie intorno agli artisti vercellesi* (Vercelli, 1883), pp. 303–05; the transcription is then revised in *Schede Vesme*, IV, 1982, pp. 1350–51 (the quotation is taken from p. 1351); the content reappears in *Gaudenzio Ferrari*, 1982, p. 190; see Gaglia 1982, p. 29.

[9] On Giuseppe, the crucial starting point remains the essay by Paola Astrua in the catalogue, together with the corresponding entries (Paola Astrua, "Giuseppe Giovenone il giovane e la sua bottega", in *Gaudenzio Ferrari*, 1982, pp. 183–86); Simone Baiocco, "Giovenone, Giuseppe il giovane", in *Dizionario biografico degli italiani*, vol. LVI (Rome, 2001), pp. 415–17; Patrizia Pivotto, "Fortuna e tramonto della cultura figurativa vercellese in territorio biellese: artisti, botteghe e committenti", in *Arti figurative a Biella e a Vercelli. Il Cinquecento*, ed. Vittorio Natale (Biella, 2003), pp. 113–28 (in particular pp. 119–21).

[10] Document of 18 October 1587: Colombo 1883, p. 325; *Schede Vesme*, IV, 1982, p. 1351; *Gaudenzio Ferrari*, 1982, p. 190.

[11] *Schede Vesme*, IV, 1982, p. 1351; *Gaudenzio Ferrari*, 1982, p. 190.

[12] The receipt of 5 December 1609, only reported by Colombo (1883, p. 327), is partially transcribed in *Schede Vesme*, IV, 1982, p. 1355; there is a reference to an inventory drafted on 25 August 1608 but it is not clear whether the drawings of interest to us were already indicated here: see Gaglia 1982, p. 29, who also refers to checks carried out on the archive conducted at the time of the exhibition by Anna Cerutti (*Gaudenzio Ferrari*, 1982, p. 33).

[13] *Schede Vesme*, IV, 1982, p. 1355.

[14] He is confirmed as having held this role between February 1634 and December 1637: *Schede Vesme*, IV, 1982, p. 1407.

[15] *Schede Vesme*, IV, 1982, pp. 1406–07.

[16] This will was, understandably, widely cited: Colombo 1883, p. 248–49; *Schede Vesme*, IV, 1982, p. 1407; Gaglia 1982, pp. 28–29; *Gaudenzio Ferrari*, 1982, p. 170 (with revision of the original by Cristina Mossetti); Piera Giovanna Tordella, "Il collezionismo dei disegni a Torino e in Piemonte da Emanuele Filiberto all'età napoleonica", in "*. . .quei leggierissimi tocchi di penna o matita. . ." Le collezioni di disegni in Piemonte*, ed. Gianni Carlo Sciolla (Milan, 1996), pp. 23–24 (who in turn quotes the original).

[17] *Schede Vesme*, IV, 1982, p. 1398; Gaglia 1982, p. 29; *Bernardino Lanino*, 1985, p. 33; document also summarised in *Bernardino Lanino e il Cinquecento a Vercelli*, ed. Giovanni Romano (Turin, 1986), p. 231.

[18] *Schede Vesme*, IV, 1982, p. 1408; *Gaudenzio Ferrari*, 1982, p. 170.

[19] Also in relation to Laura, the family tree drafted by Alessandro Baudi di Vesme remains valuable (*Schede Vesme*, IV, 1982, pp. 1436–37): she was baptised on 13 November 1548 (ibid., p. 1392); still unmarried as of 1576, at the time of the drafting of her father's will (ibid., p. 1399), on 9 December 1588 she is referred to as the widow of Giorgio Soleri (ibid., p. 1403); she died on 6 June 1596 (ibid., p. 1405).

[20] *Gaudenzio Ferrari*, 1982, entry 53 by G. Romano, pp. 256–57 (quotation on p. 257). On the proposal in favour of Soleri: *Tesori dal Marchesato Paleologo*, eds. Bruno Ciliento and Alessandra Guerrini, exhibition catalogue, Fondazione Ferrero, Alba, 19 October – 8 December 2003 (Alba-Savigliano, 2003), entry 15 by Carlenrica Spantigati, pp. 90–93; *"Il nostro pittore fiamengo". Giovanni Caracca alla corte dei Savoia (1568-1607)*, eds. Paola Astrua, Anna Maria Bava and Carla Enrica Spantigati, exhibition catalogue, Galleria Sabauda, Turin, 21 September 2005 – 8 January 2006 (Turin, 2005), entry 5 by Clelia Arnaldi di Balme, pp. 78–79. For Soleri, we may begin again from the documents cited in *Schede Vesme*, III, 1968, pp. 993–95; Giovanni Romano, "Artisti alla corte di Carlo Emanuele I: la costruzione di una nuova tradizione figurativa", in *Le collezioni di Carlo Emanuele I di Savoia*, ed. Giovanni Romano (Turin, 1995), pp. 13–62 (in particular pp. 36–37); Carlo Prosperi, *Artisti e maestranze in Monferrato nei secoli XVI e XVII. Ricerche d'archivio* (Acqui Terme, 2019).

[21] Giuseppe Colombo, *Vita ed opere di Gaudenzio Ferrari pittore con documenti inediti* (Rome-Turin-Florence, 1881), p. 242; the information had been mentioned also by father Della Valle: see Guglielmo Della Valle, *Notizie degli artefici piemontesi*, ed. Gianni Carlo Sciolla (Turin, 1990), p. 52. See also Gaglia 1982, p. 30; *Il Rinascimento di Gaudenzio Ferrari*, eds. Giovanni Agosti and Jacopo Stoppa, exhibition catalogue, Varallo, Vercelli, Novara, 24 March – 1 July 2018 (Milan, 2018), entry 64 by G. Renzi, p. 410. The figure of Soleri was also referenced in this context as regards the *Album Abrate*, the events of which should be read more and more in parallel to those of the Albertina group: Antonella Chiodo, "Riscoprendo l'*Album Abrate*. Dalla formazione alla dispersione di un album di disegni del Seicento", in *Libri e album di disegni 1550-1800. Nuove prospettive metodologiche e di esegesi storico-critica*, conference proceedings, Rome, Koninklijk Nederlands Instituut and Accademia di Belle Arti, 30 May – 1 June 2018, ed. Vita Segreto (Rome, 2018), pp. 139–48.

[22] Giuseppe Roberti, "Il carteggio erudito fra Giuseppe Vernazza e Giovanni Antonio Ranza", in *Atti della Reale Accademia delle Scienze di Torino*, vol. XXIX, 1894, pp. 810–32, note on p. 819; *Schede Vesme*, IV, 1982, p. 1408.

[23] *Bernardino Lanino*, 1985, entry 16 by C. Mossetti, pp. 78–80.

[24] Anna Maria Bava, "La collezione di pittura e i grandi progetti decorativi", in *Le collezioni*, 1995, pp. 211–64 (in particular pp. 223, 237).

[25] Massimo Romeri, "Gaudenzio Ferrari nell'età di Federico Borromeo e di Carlo Emanuele I: Milano e Torino", in *Scambi artistici tra Torino e Milano. 1580–1714*, conference proceedings, Turin, 28–29 May 2015 (Milan, 2016), pp. 183–97 (in particular pp. 185–86).

[26] *Il Rinascimento*, 2018, entry 65 by G. Renzi, pp. 415–21 (in particular p. 415, with photograph on p. 418). Reference is made here to the aforementioned quotation by Ranza, but with a citation of the *Lamentation* that must be considered only indirect.

[27] This specific information was recovered by Tordella 1996, pp. 17–18.

[28] *Gaudenzio Ferrari*, 1982, entry 25 by G. Galante Garrone, pp. 159–61; *Bernardino Lanino*, 1985, entry 13 by G. Galante Garrone, pp. 68–70; Tordella 1996, pp. 18–19.

[29] In particular with the early quotations in the writings of Federico Zuccari: Giovanni Agosti, *Disegni del Rinascimento in Valpadana*, exhibition catalogue (Florence, 2001), p. 6; Giovanni Agosti, "Gaudenzio, per adesso", in *Il Rinascimento*, 2018, note 27.

[30] Gelsomina Spione, "La tutela delle collezioni", in *Le collezioni*, 1995, pp. 333–47 (in particular pp. 338–41). See also Bava 1995, pp. 244–45.

[31] *Schede Vesme*, III, 1968, p. 751.

[32] *Schede Vesme*, III, 1968, pp. 974–75; Spione 1995, p. 340; Tordella 1996, pp. 16–17.

[33] Simone Amerigo, "Gaudenzio Ferrari nell'età di Federico Borromeo e di Carlo Emanuele I: Varallo, Novara e Vercelli", in *Scambi artistici*, 2016, pp. 199–207 (in particular p. 203): it very clearly refutes the idea that the drawings brought by Secondiano are those of "the group of drawings today at the Albertina, documented as still being in Vercelli in 1636", making reference to the date of the will of Pietro Antonio Lanino referred to above. But the match between that group and what we see today remains, unfortunately, entirely to be demonstrated.

[34] I refer back to the transcription of the inventory compiled by Anna Maria Bava in *Le collezioni*, 1995, pp. 53–62 (I quote from p. 60).

[35] Tordella 1996, p. 24; Agosti 2001, pp. 4–6.

[36] *Gaudenzio Ferrari*, 1982, entry 5 by M. di Macco, pp. 80–83; for the Giovenone drawings, see also Agosti 2001, pp. 273–76.

[37] The Dal Pozzo collection was illustrated by Mauro Natale on the occasion of the conference on Lanino held in Vercelli in 1985; for a summary on the drawings, see Tordella 1996, p. 26.

[38] Michela di Macco, "Quadreria di palazzo e pittori di corte. Le scelte ducali dal 1630 al 1684", in *Figure del Barocco in Piemonte. La corte, la città, i cantieri, le province*, ed. Giovanni Romano (Turin, 1988), p. 71. The identification of the cartoons in the 1682 inventory was the focus of the author's speech at the aforementioned 1985 conference on Lanino. The transcription of the part of the inventory corresponding to the drawings is in Tordella 1996, pp. 33–35. See also Michela di Macco, "'Critica occhiuta': la cultura figurativa *(1630-1678)*", in *Storia di Torino*, IV, *La città fra crisi e ripresa (1630-1730)*, ed. Giuseppe Ricuperati (Turin, 2002), pp. 377–430 (in particular pp. 417–19).

[39] Romano 1985, p. 22 and note 33 on p. 26; *Il Rinascimento*, 2018, entry 63 by S. Bruzzese, pp. 408–09.

[40] Gaspare De Gregory, *Istoria della vercellese letteratura ed arti* (Turin, 1819–24, part II, 1820), p. 238; Tordella 1996, p. 24.

[41] Enrica Pagella and Lucia Piovano, "Bernardino Lanino tra Manierismo e Controriforma", in *Bernardino Lanino e il Cinquecento a Vercelli*, ed. Giovanni Romano (Turin, 1986), pp. 163–217 (in particular pp. 194–201). Very useful in this regard are the sections by Antonella Chiodo in "La civiltà figurativa nel Seicento e nel Settecento", eds. Massimiliano Caldera and Gelsomina Spione, in *Storia di Vercelli in età moderna e contemporanea*, ed. Edoardo Tortarolo, vol. I (Turin, 2011), pp. 454–65.

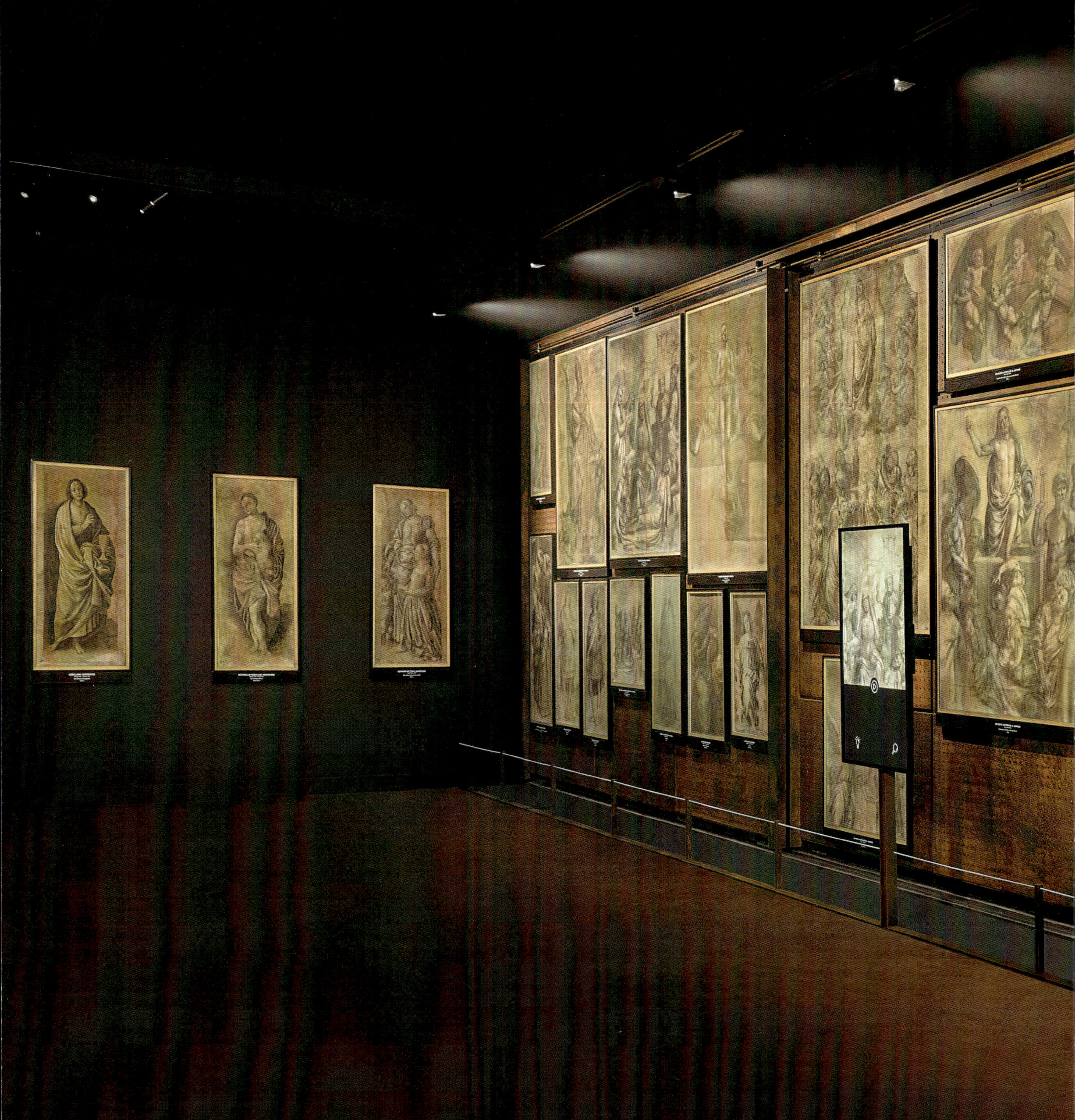

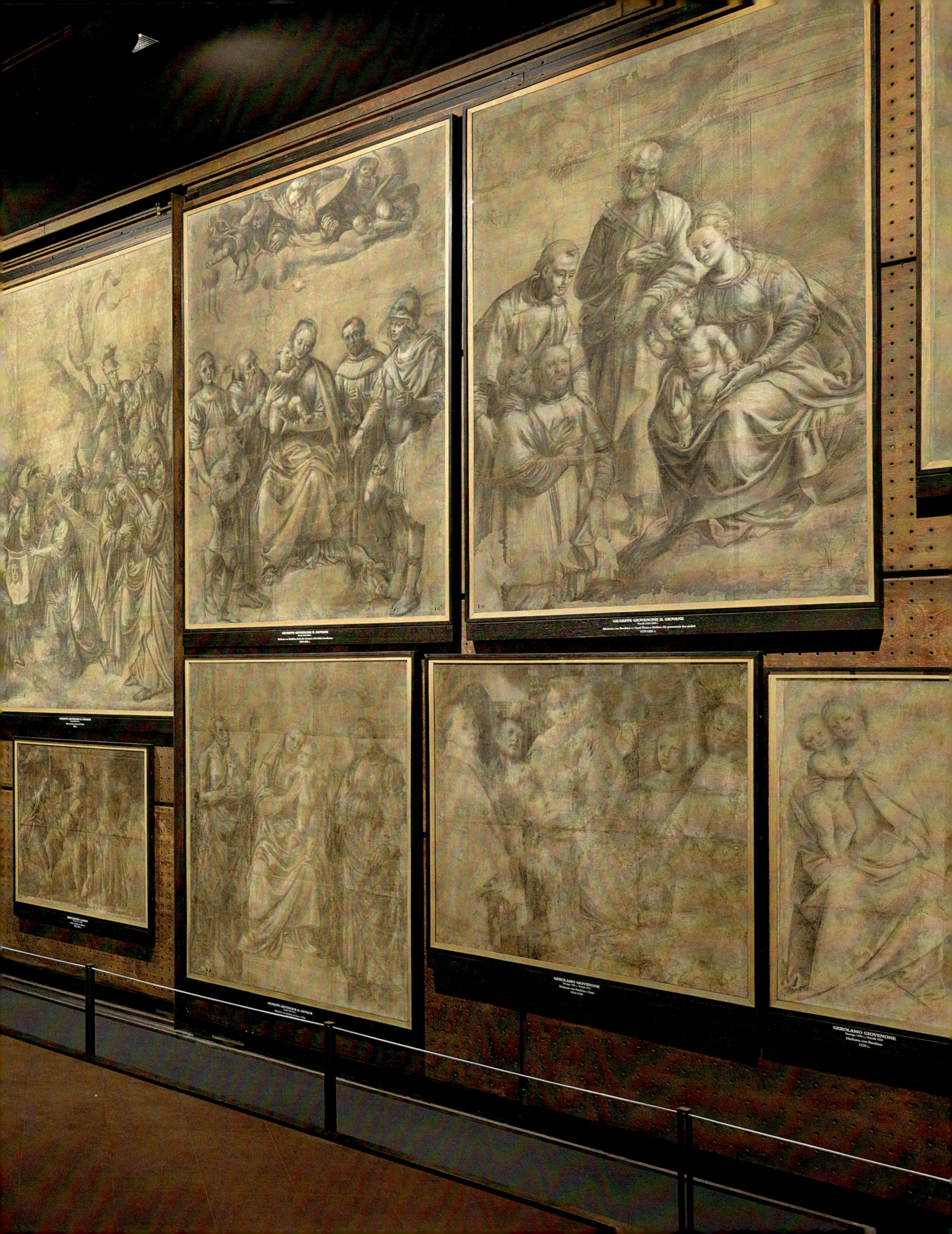
GIUSEPPE GIOVENONE IL GIOVANE
GEROLAMO GIOVENONE
GEROLAMO GIOVENONE
Madonna con Bambino
1530 c.

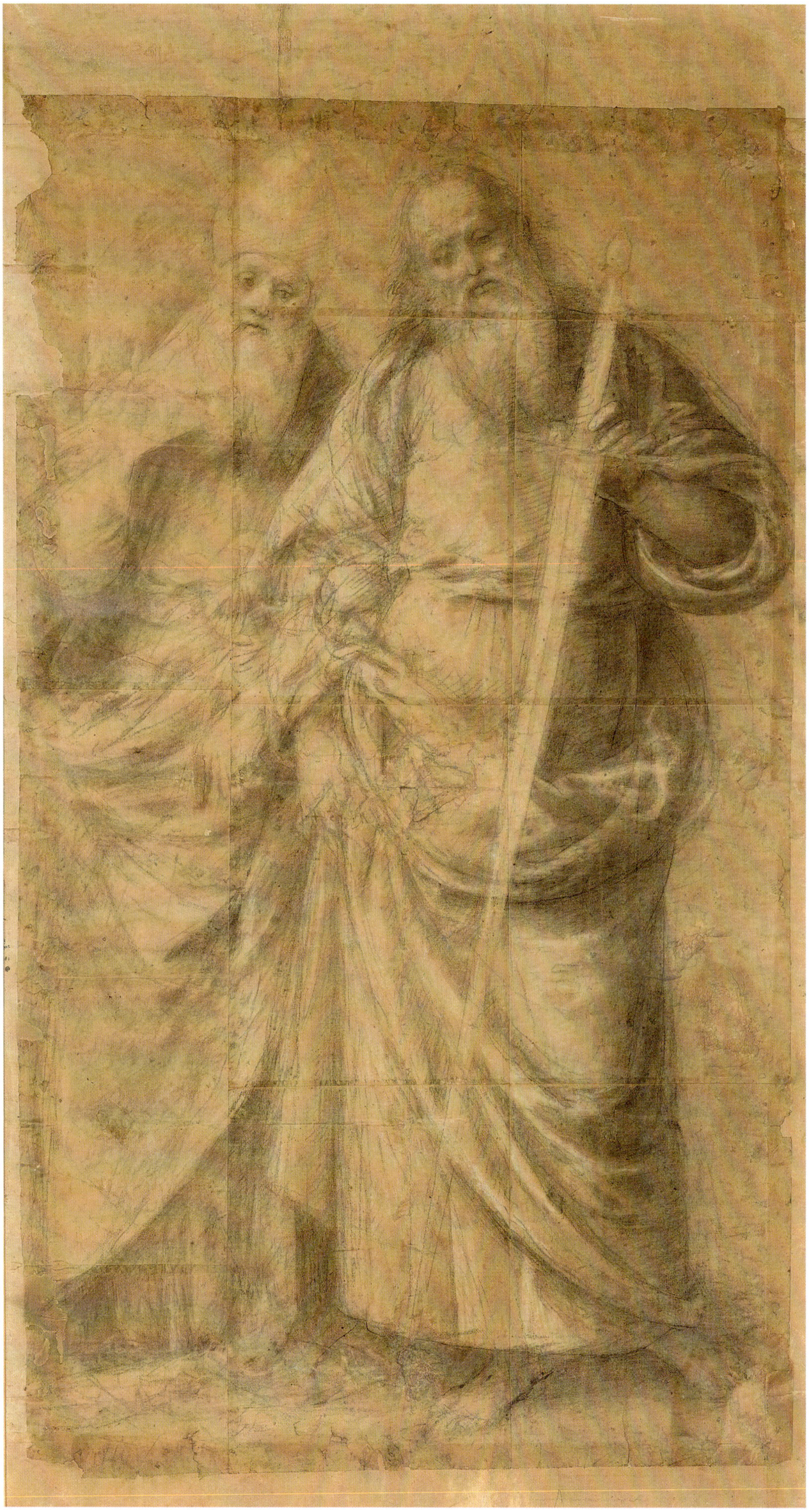

1

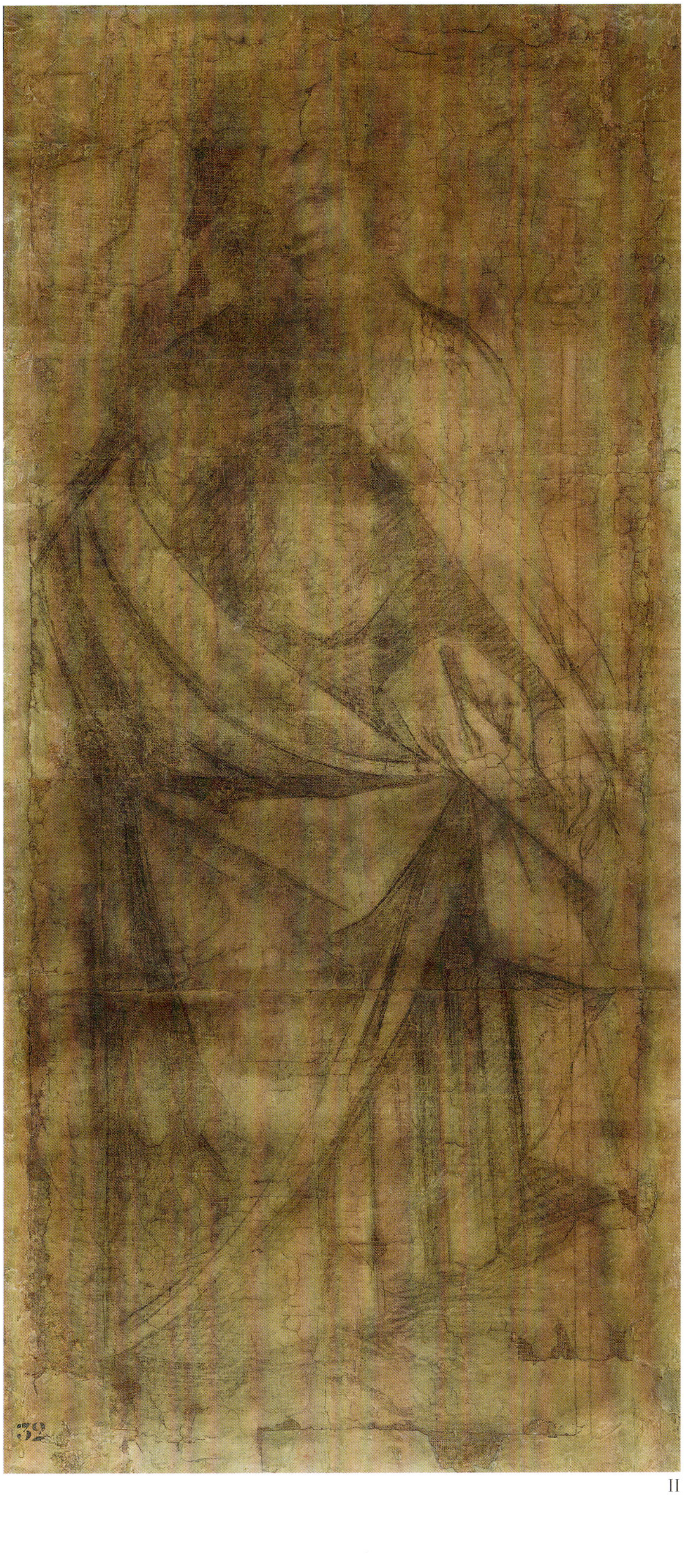

II

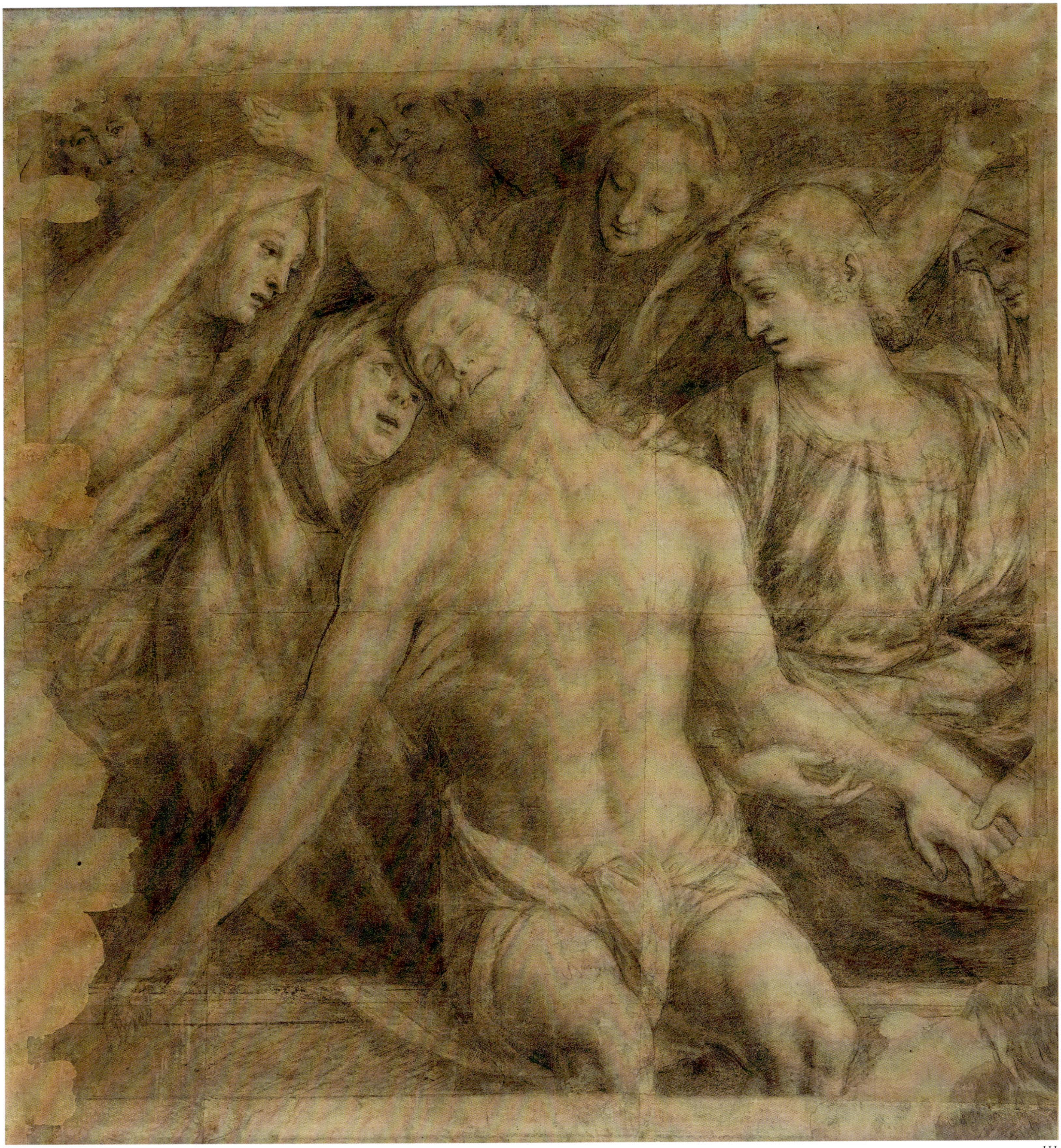

III

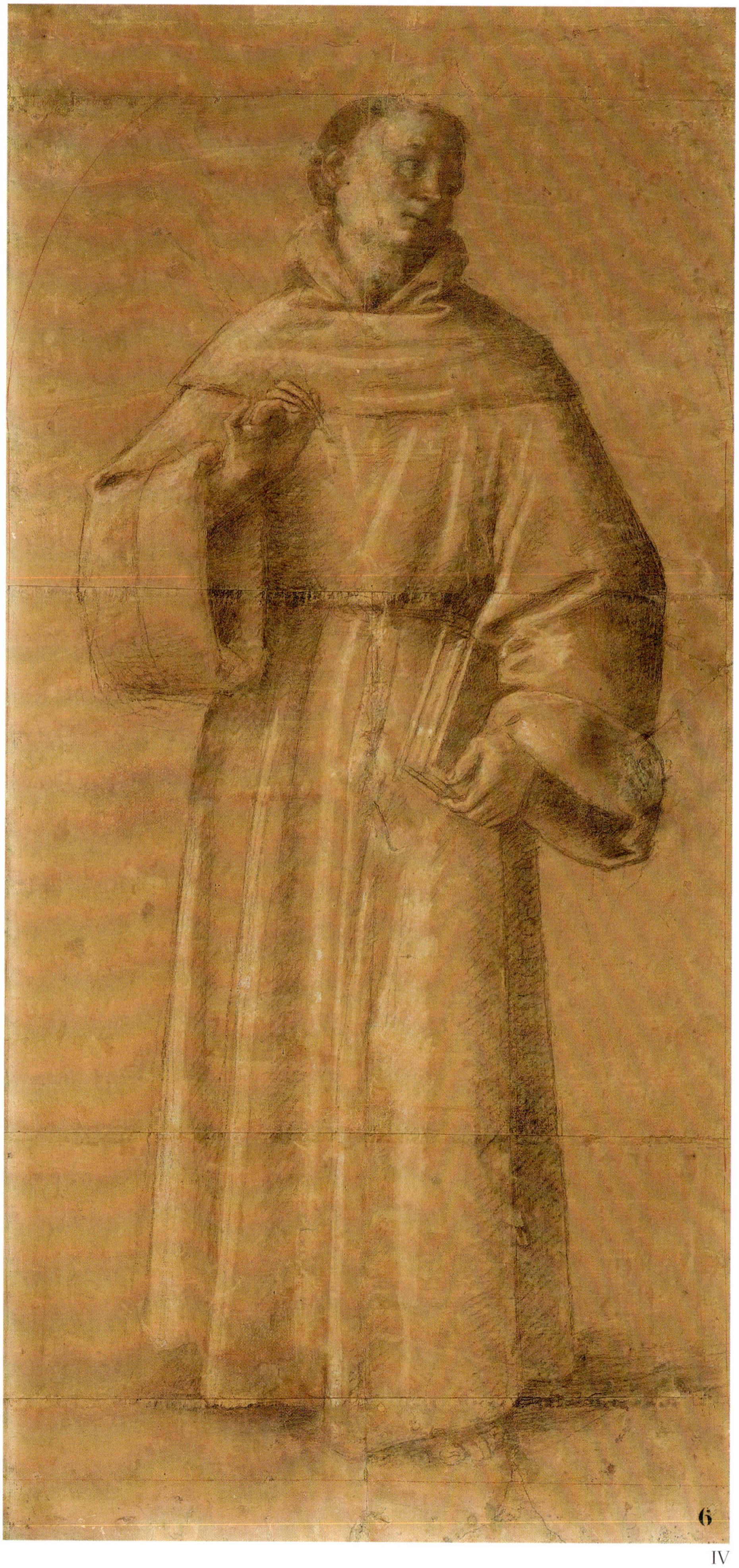

IV

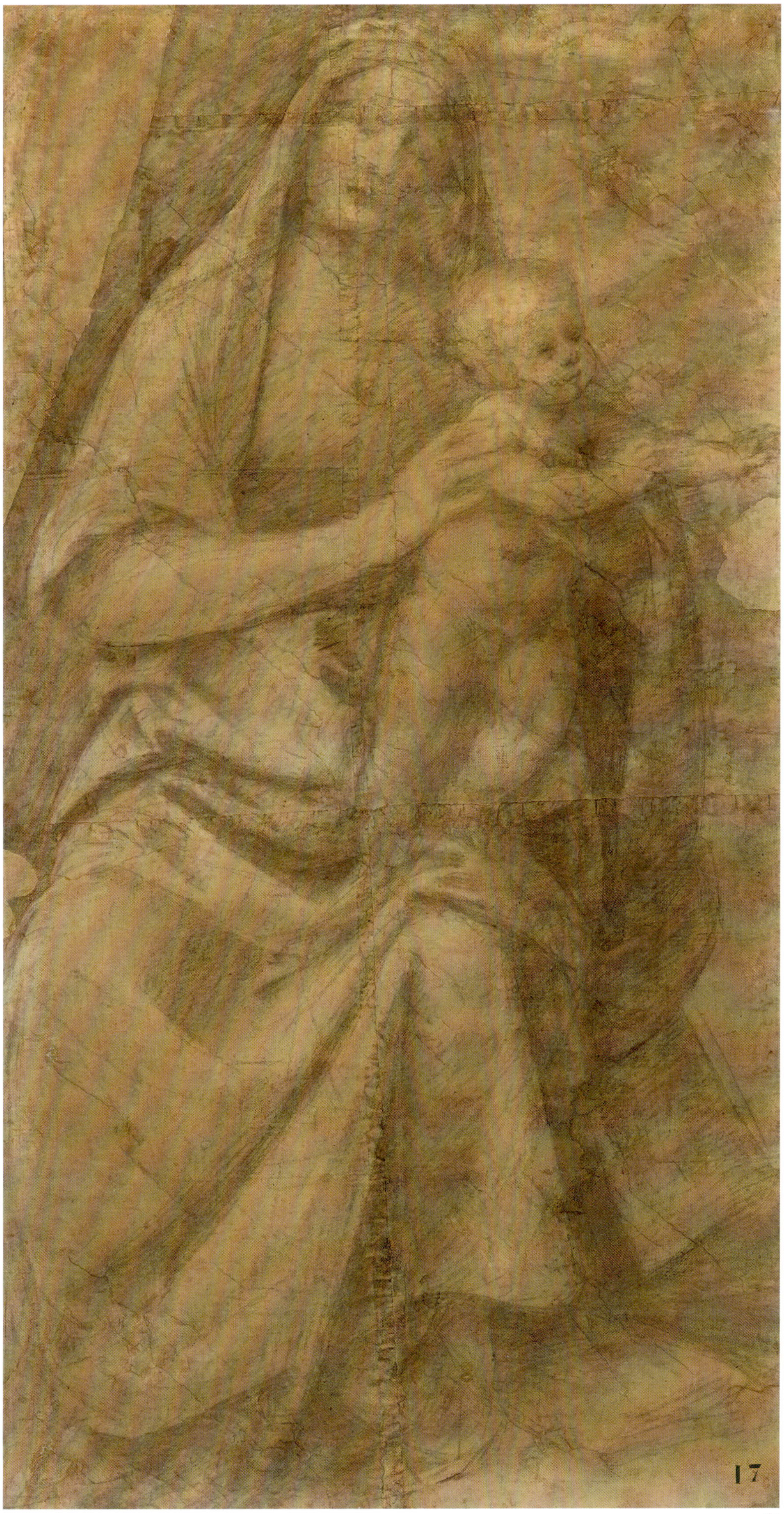

V

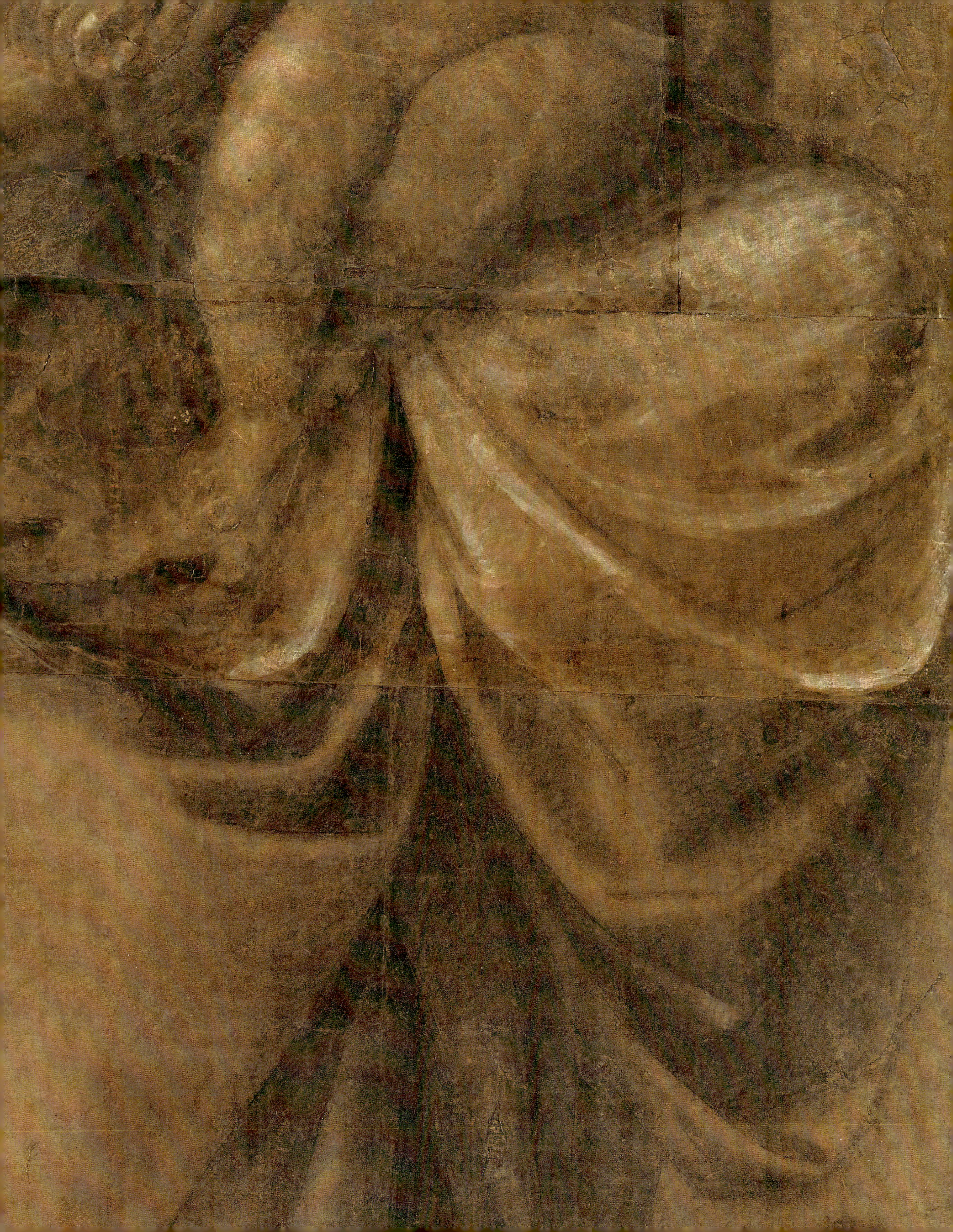

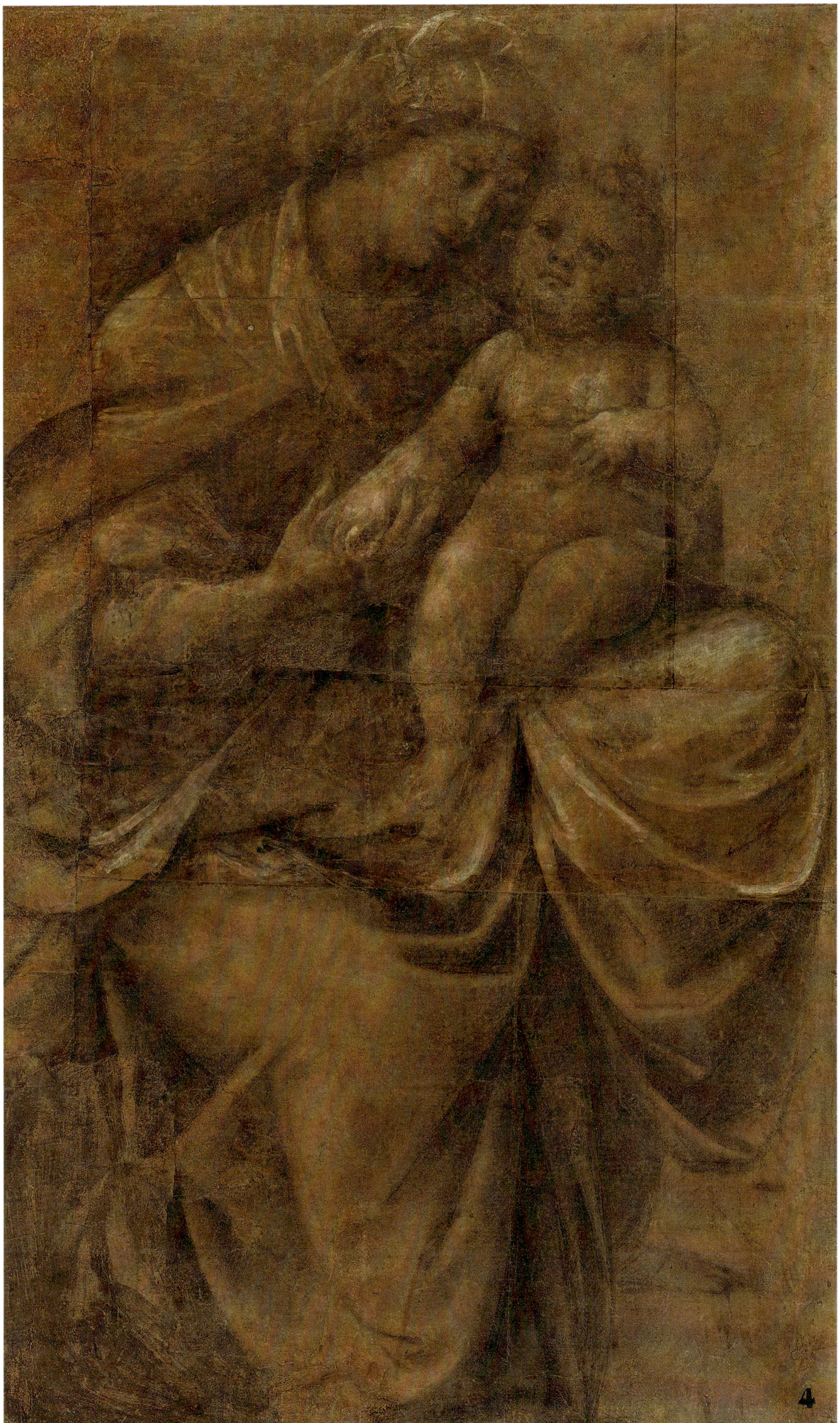

VI

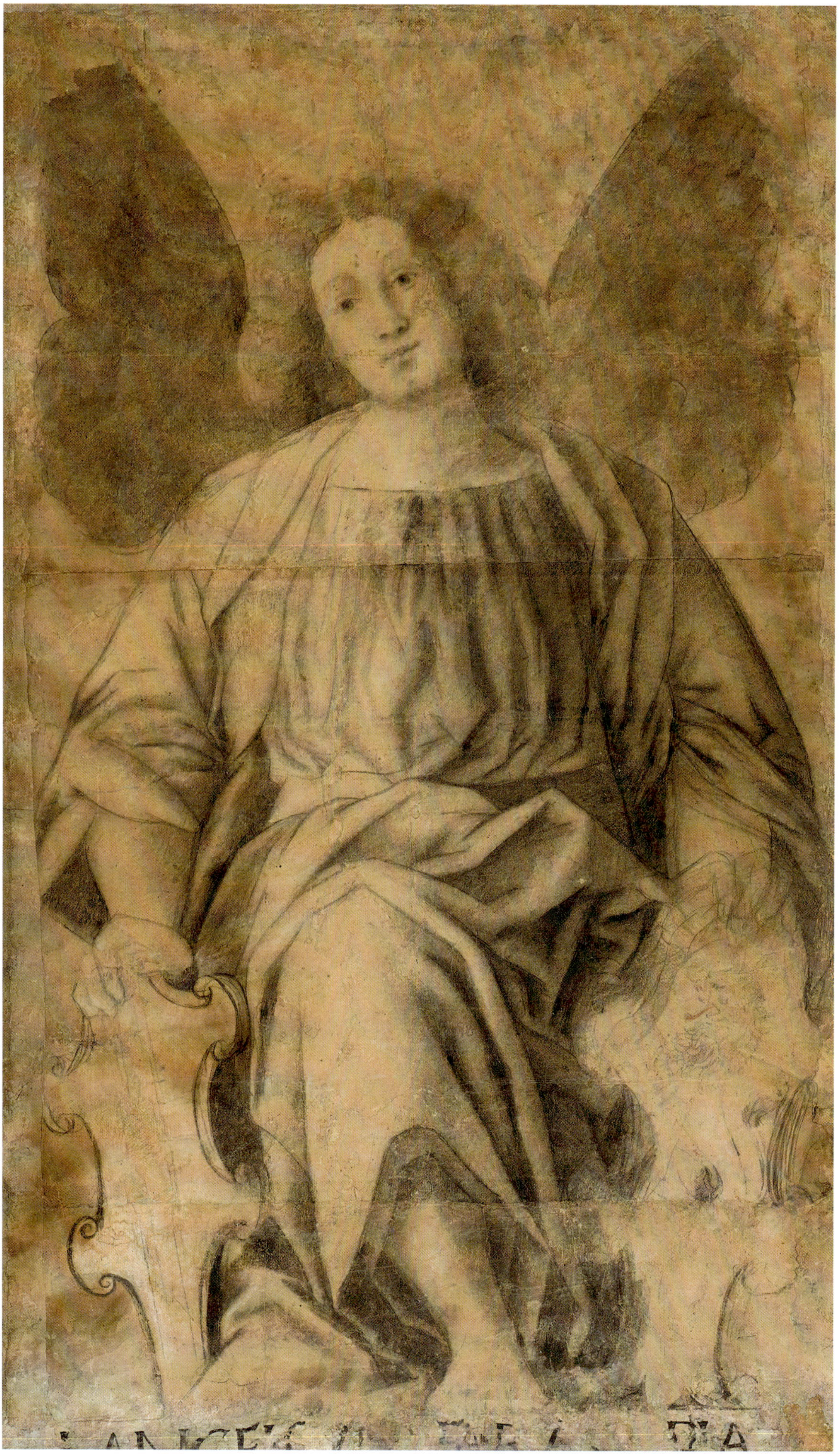

VII

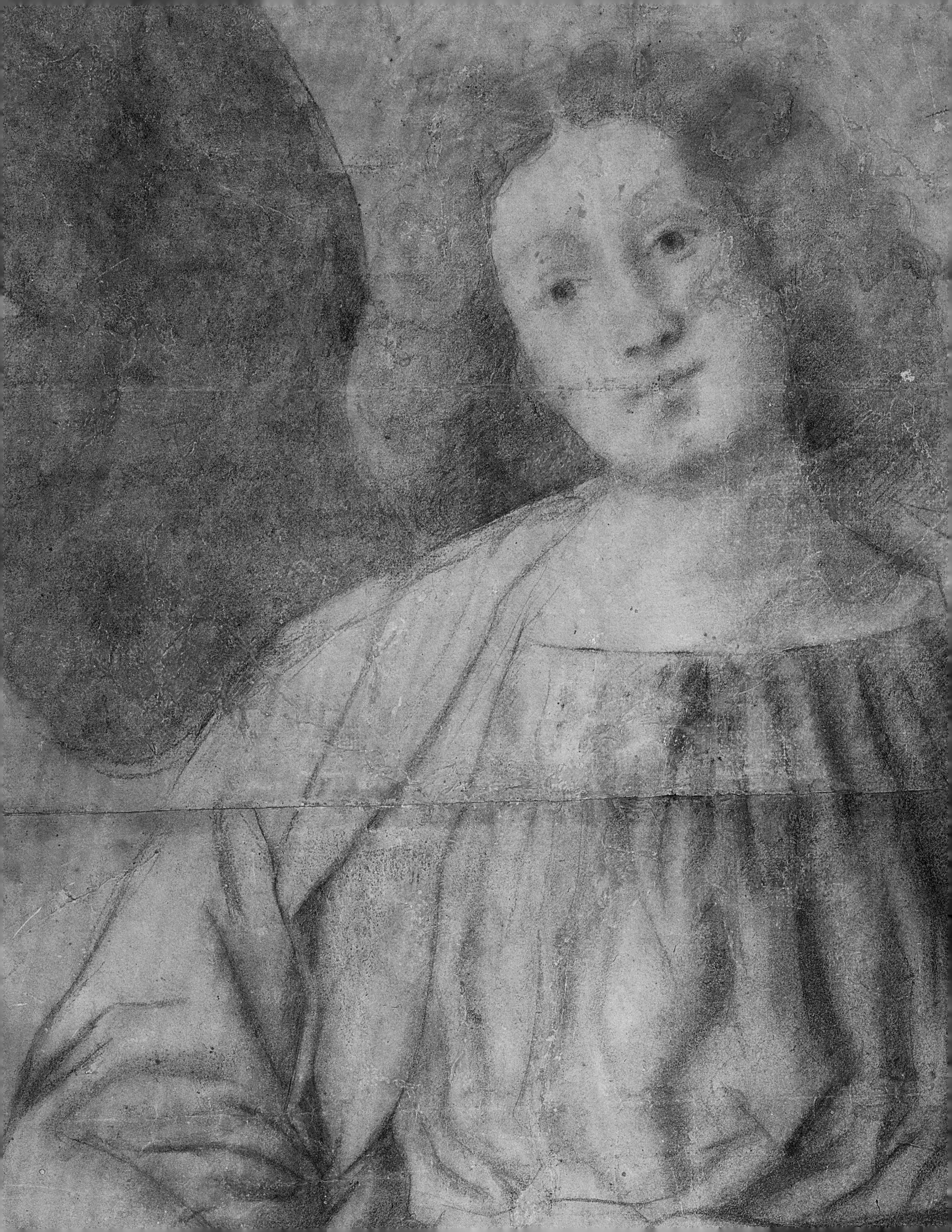

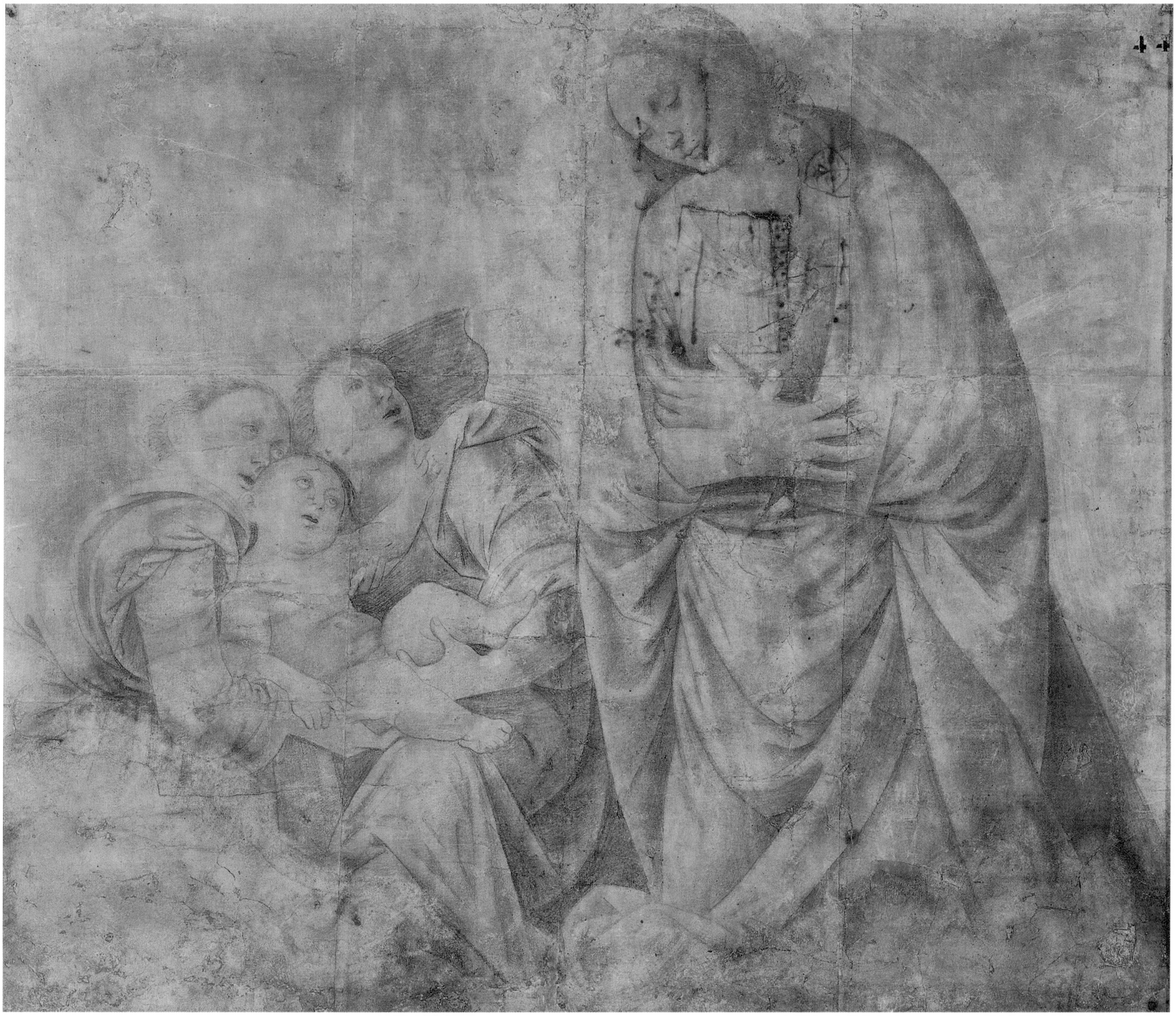

VIII

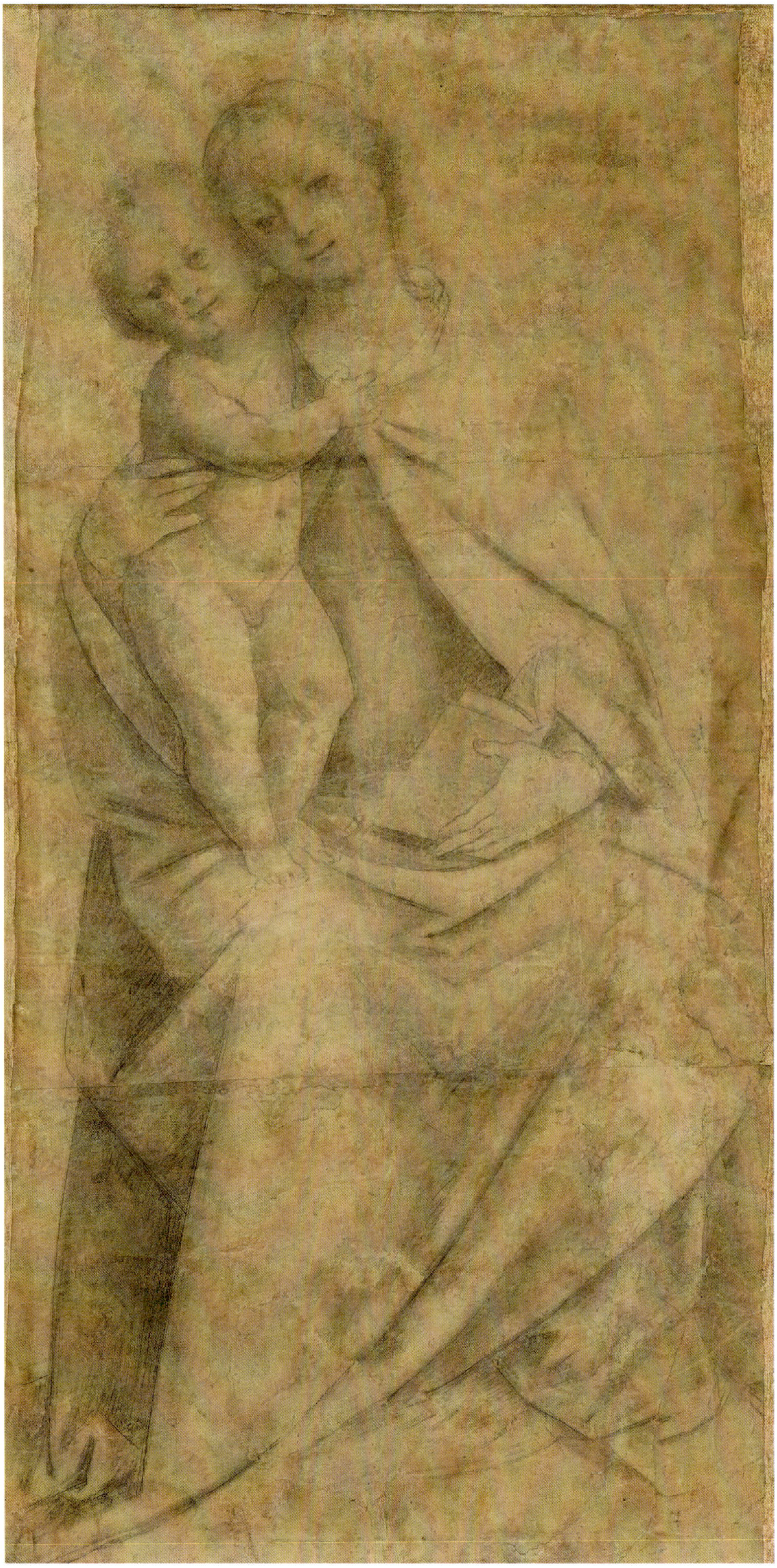

IX

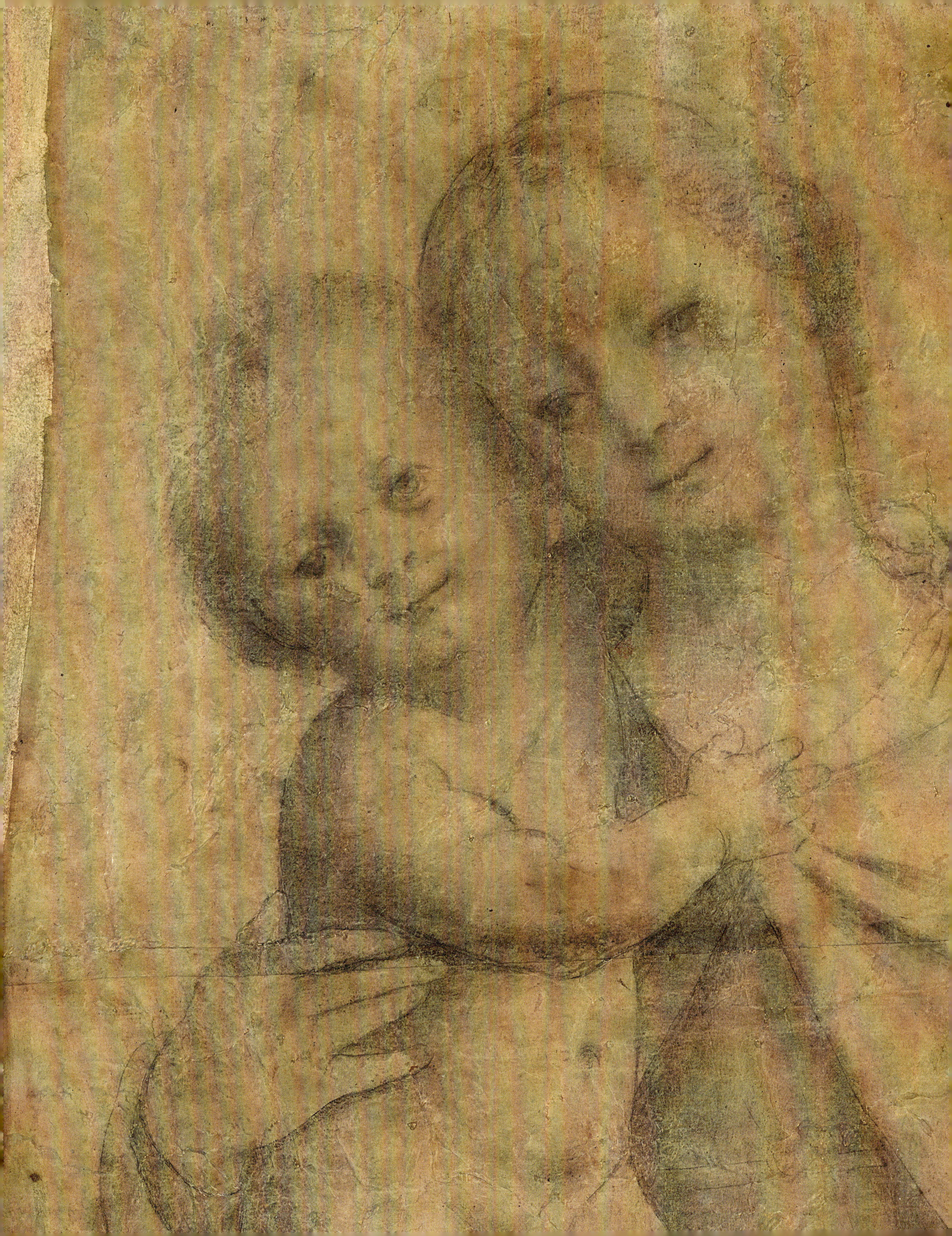

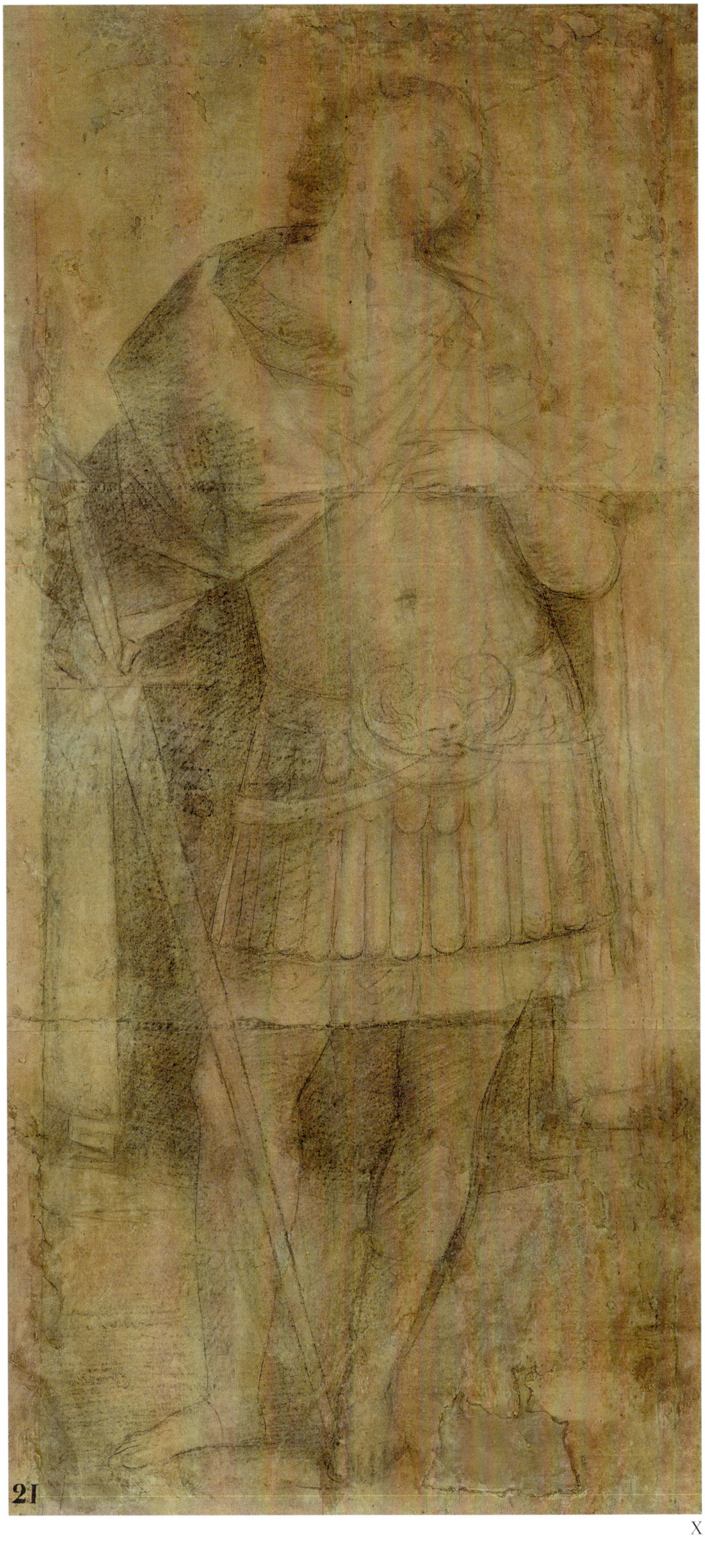

X

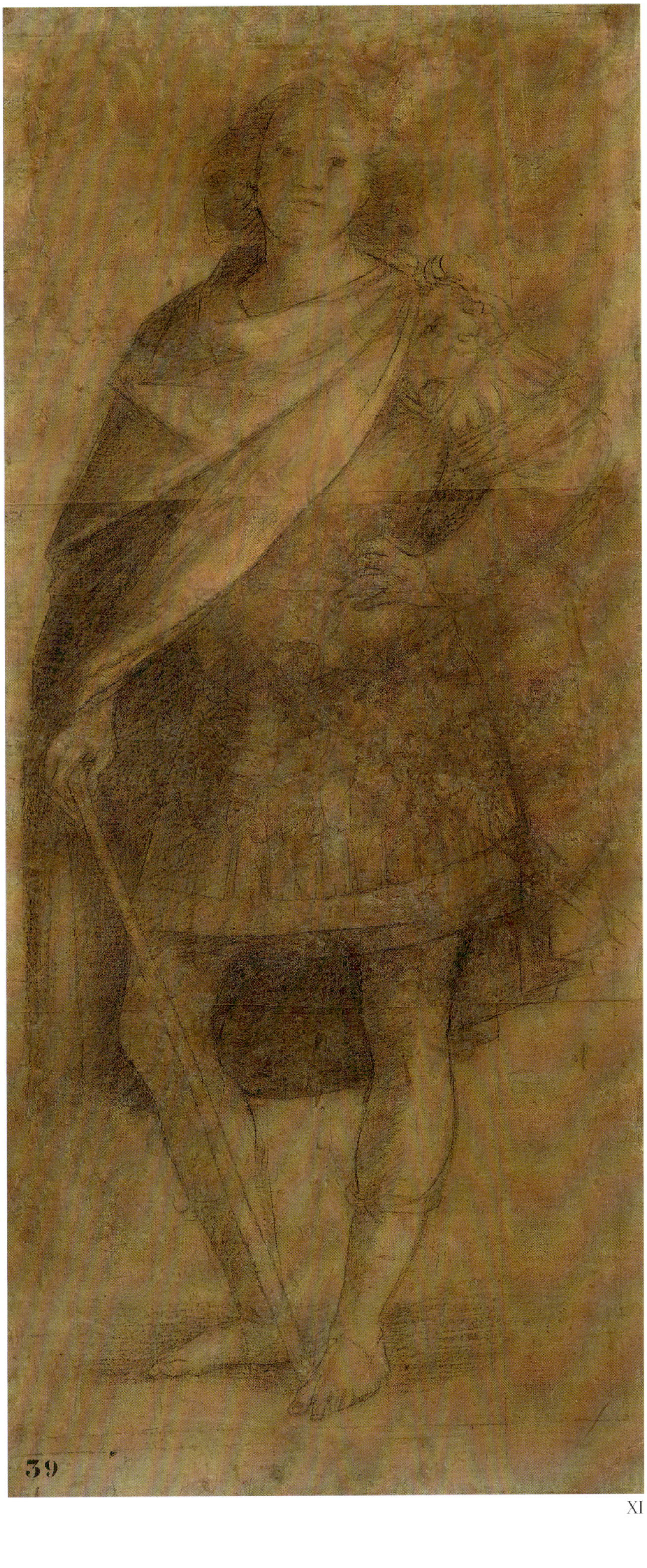

XI

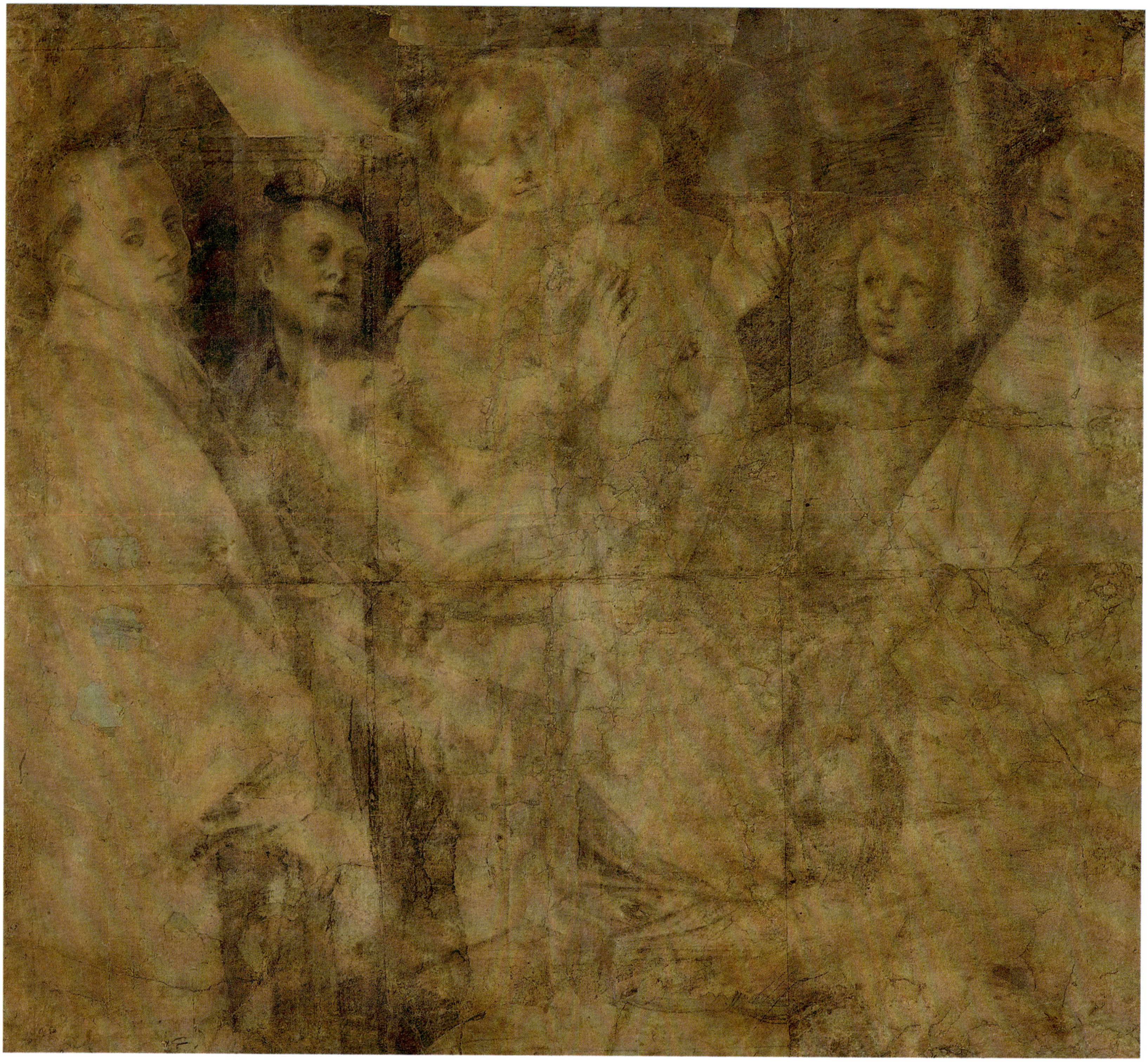

XII

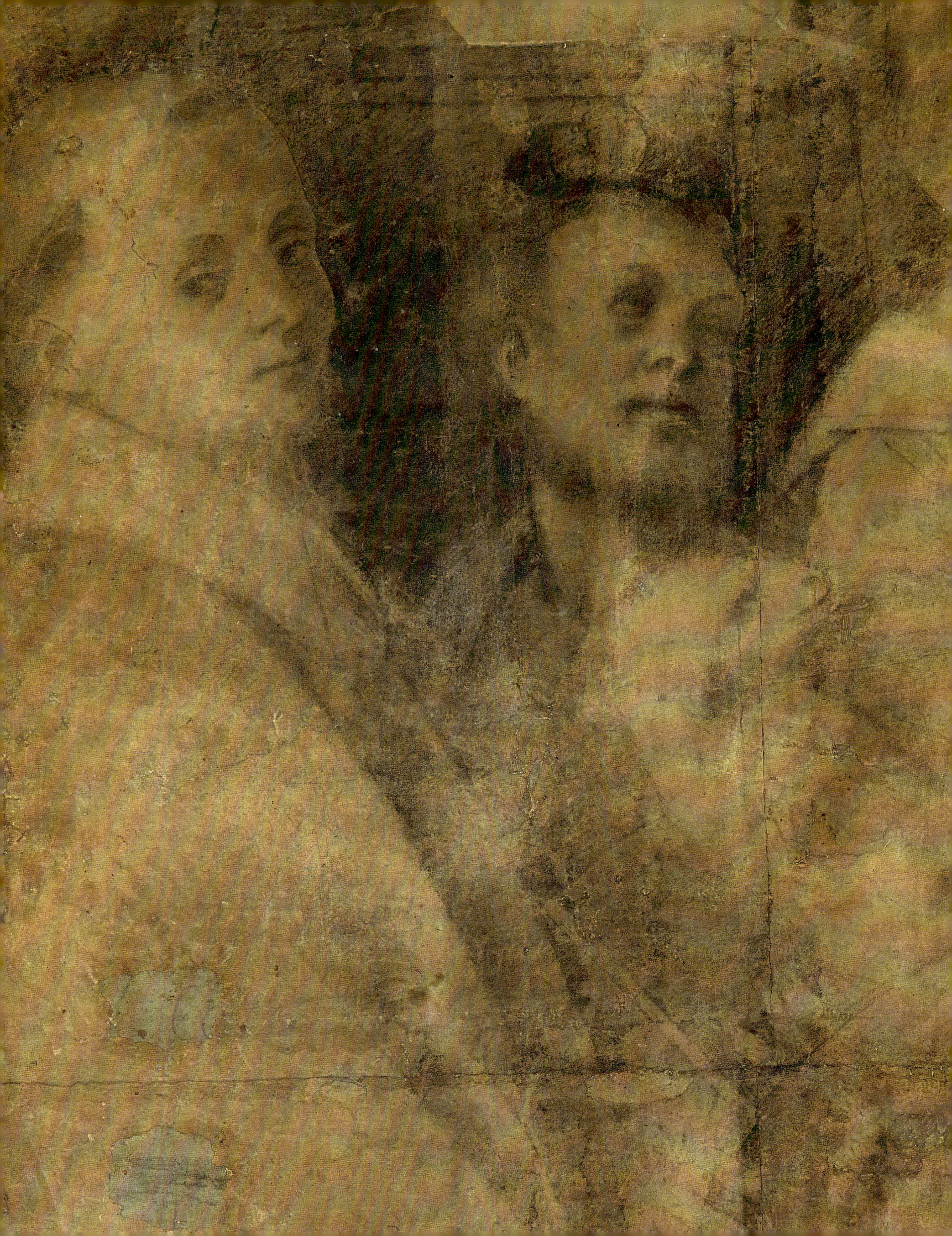

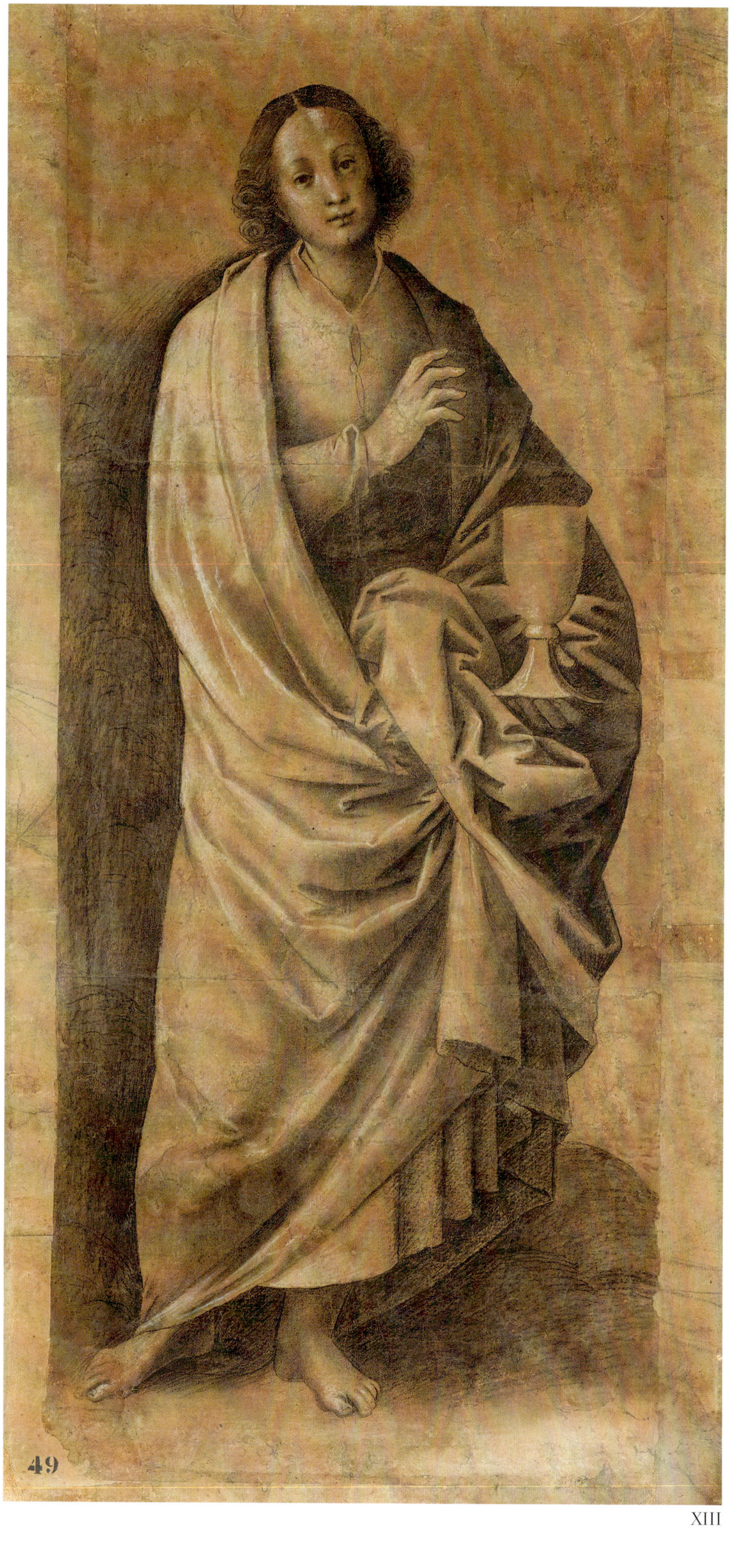

XIII

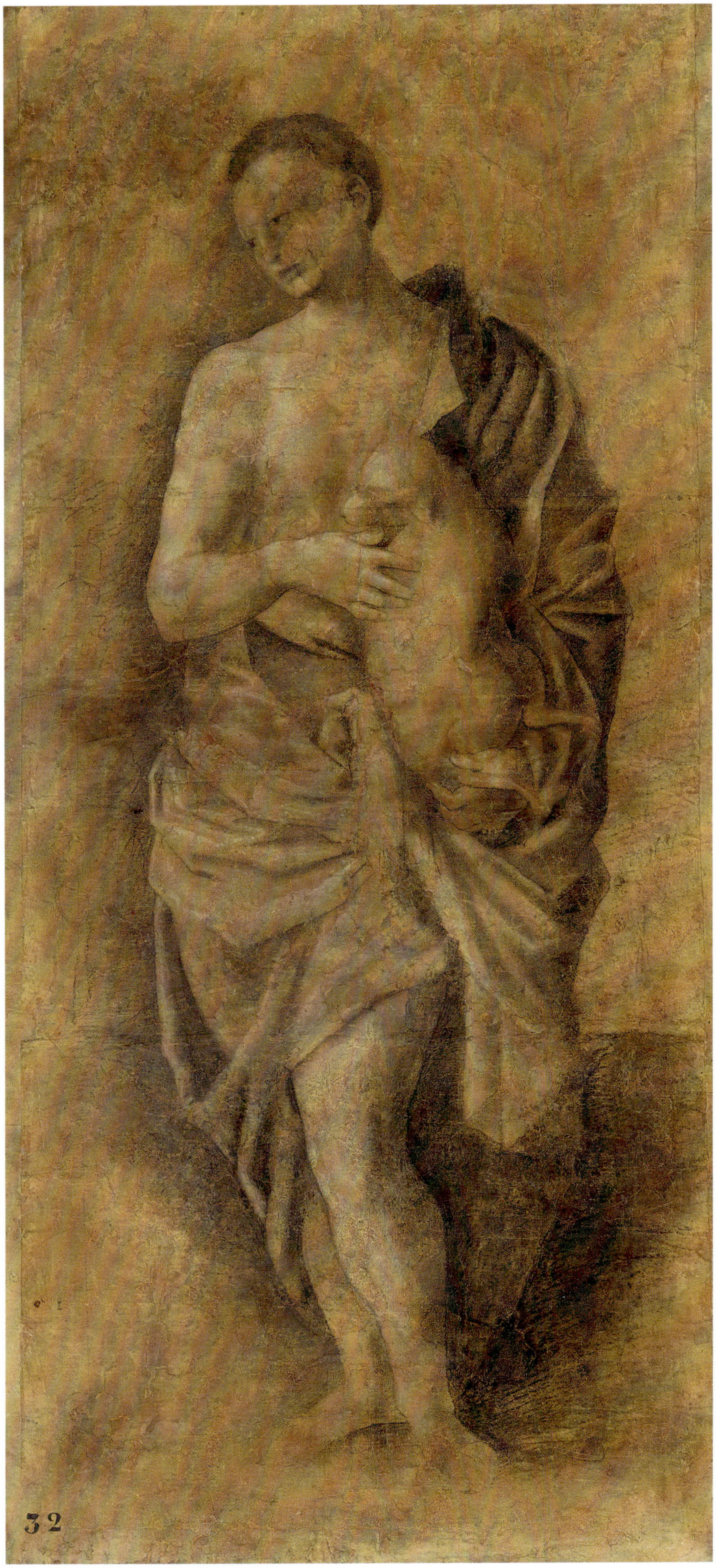

XIV

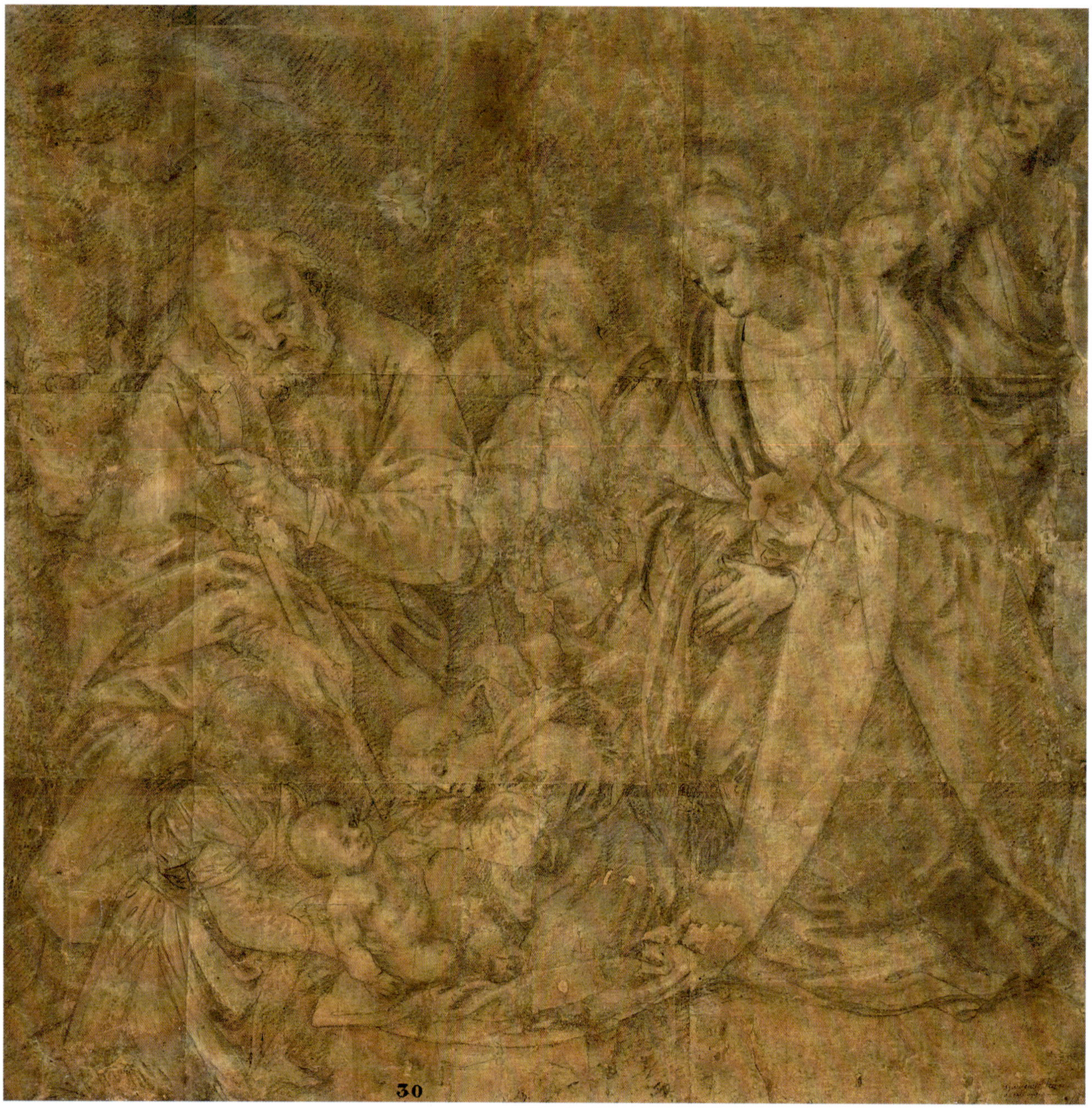

XV

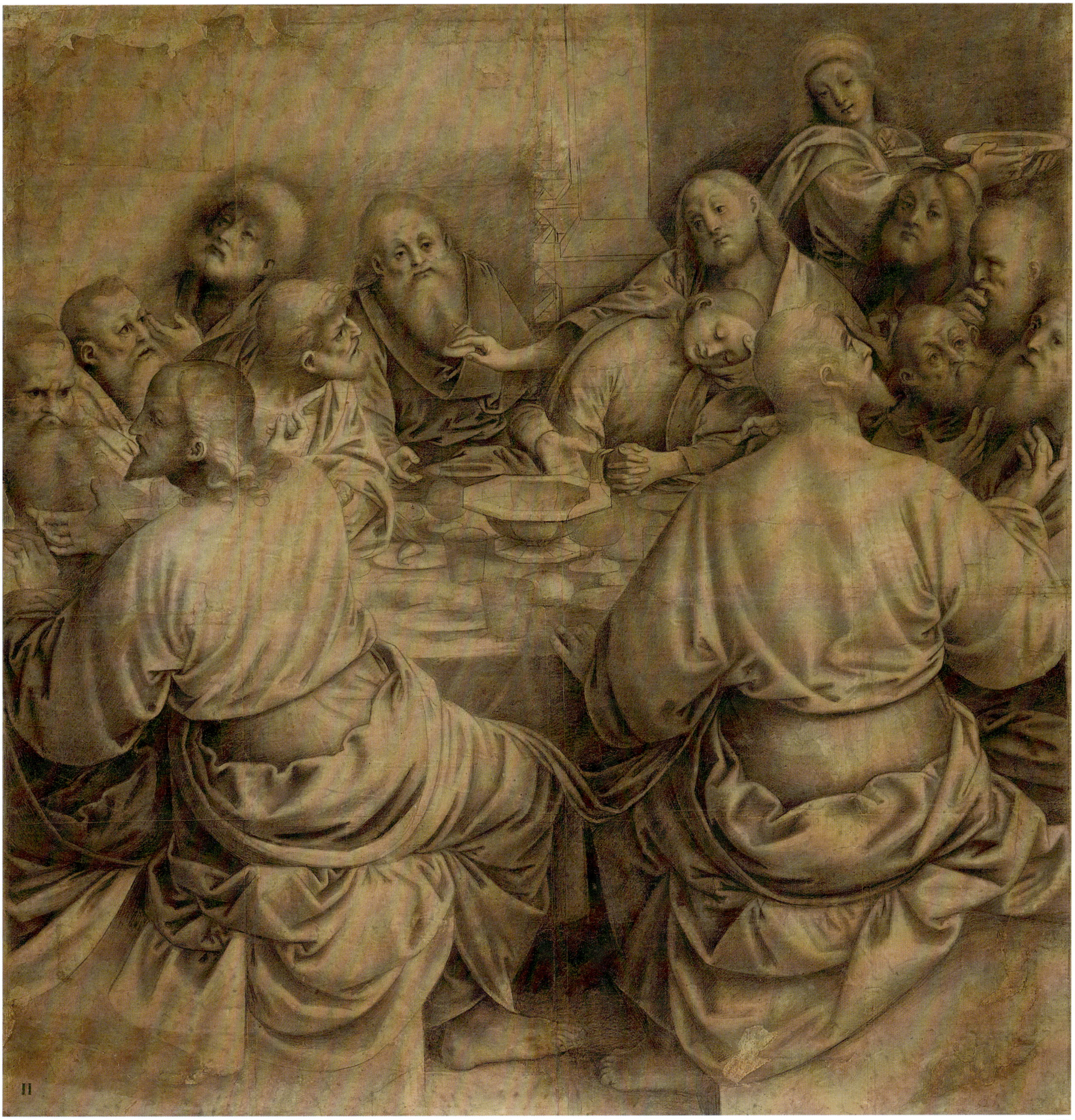

XVI

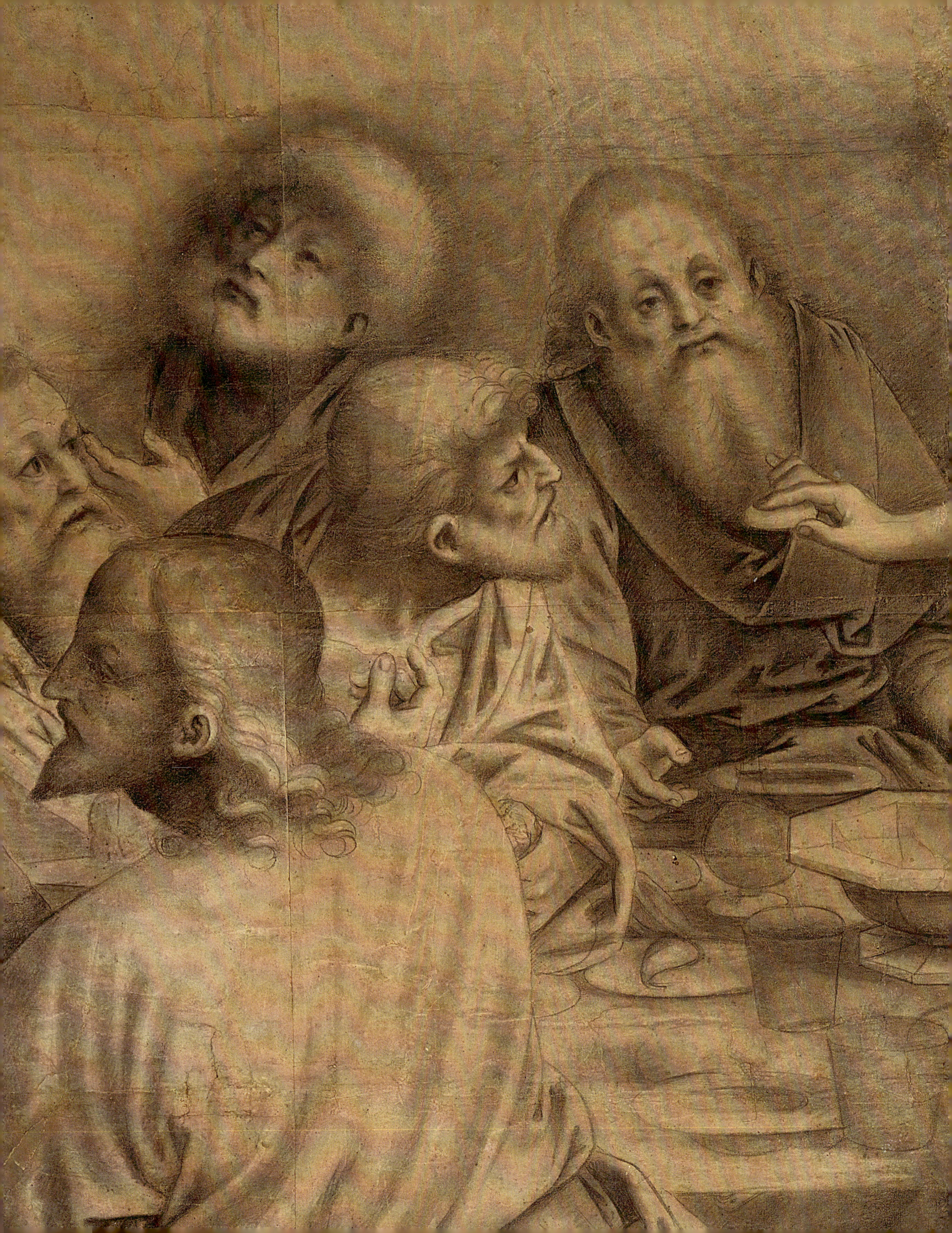

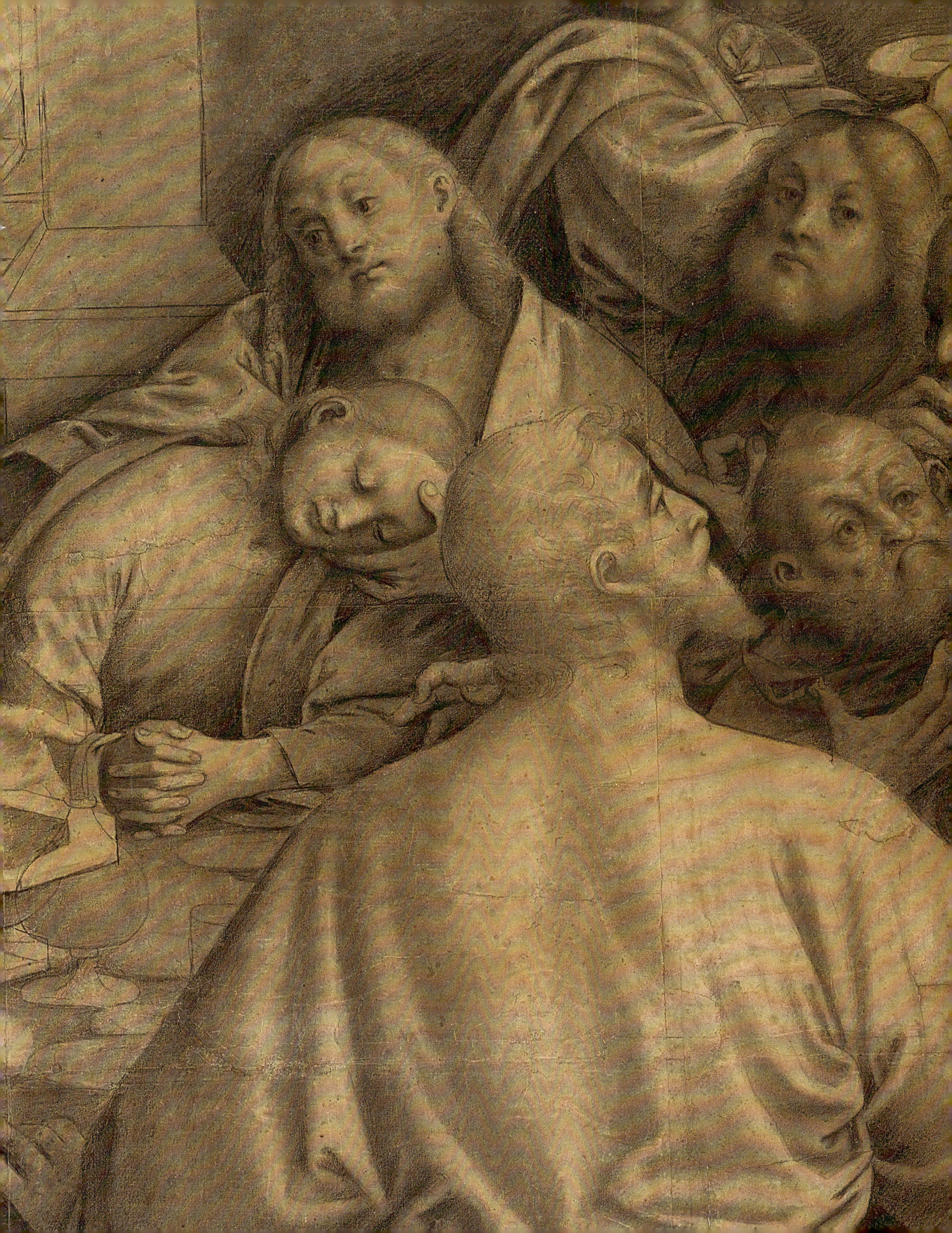

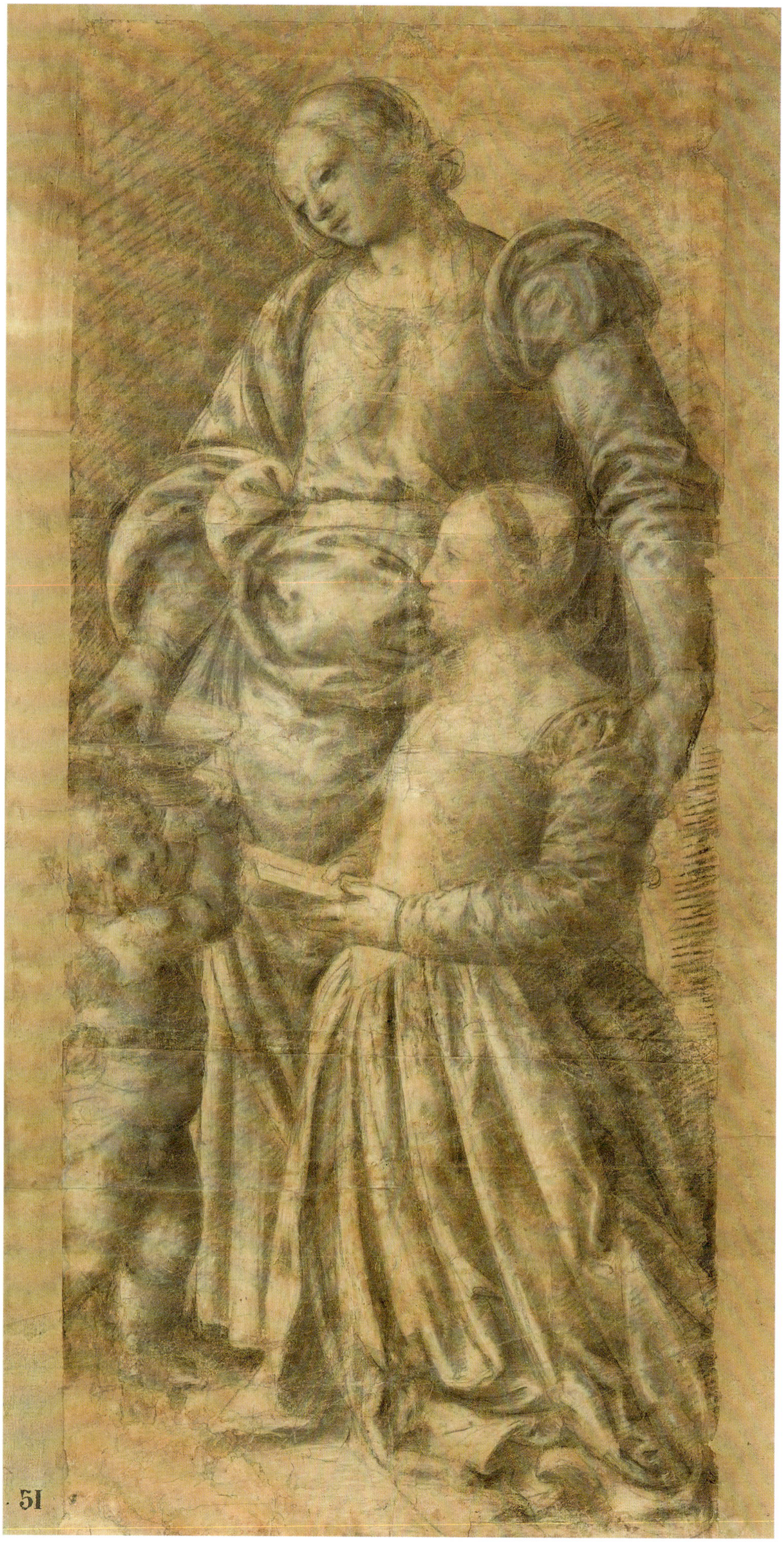

XVII

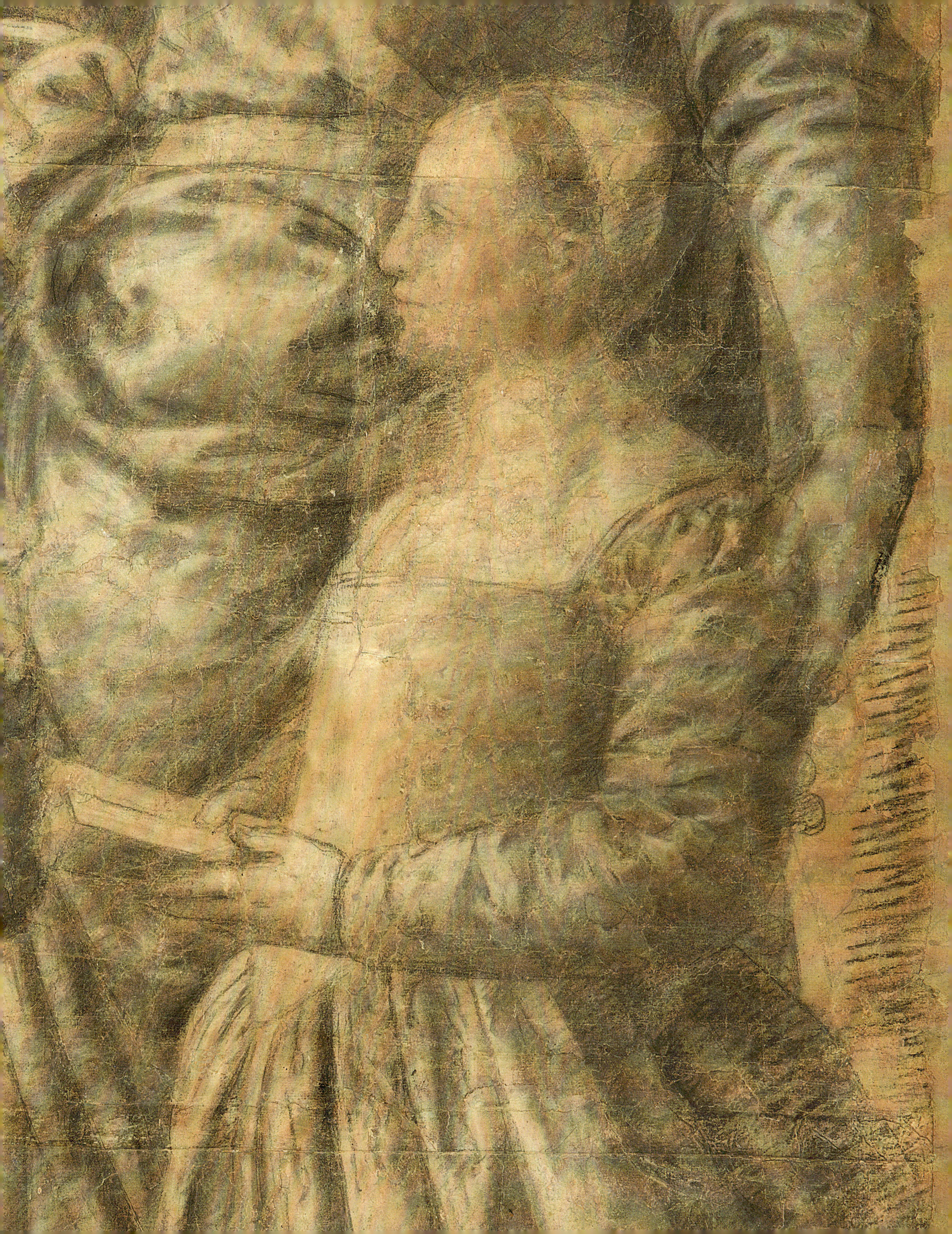

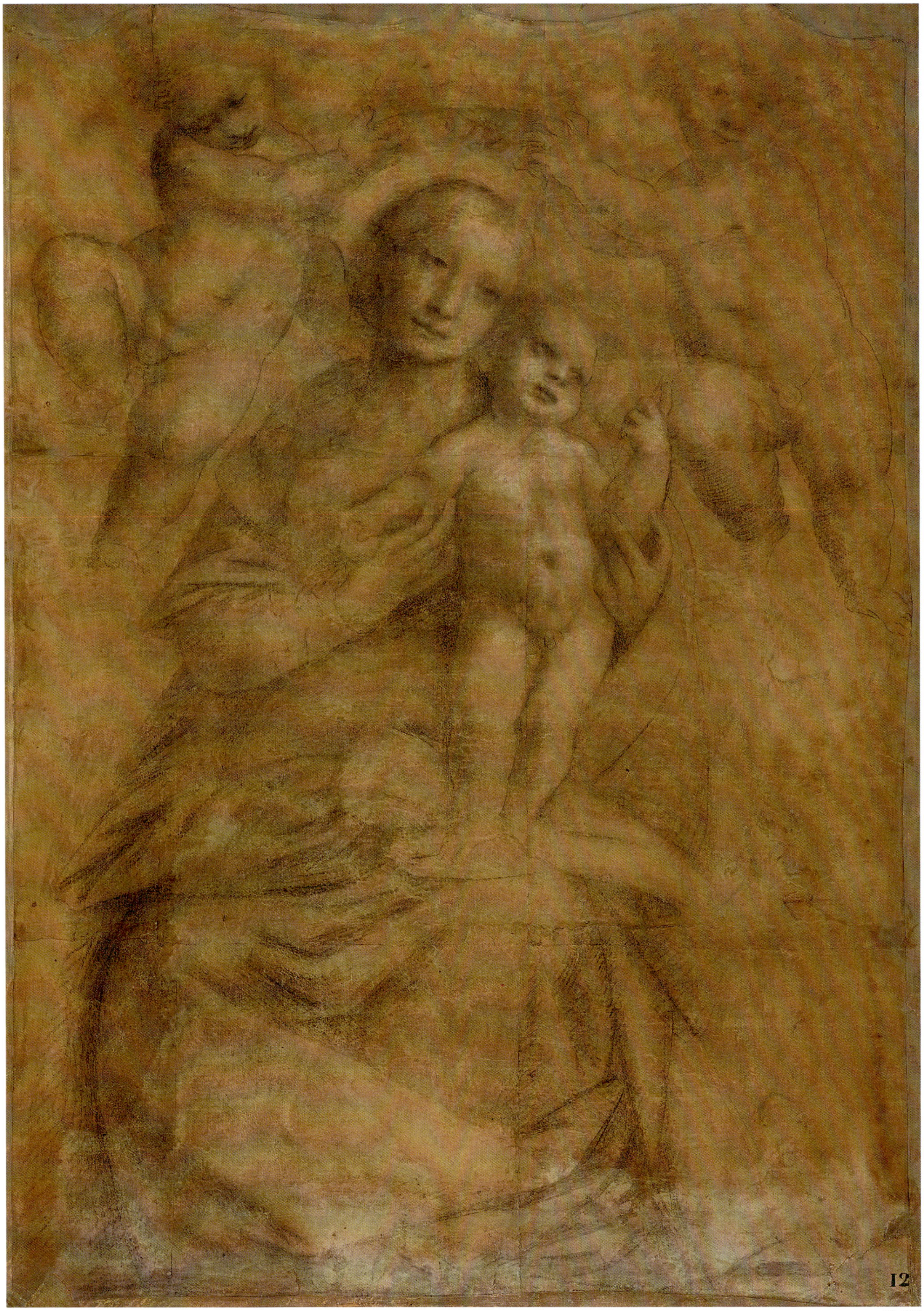

XVIII

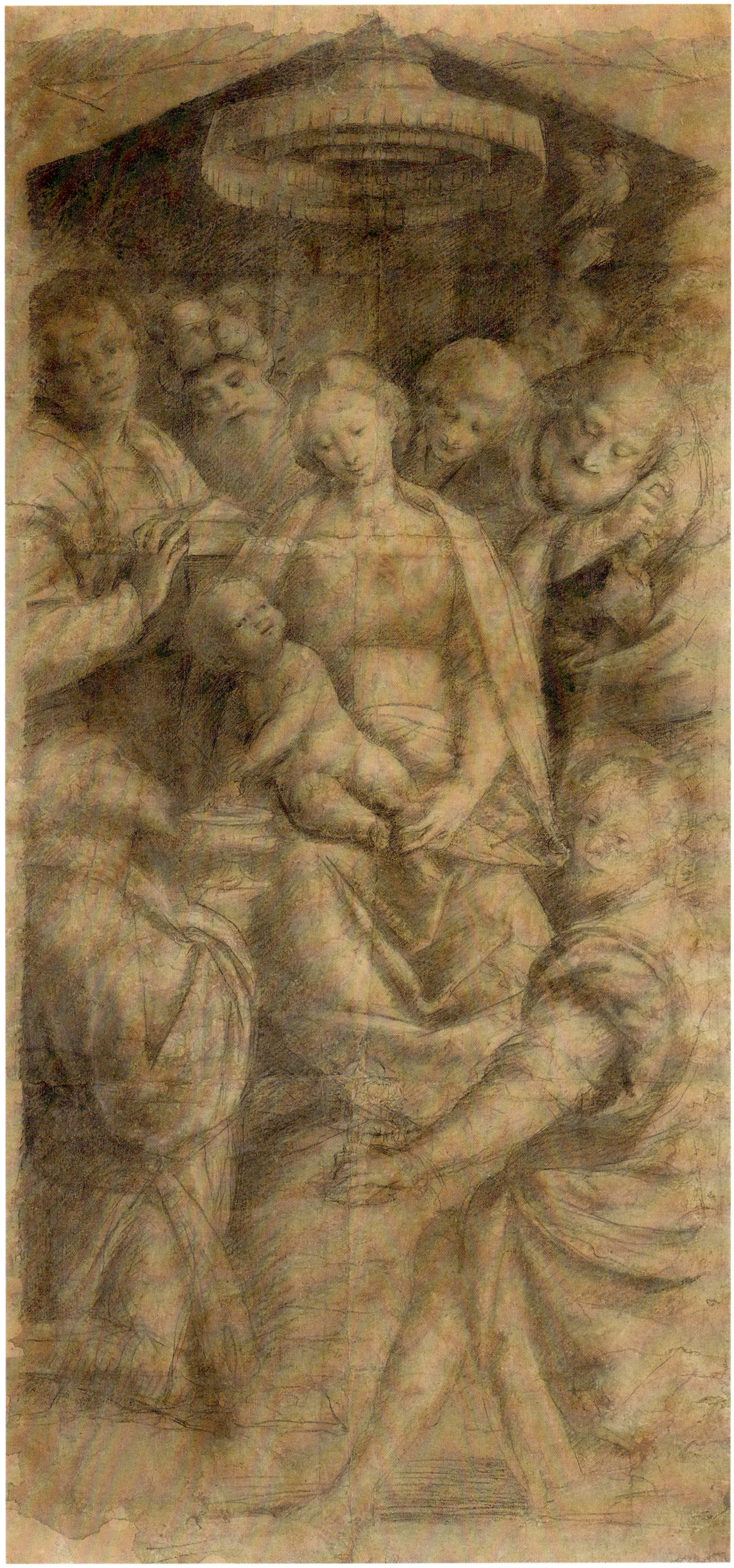

XIX

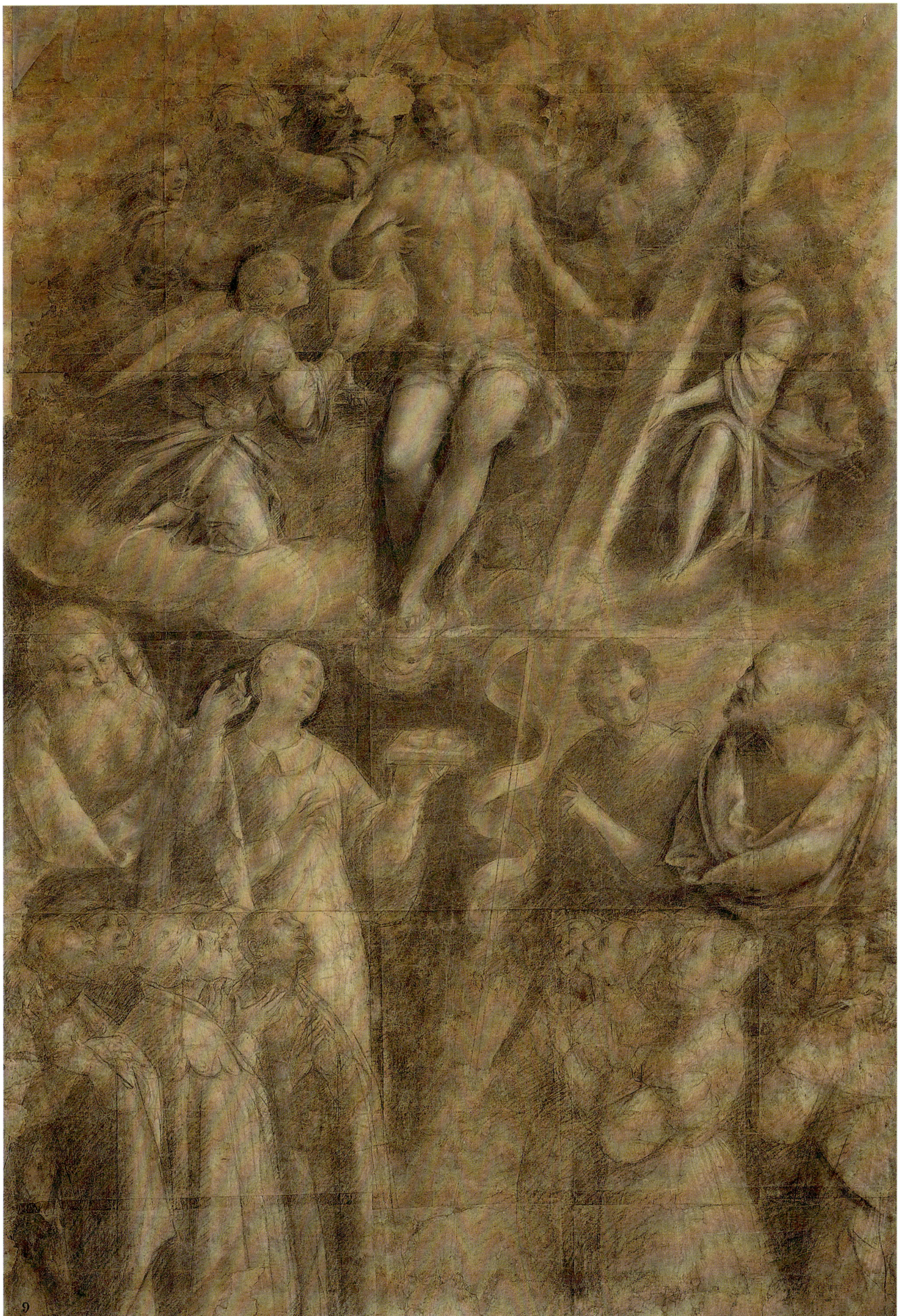

XX

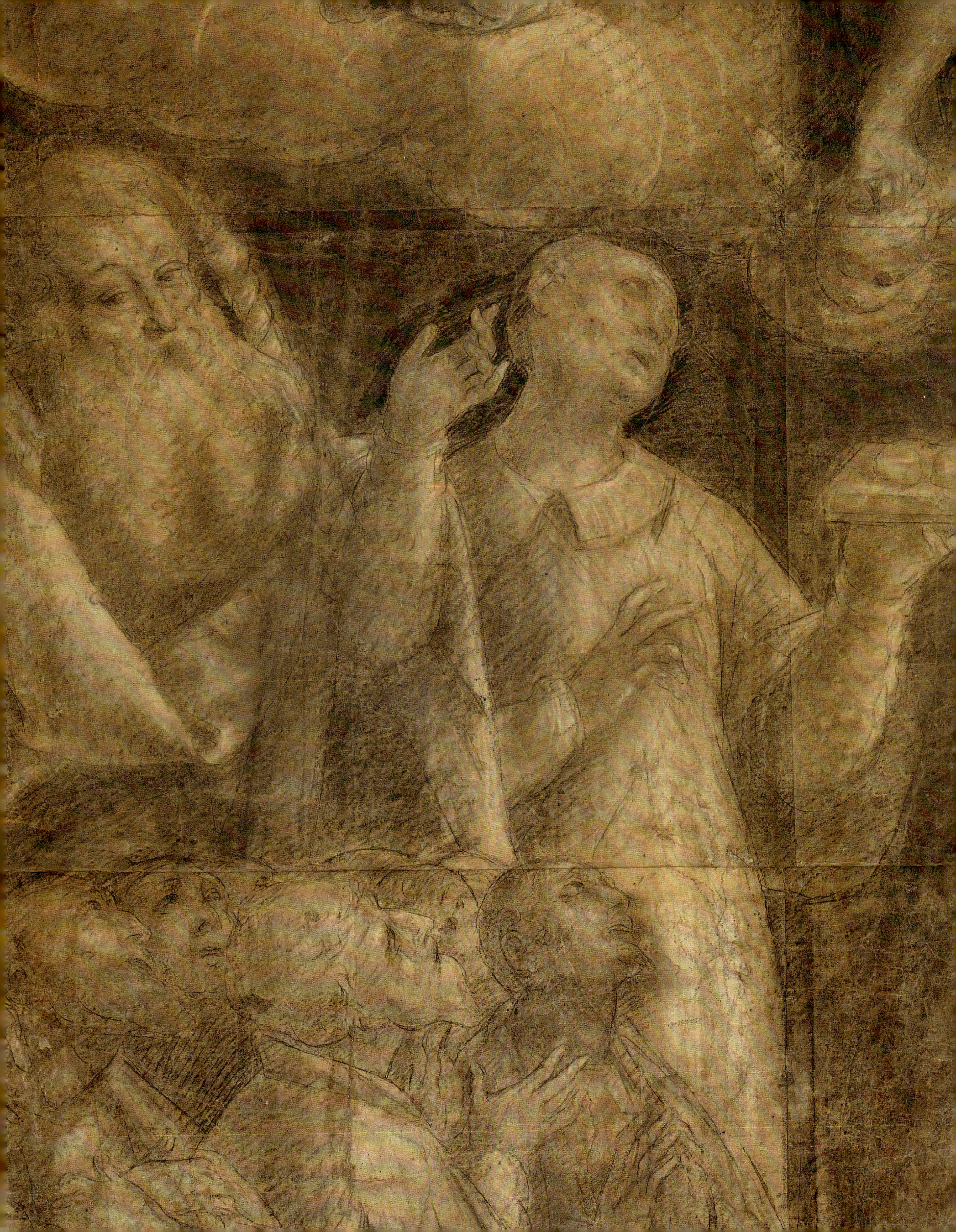

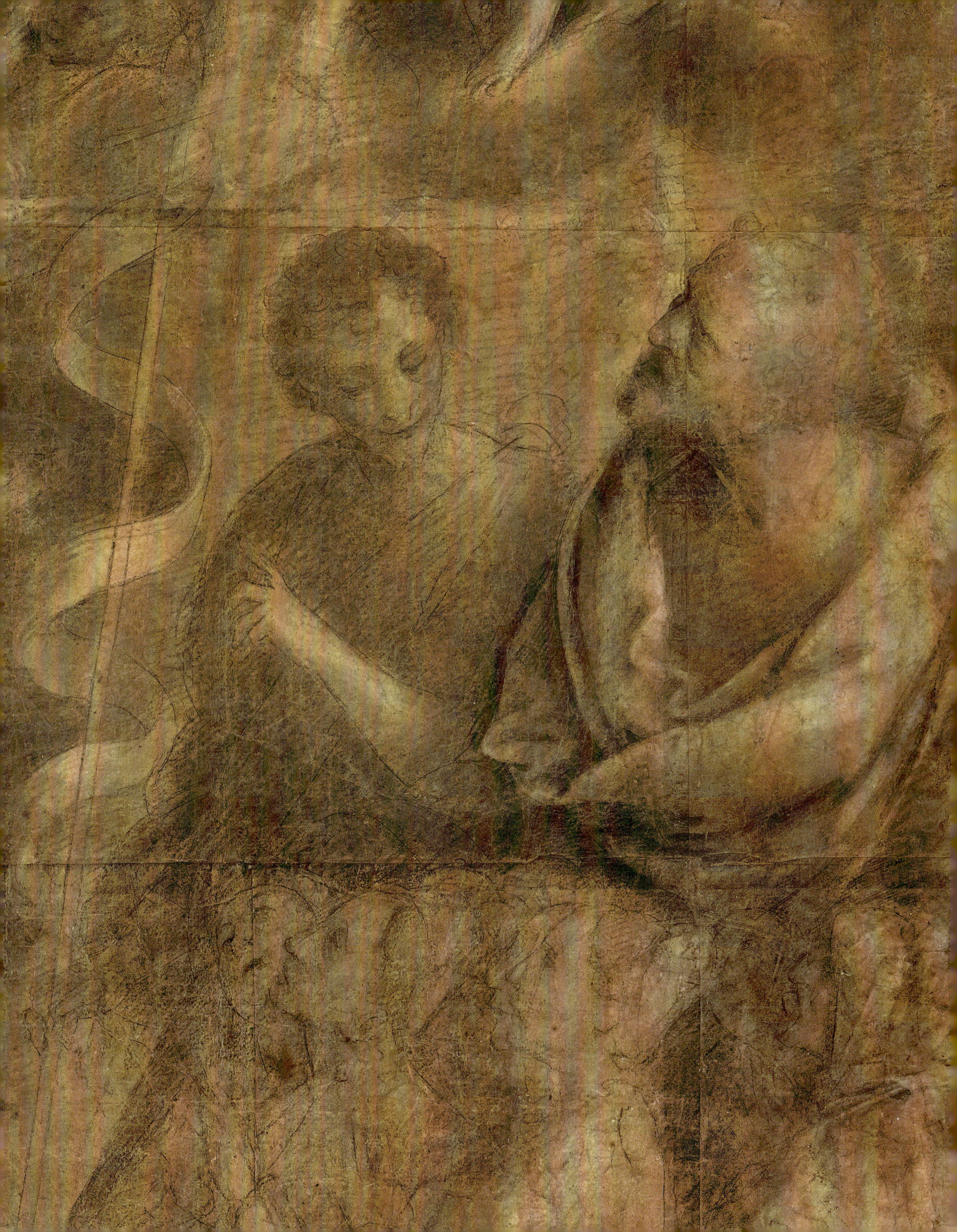

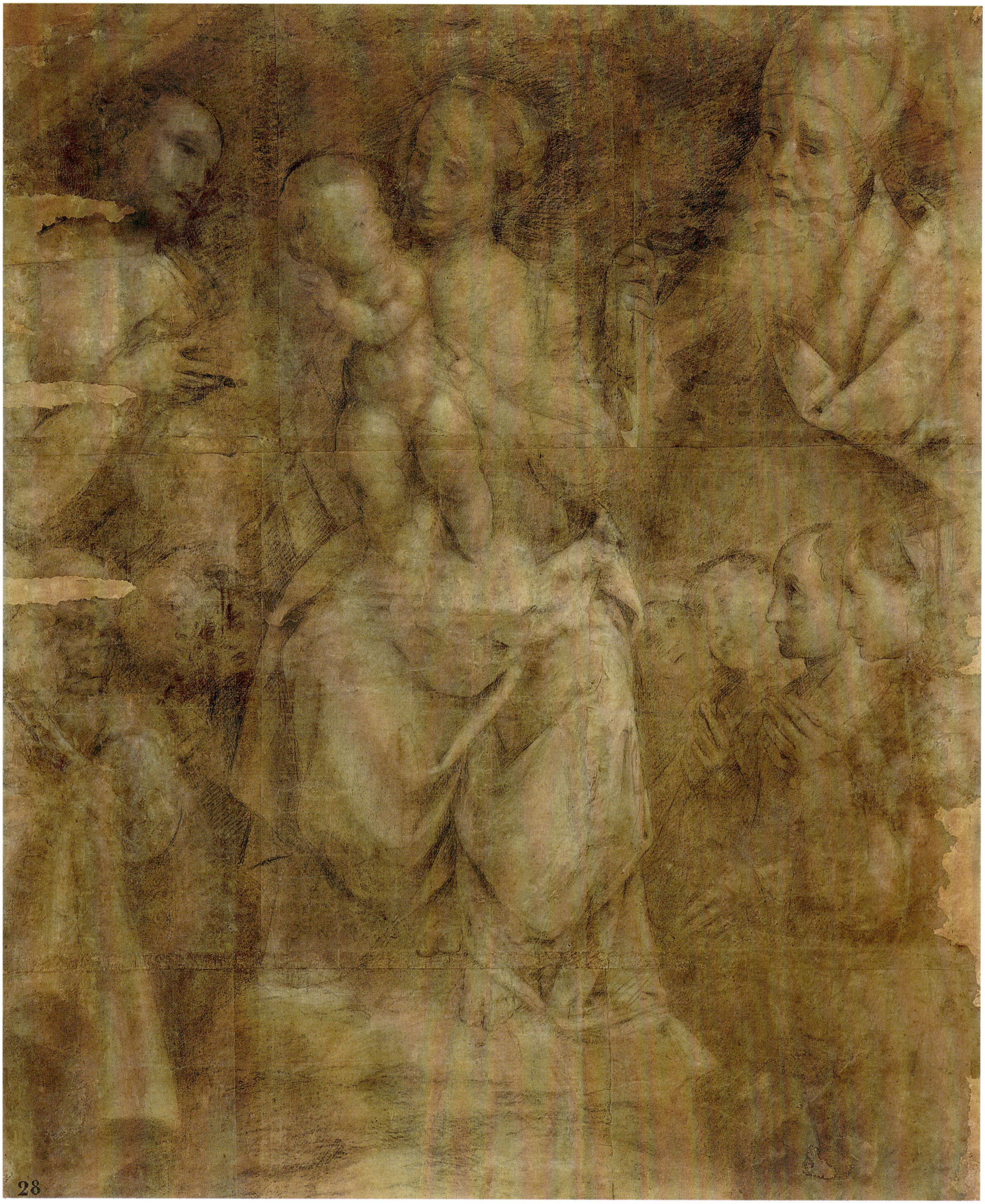

XXI

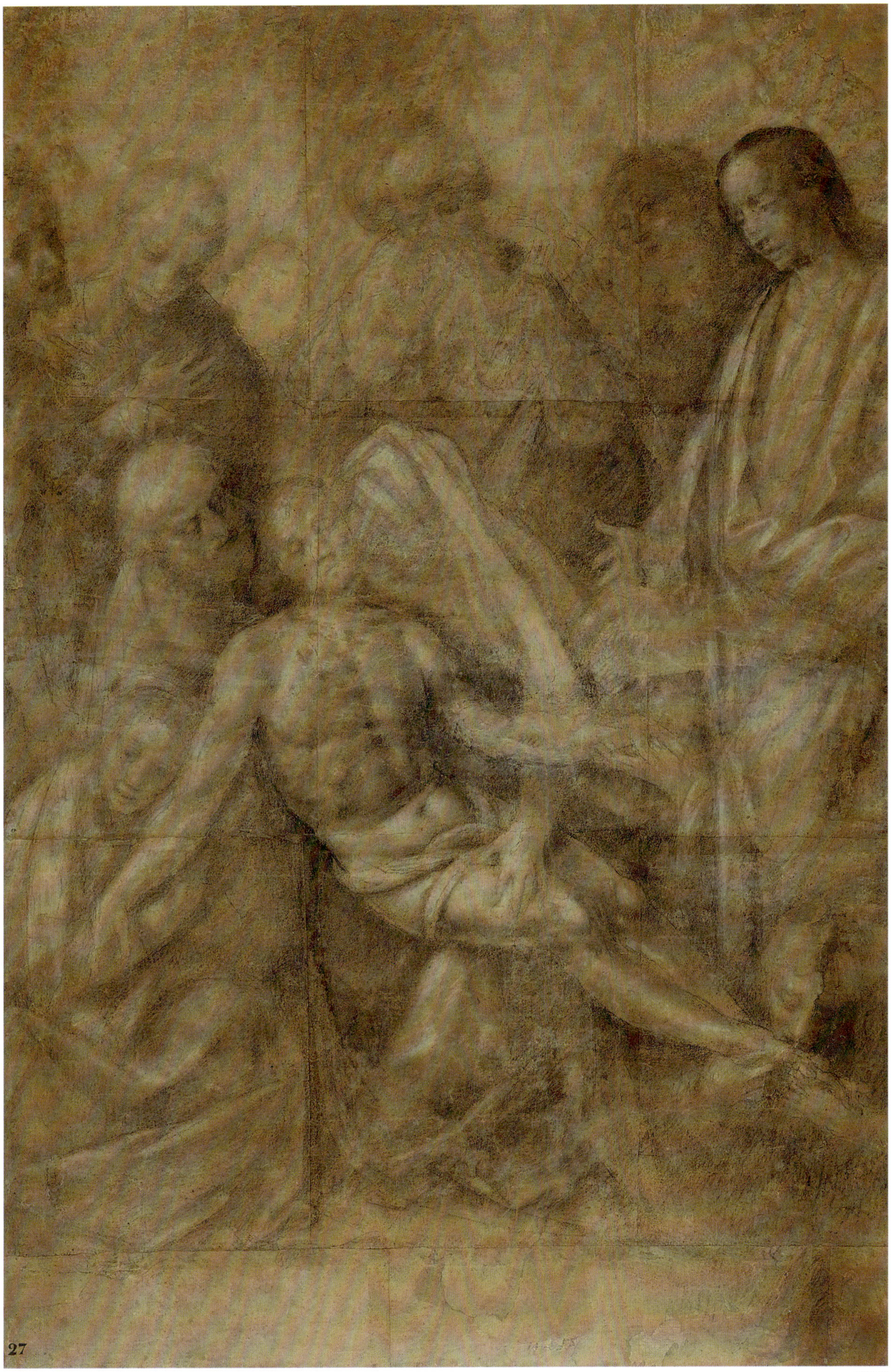

27

XXII

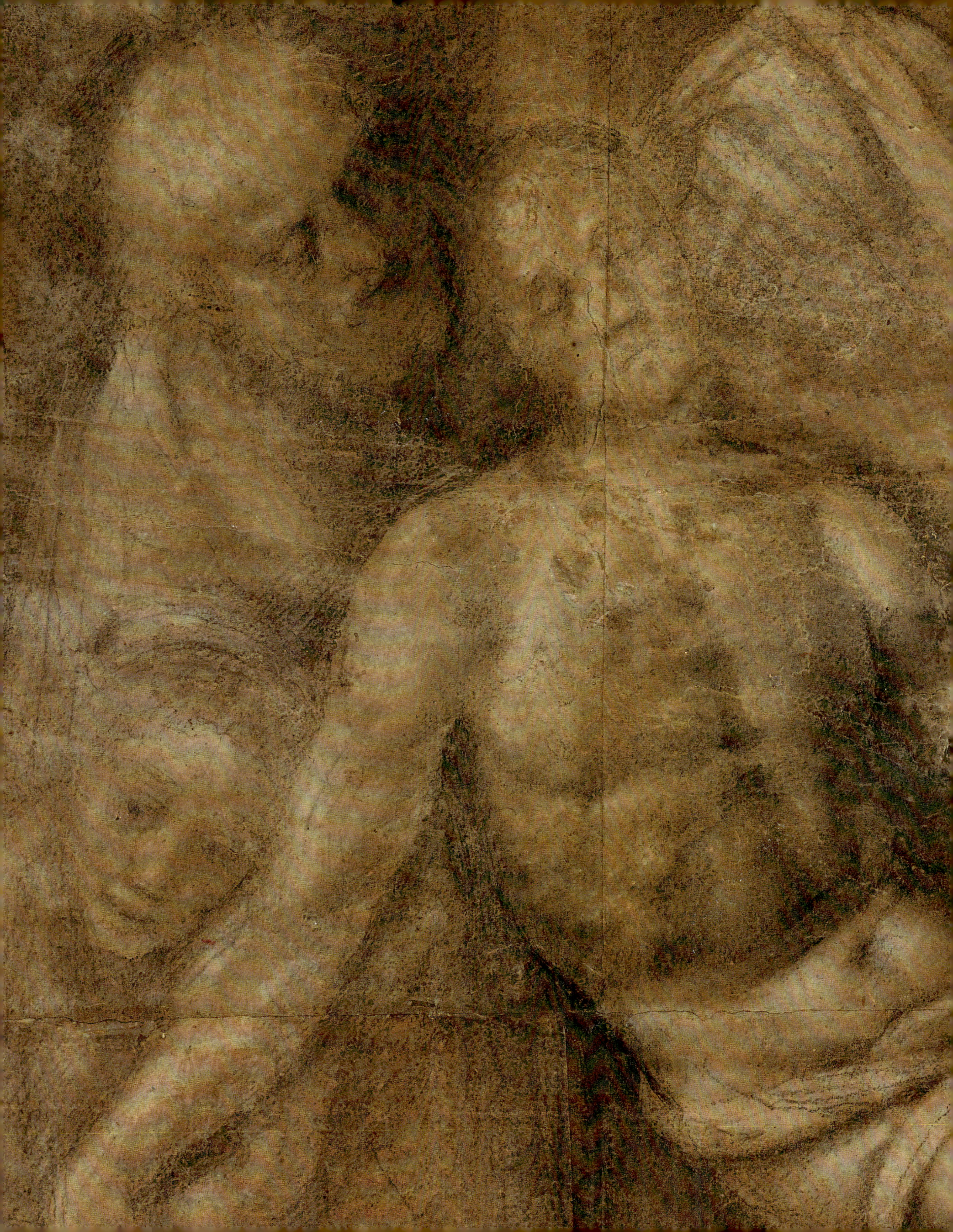

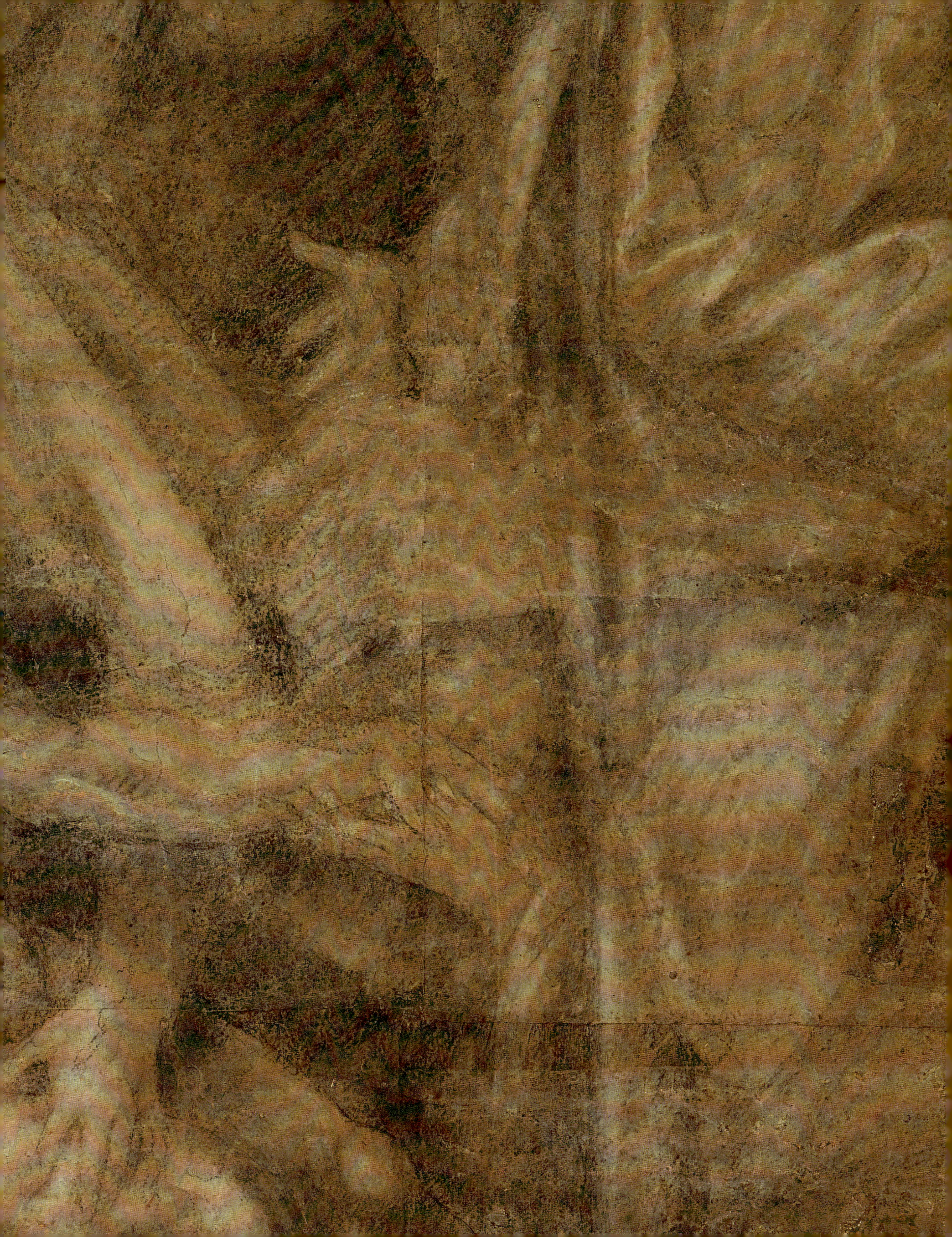

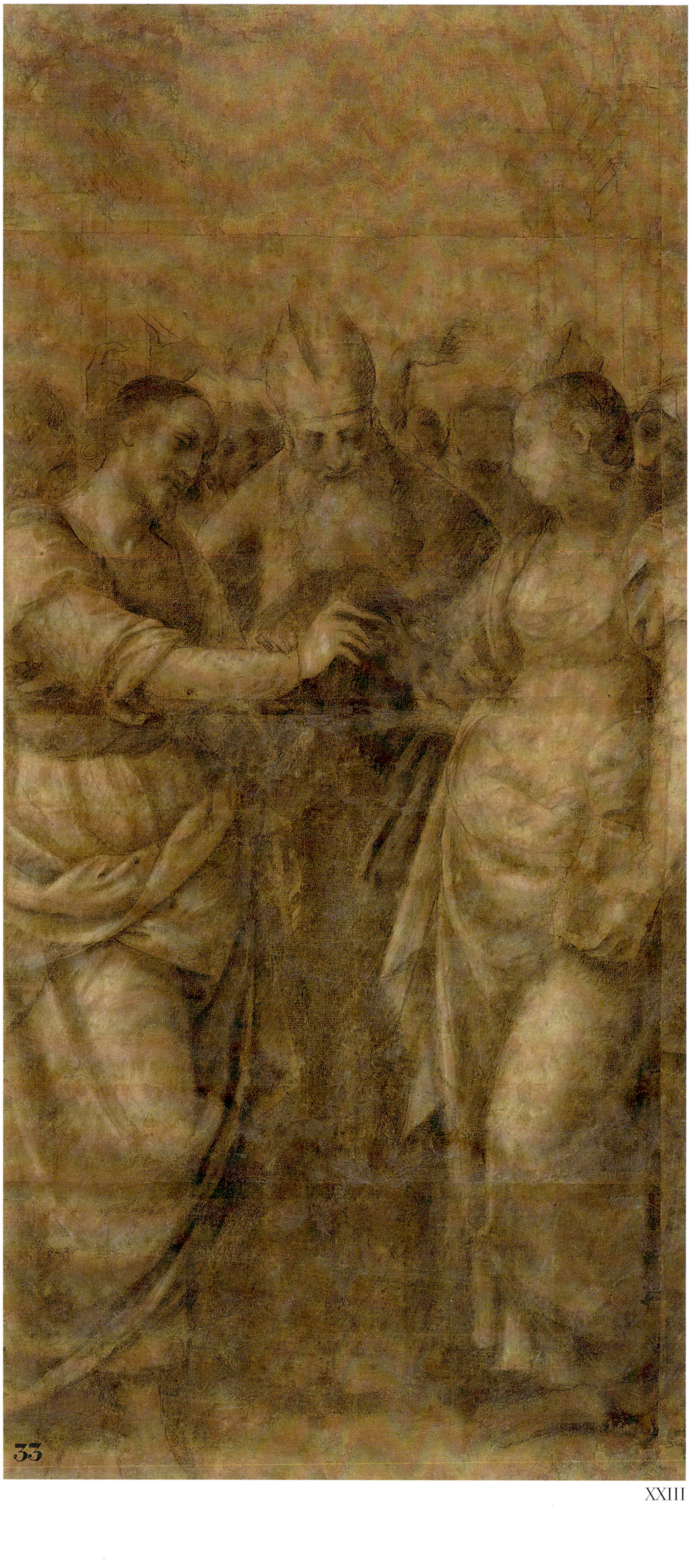

XXIII

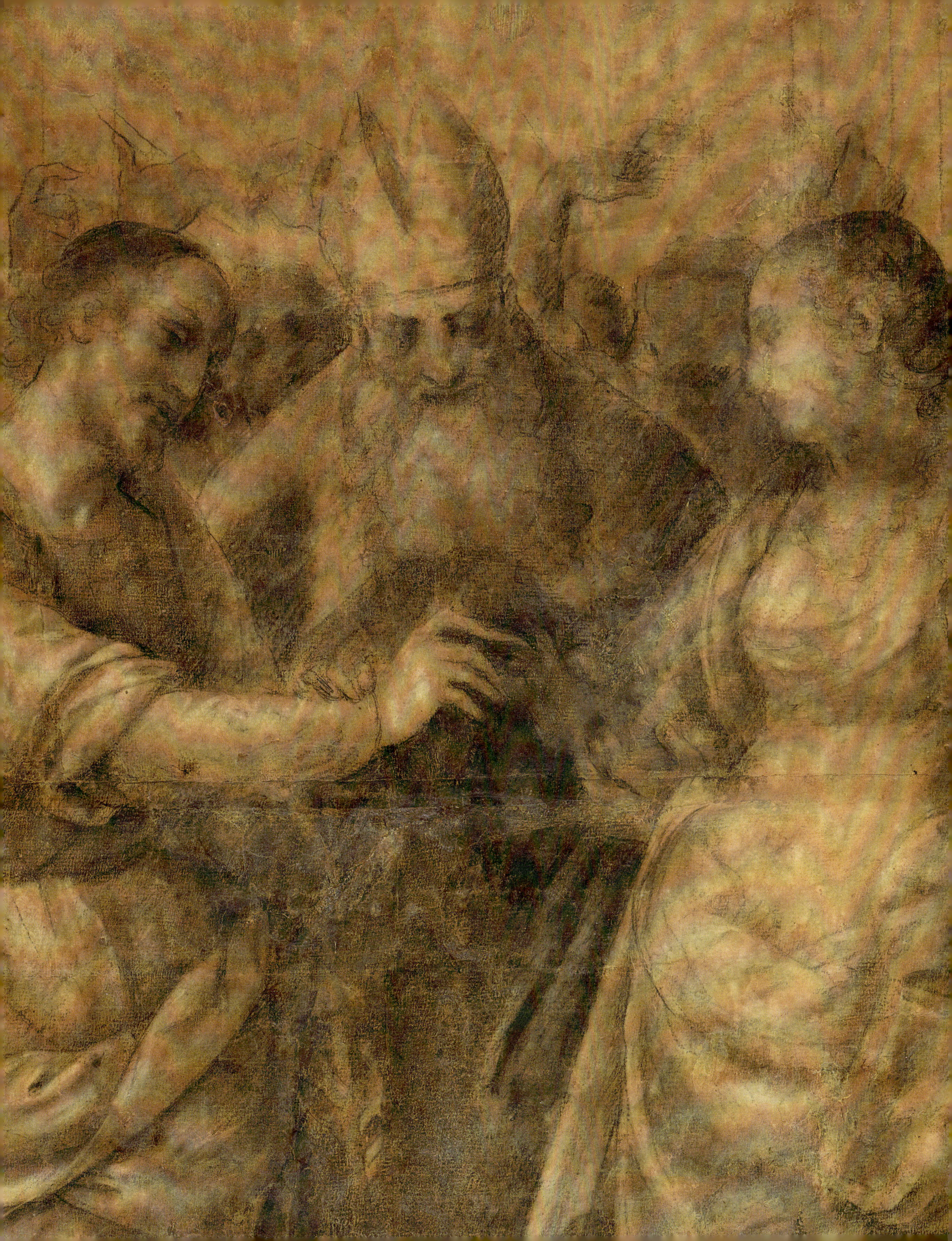

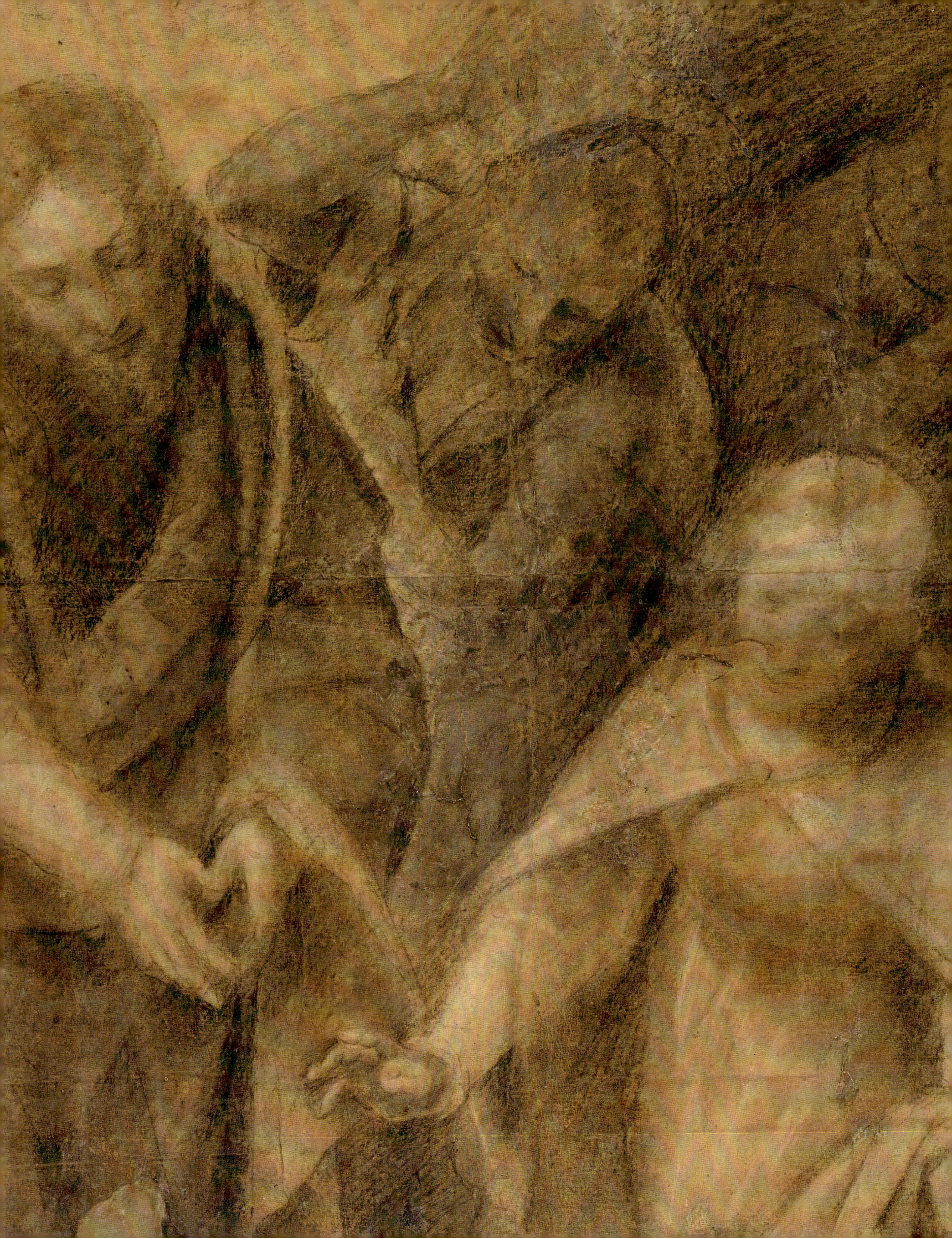

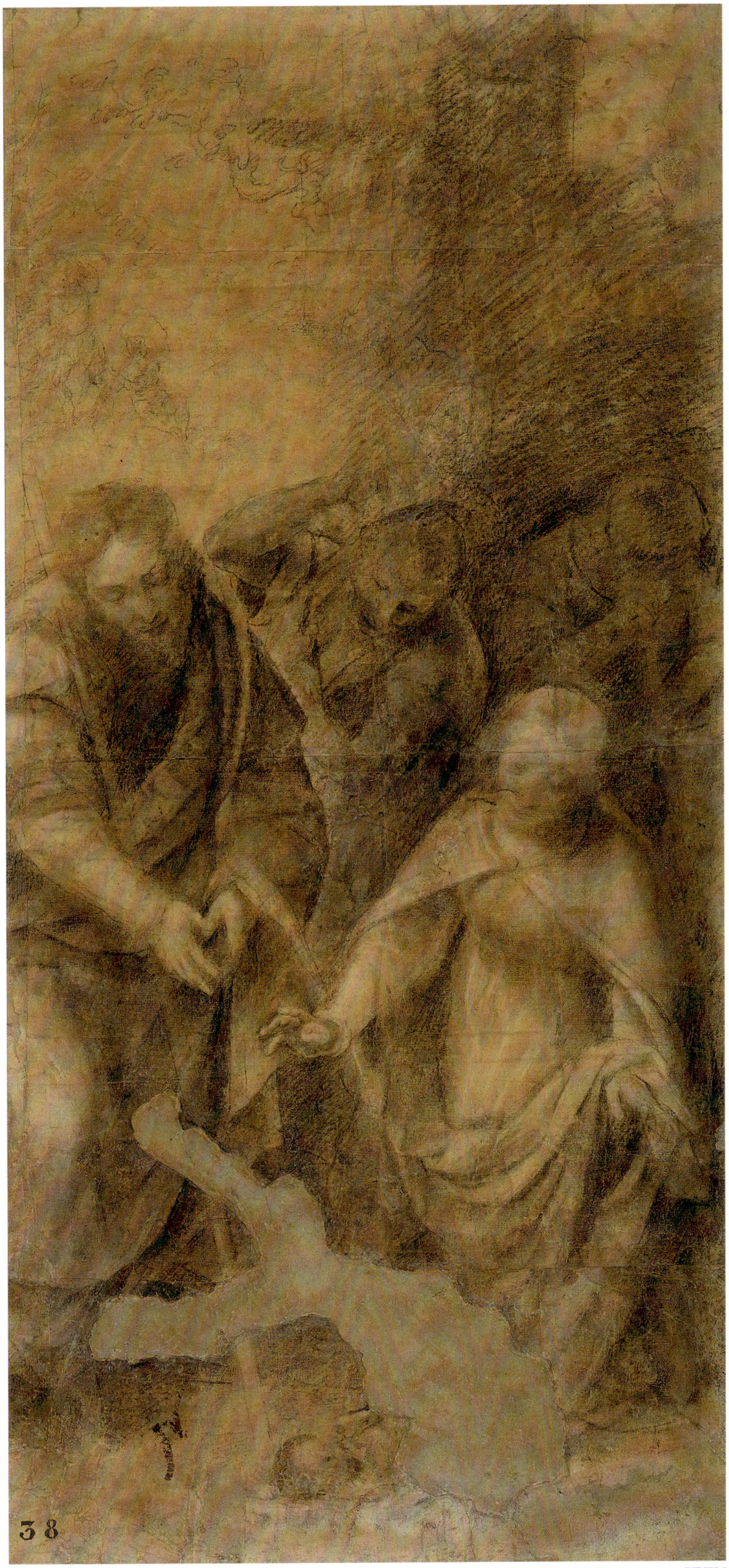

XXIV

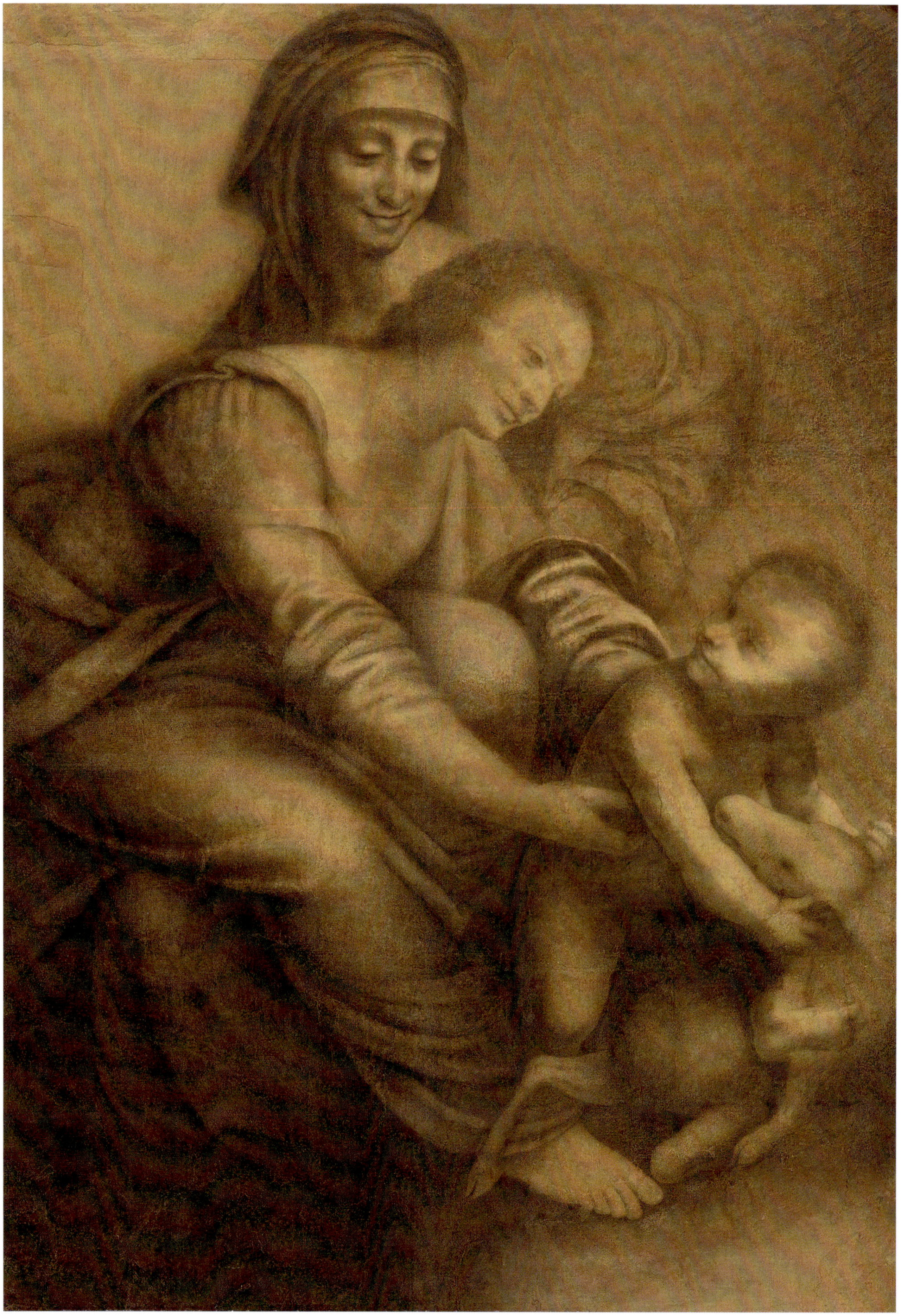

XXV

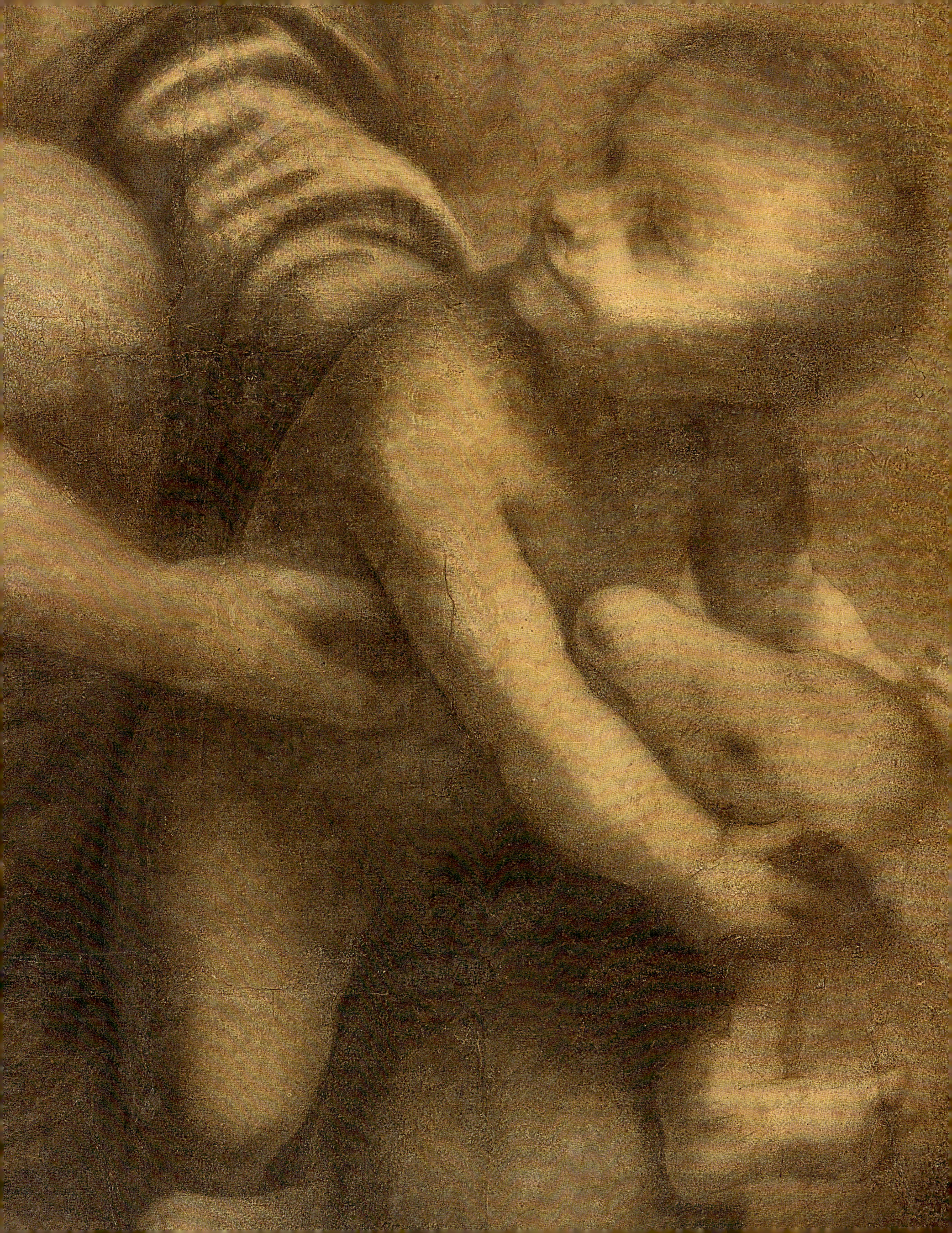

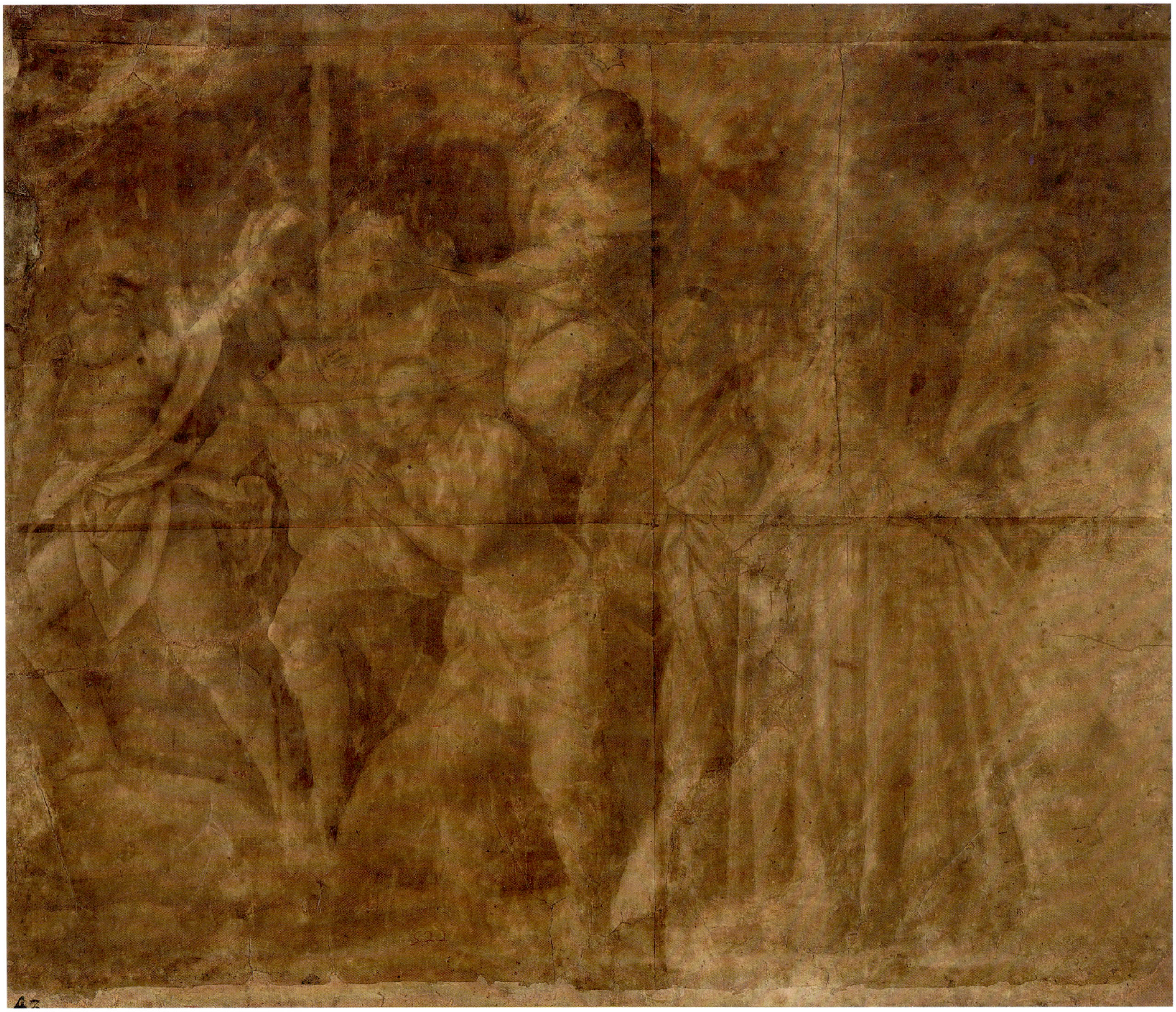

XXVI

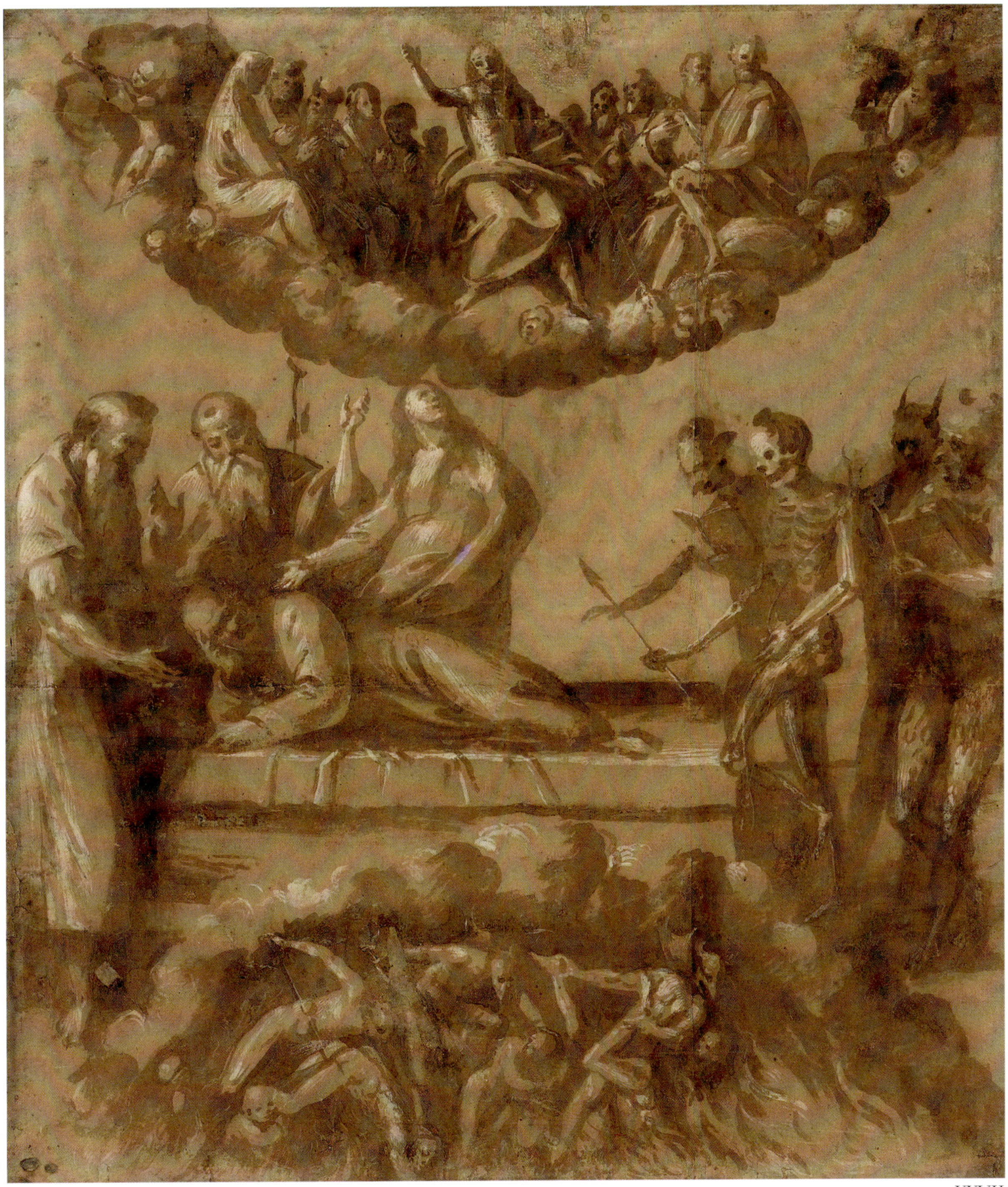

XXVII

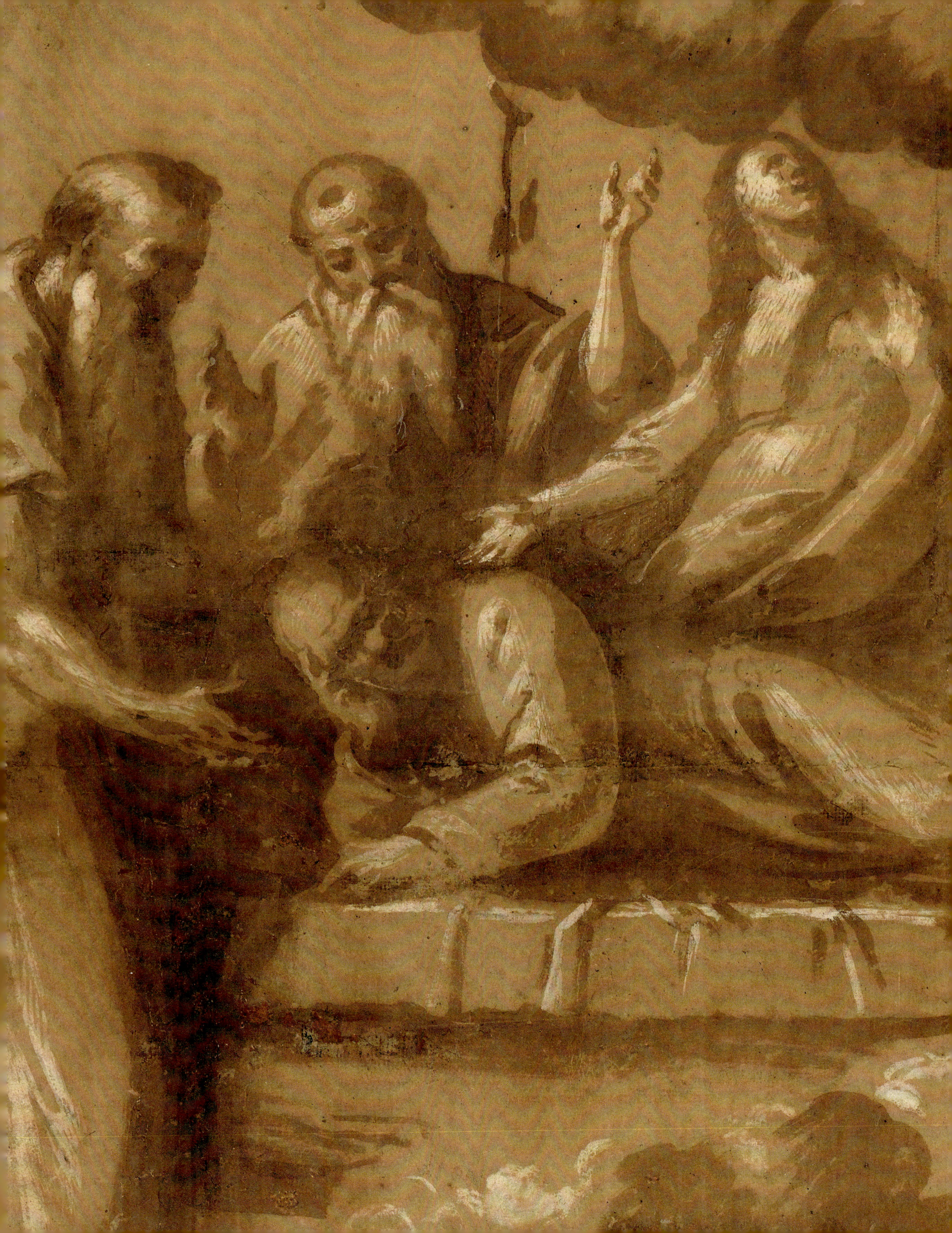

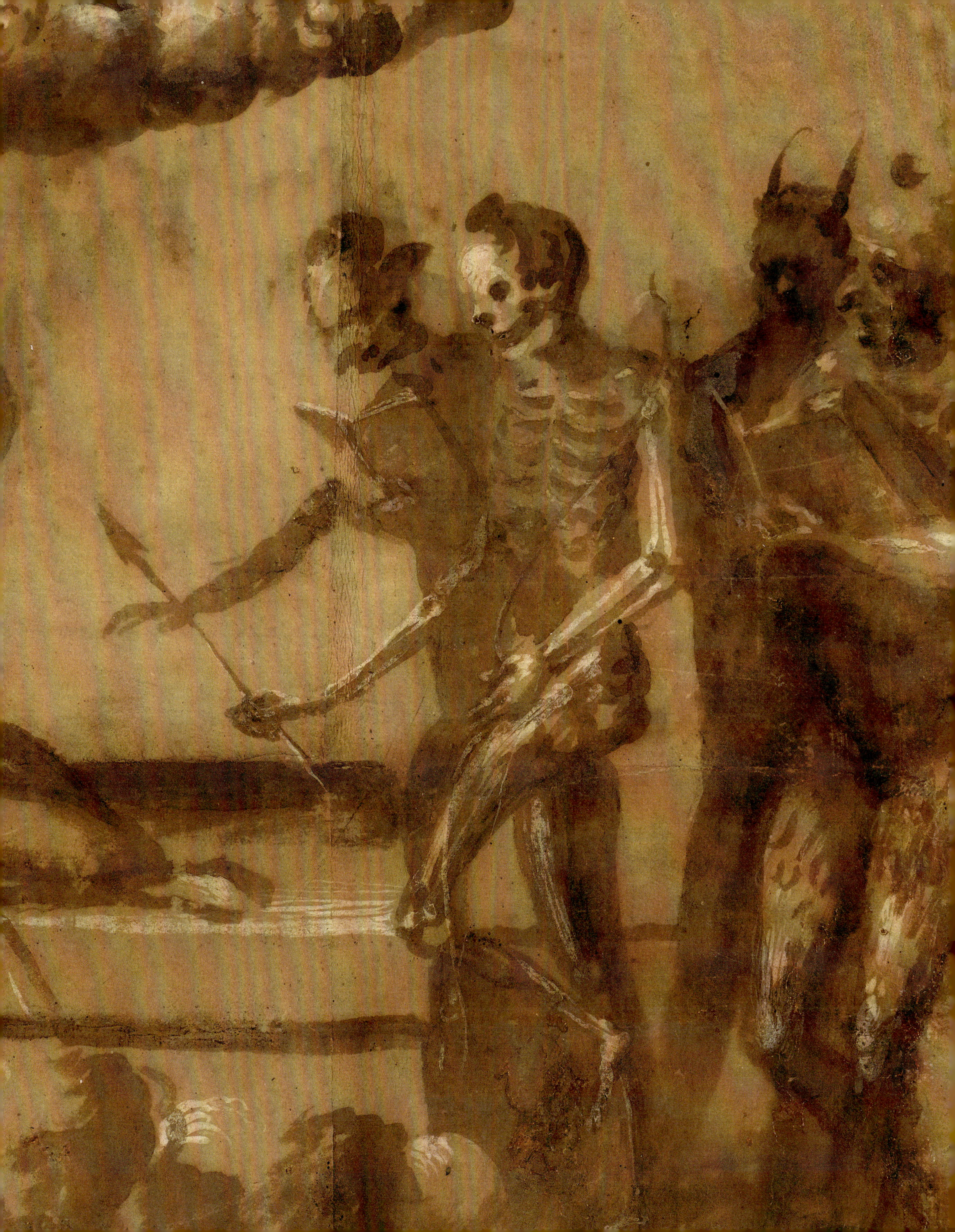

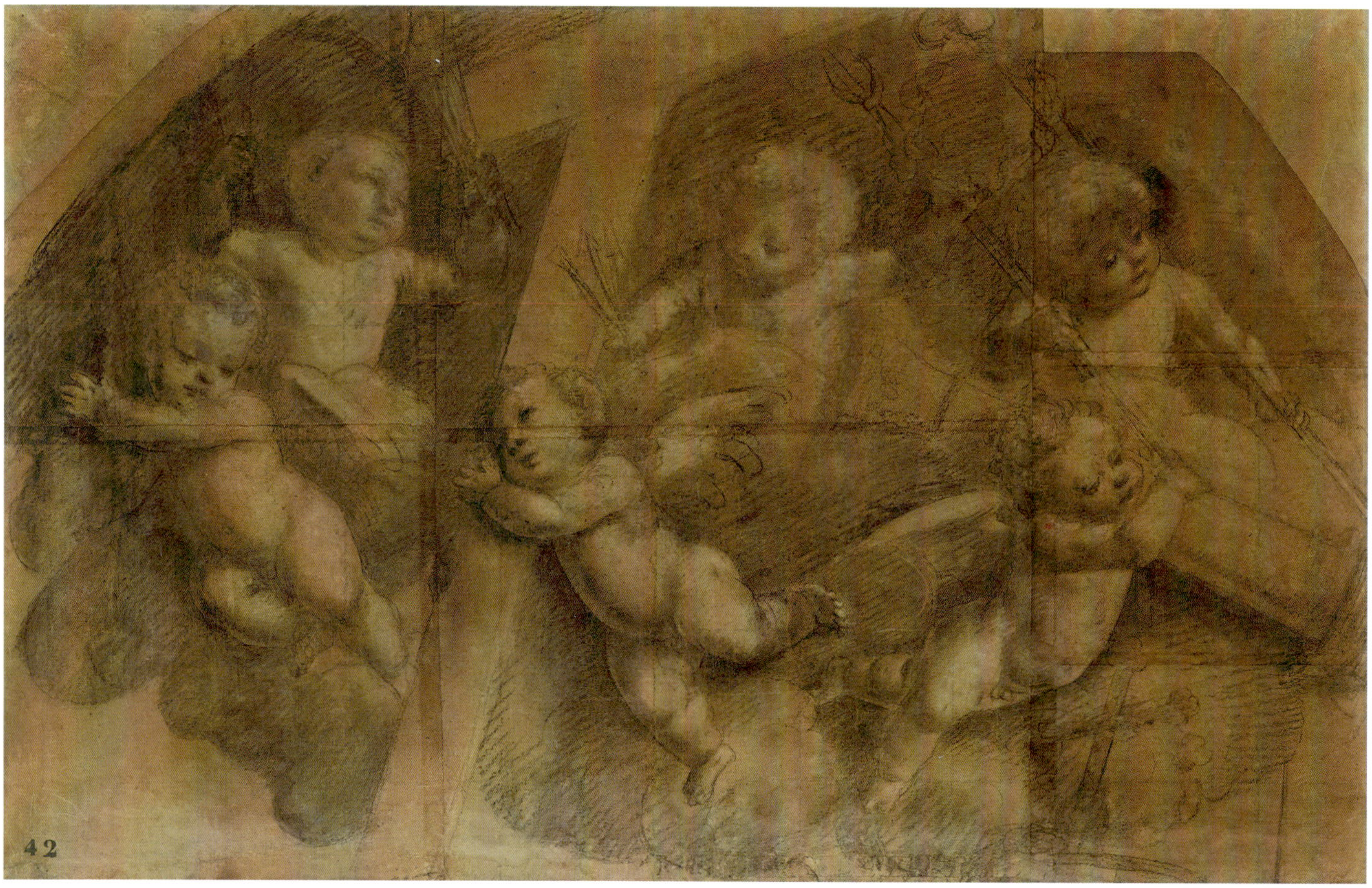

XXVIII

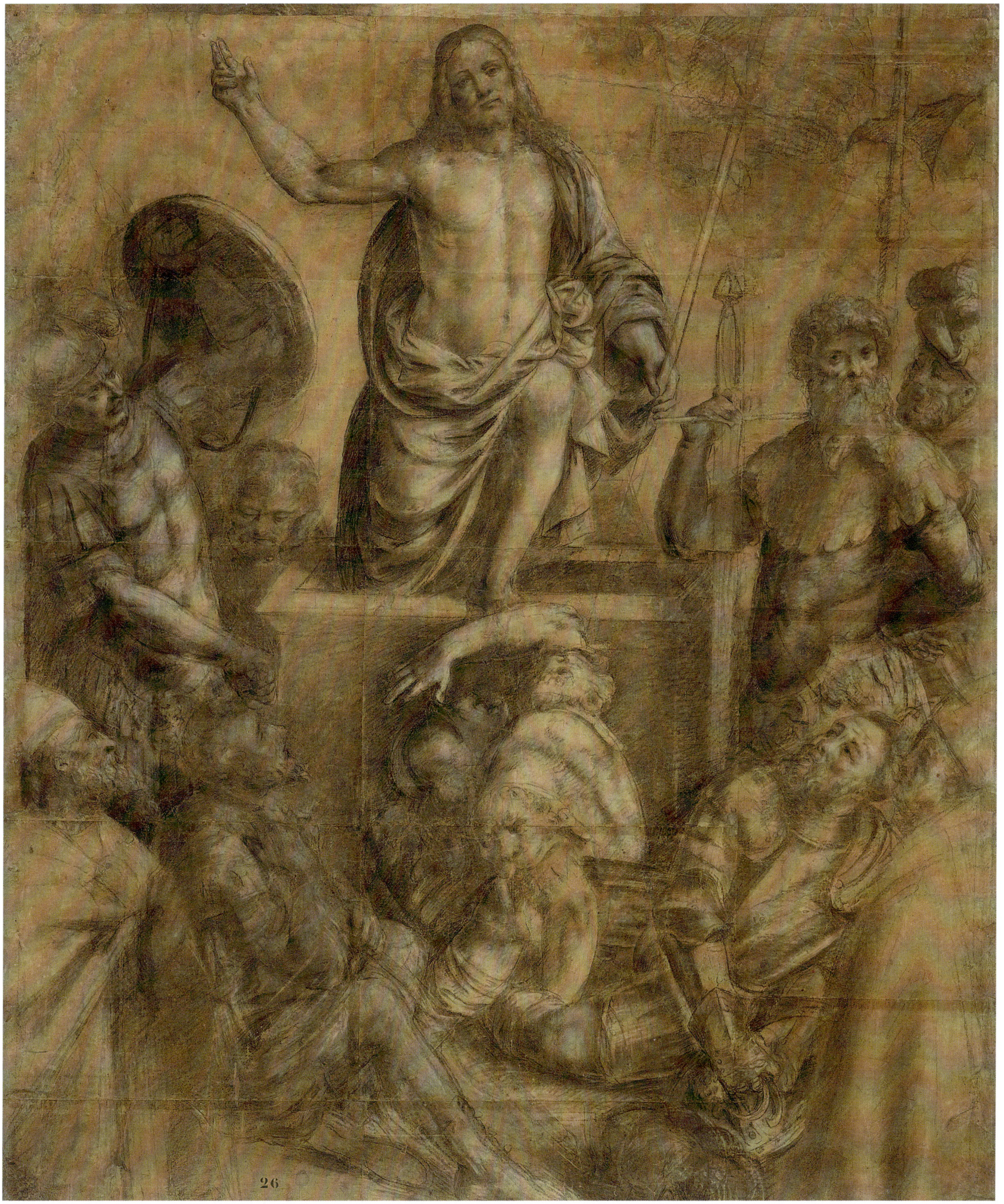

XXIX

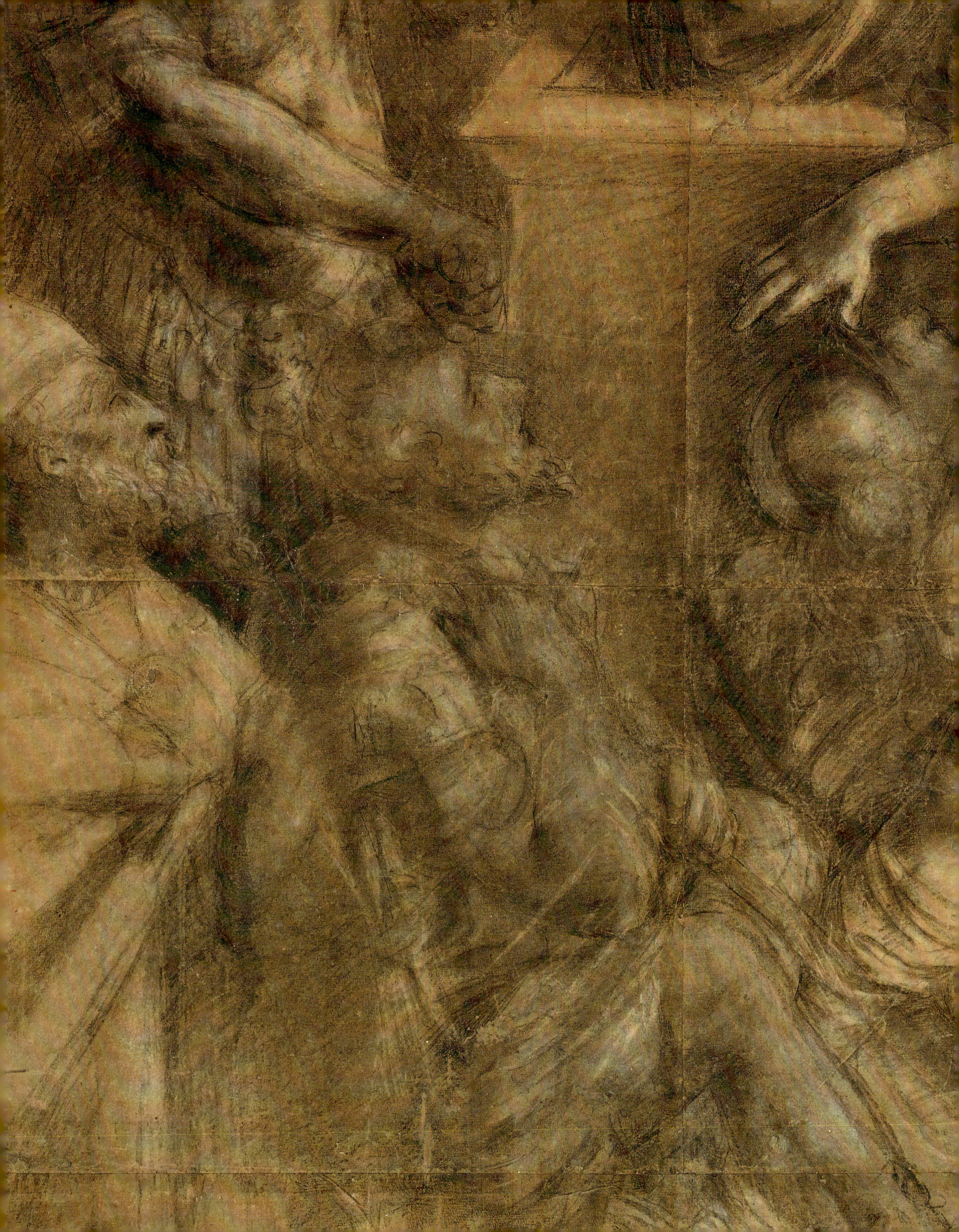

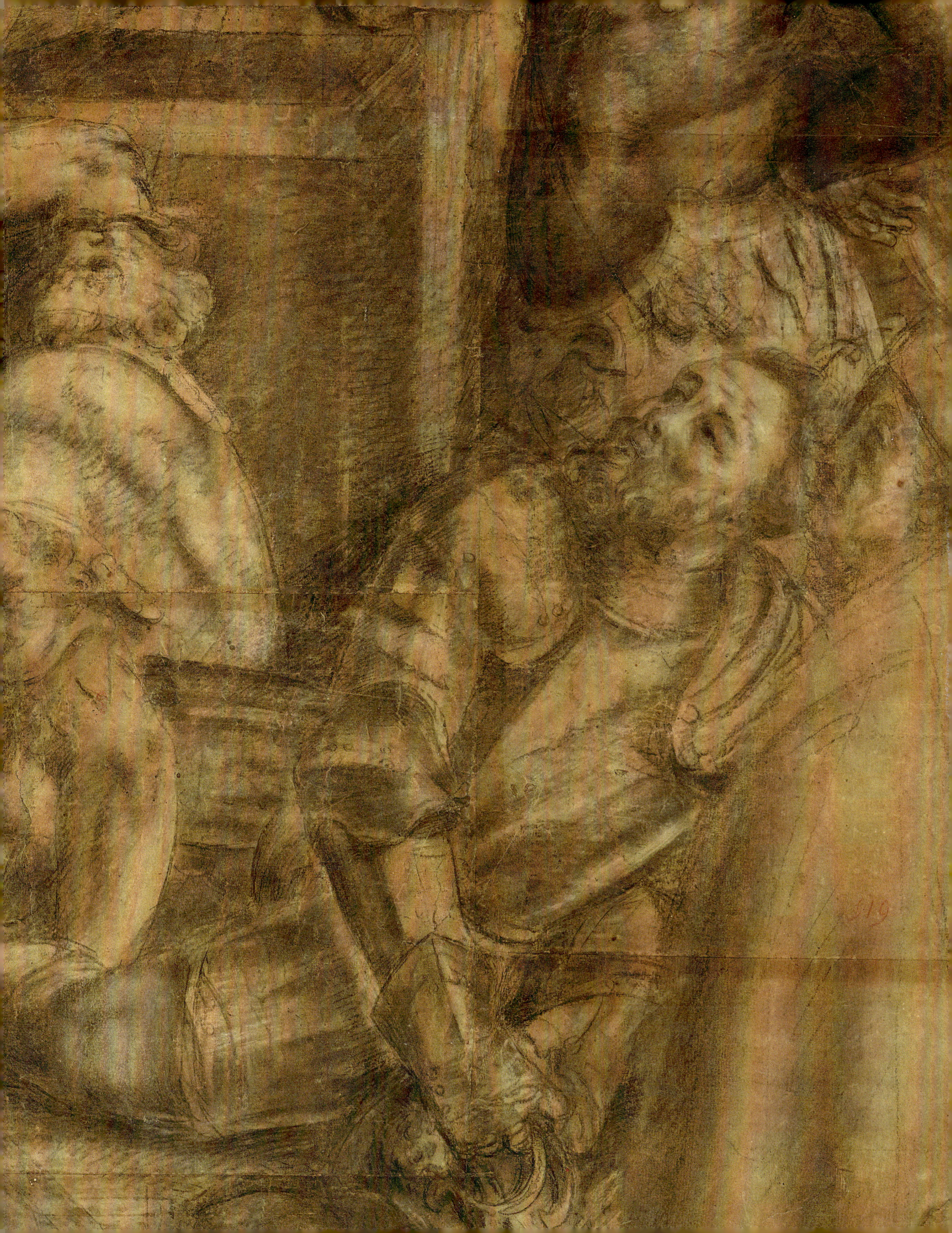

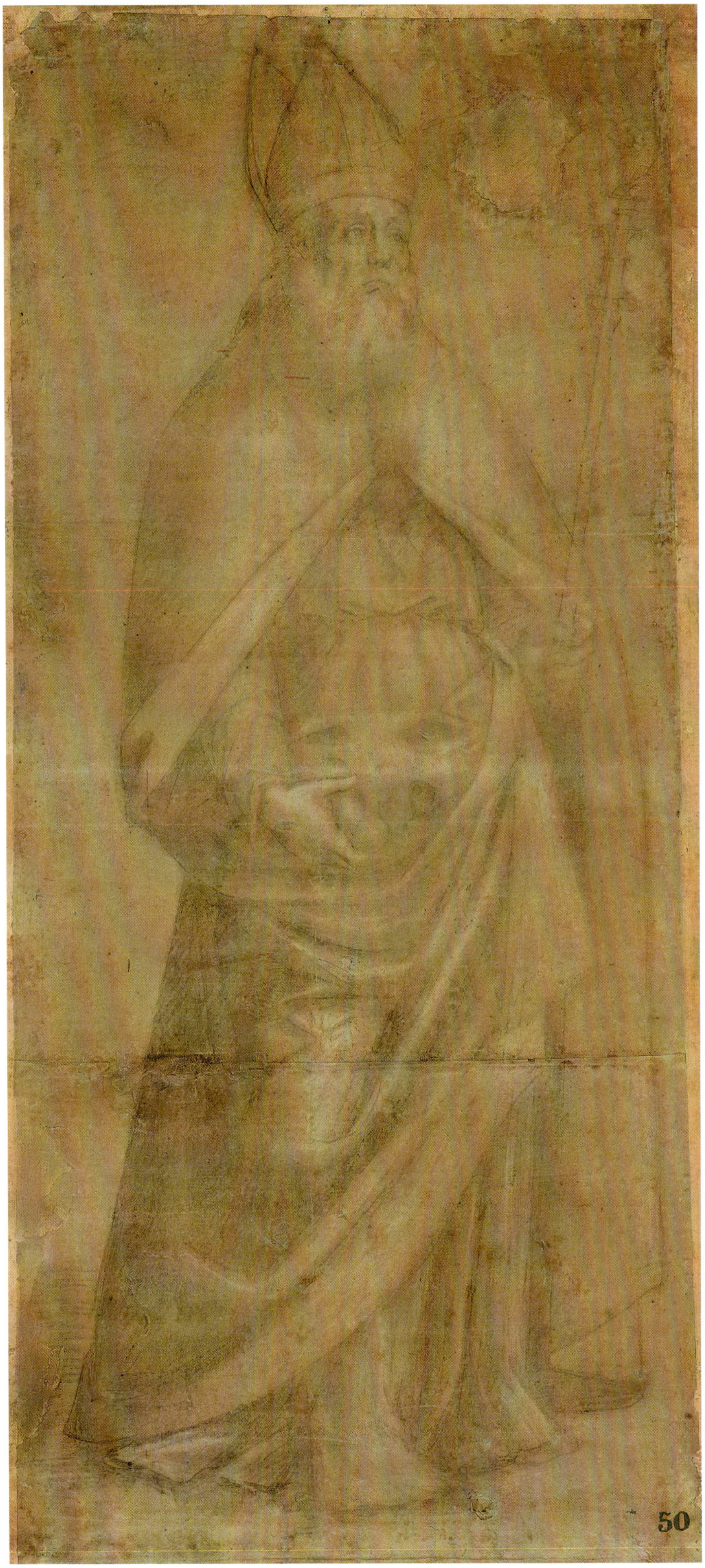

XXX

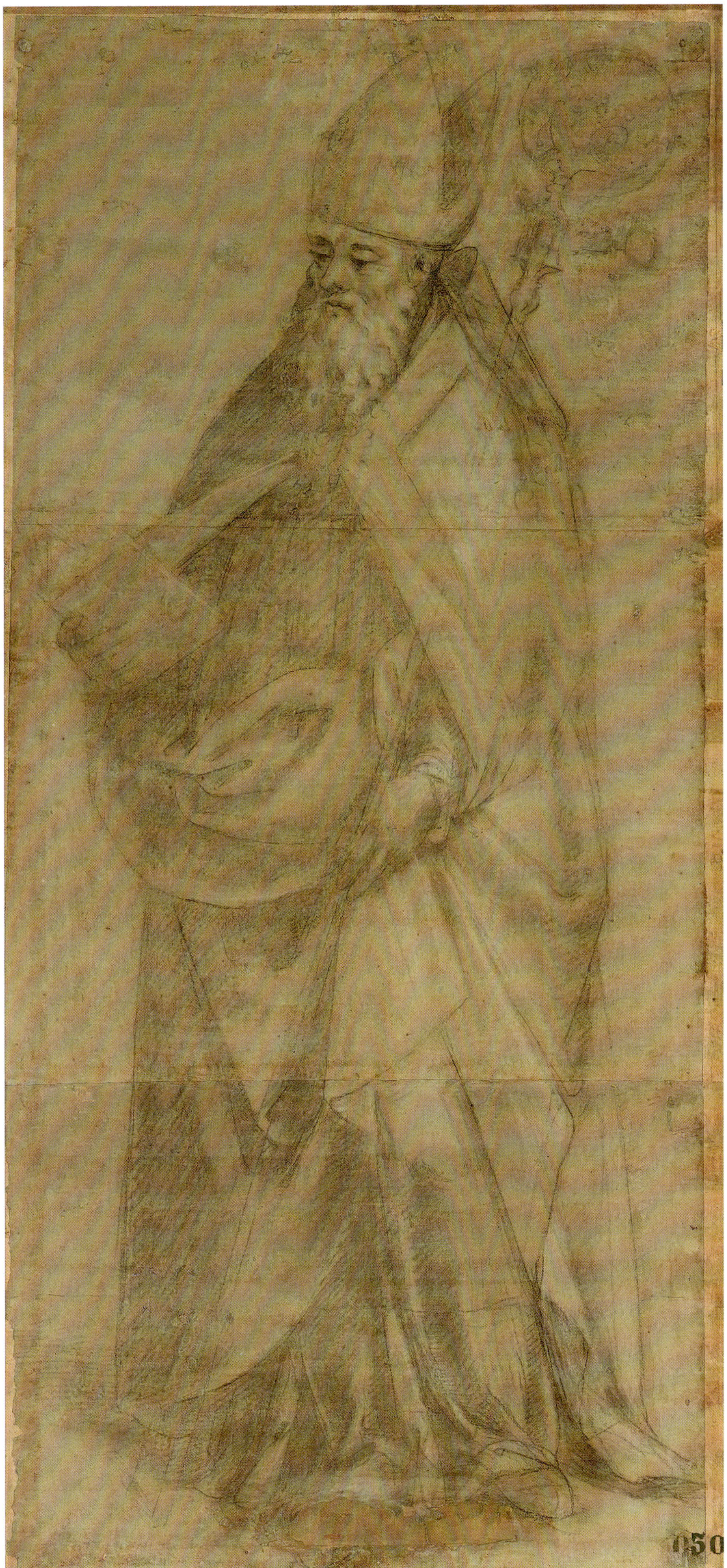

XXXI

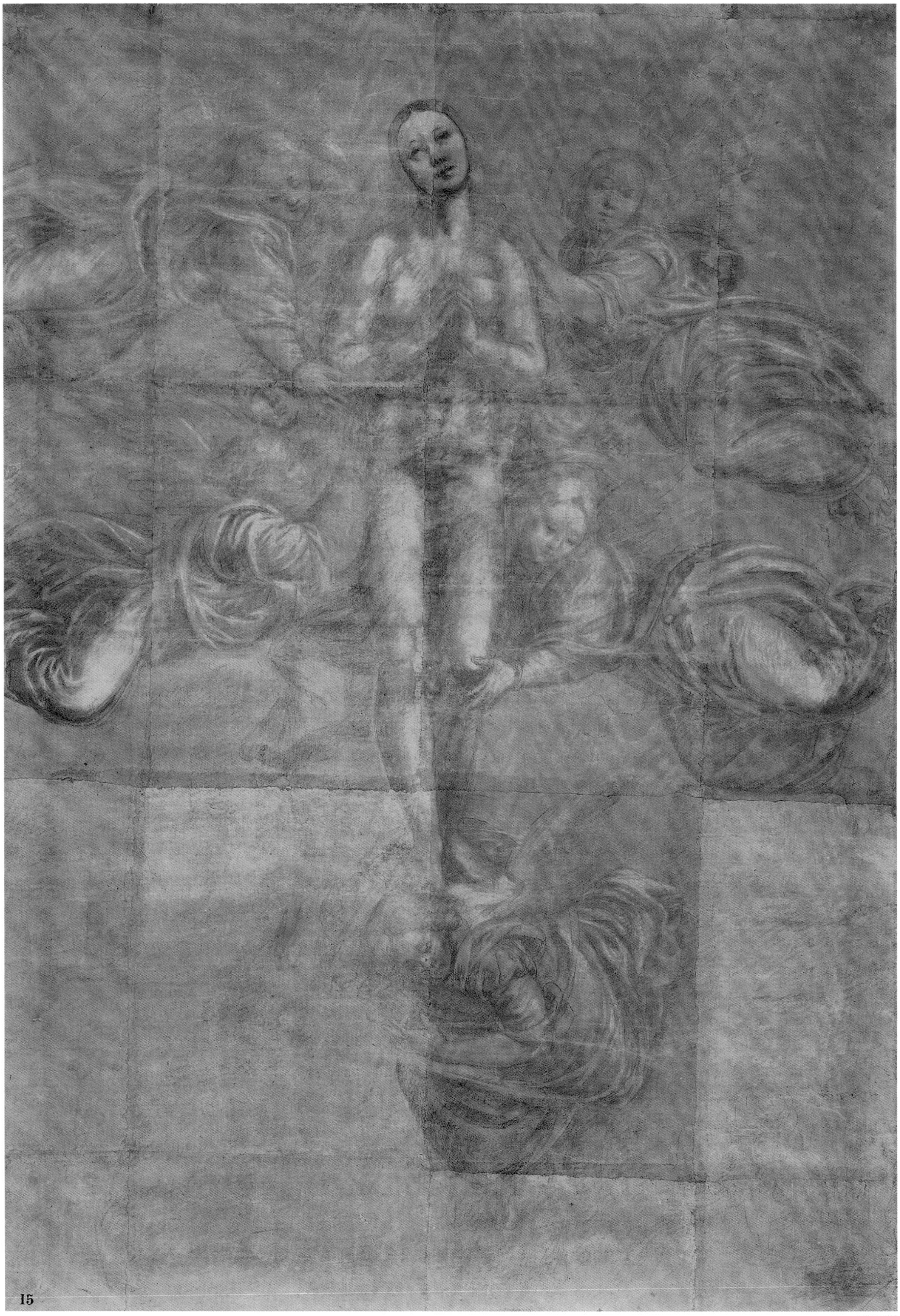

15

XXXII

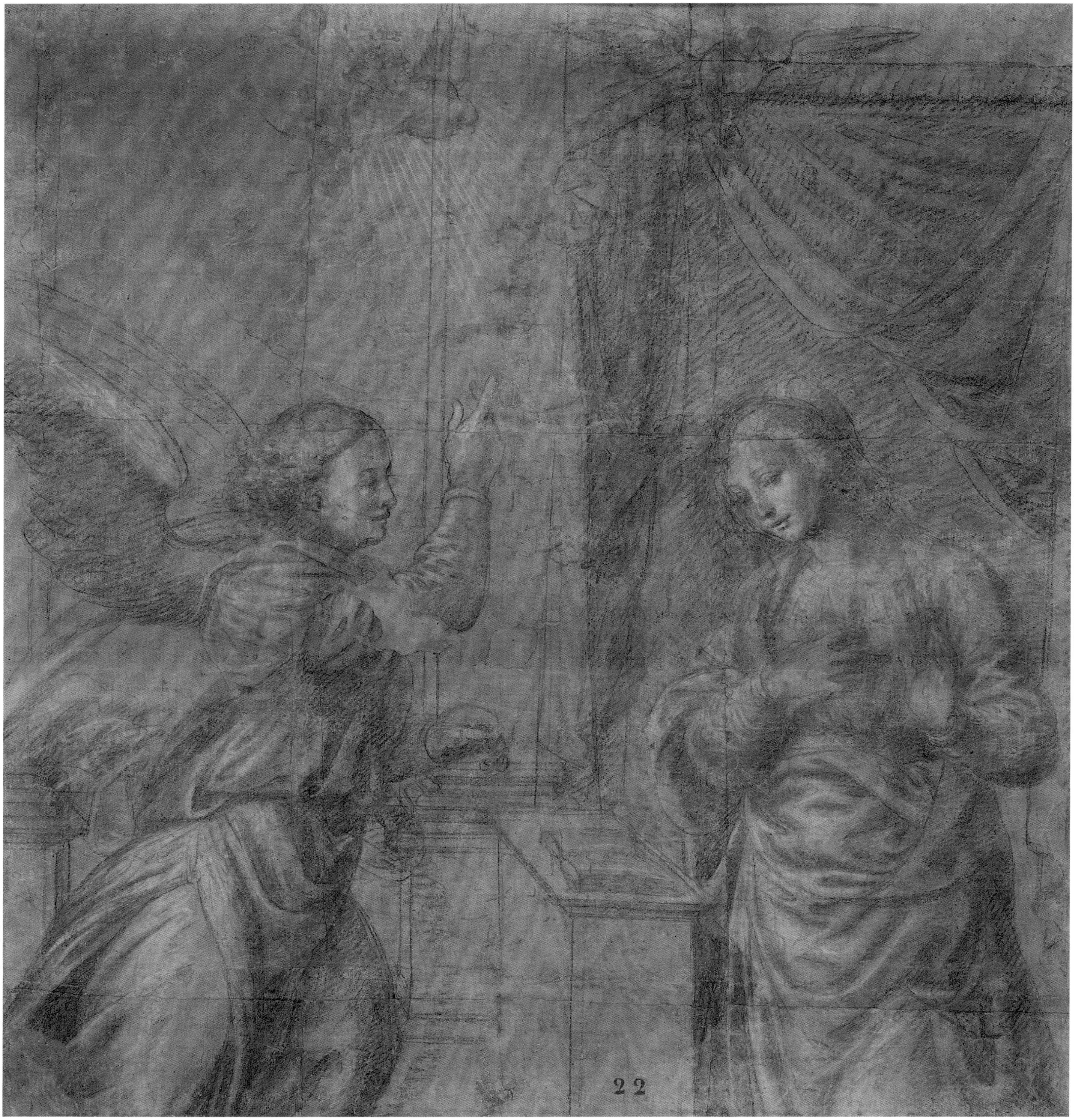

XXXIII

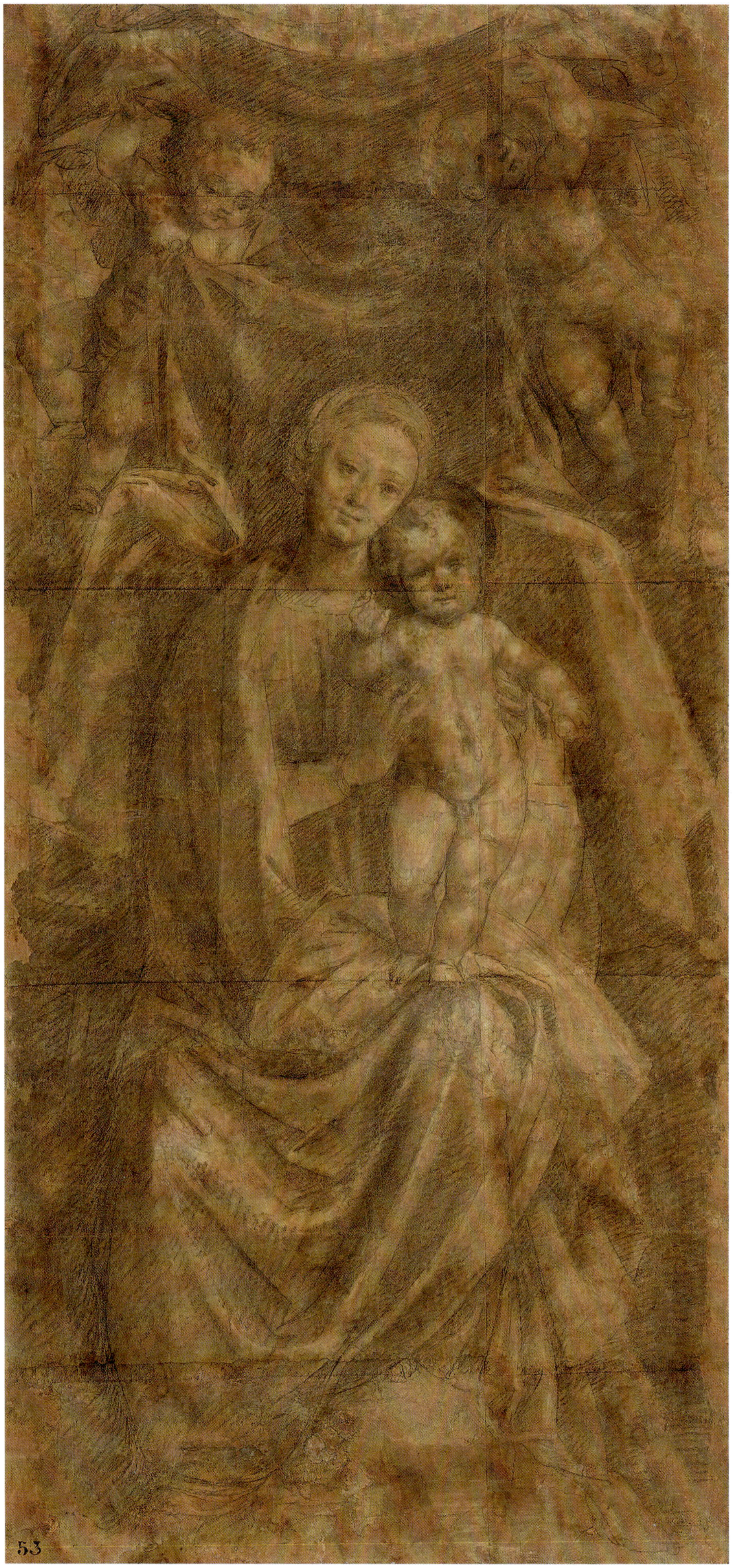

XXXIV

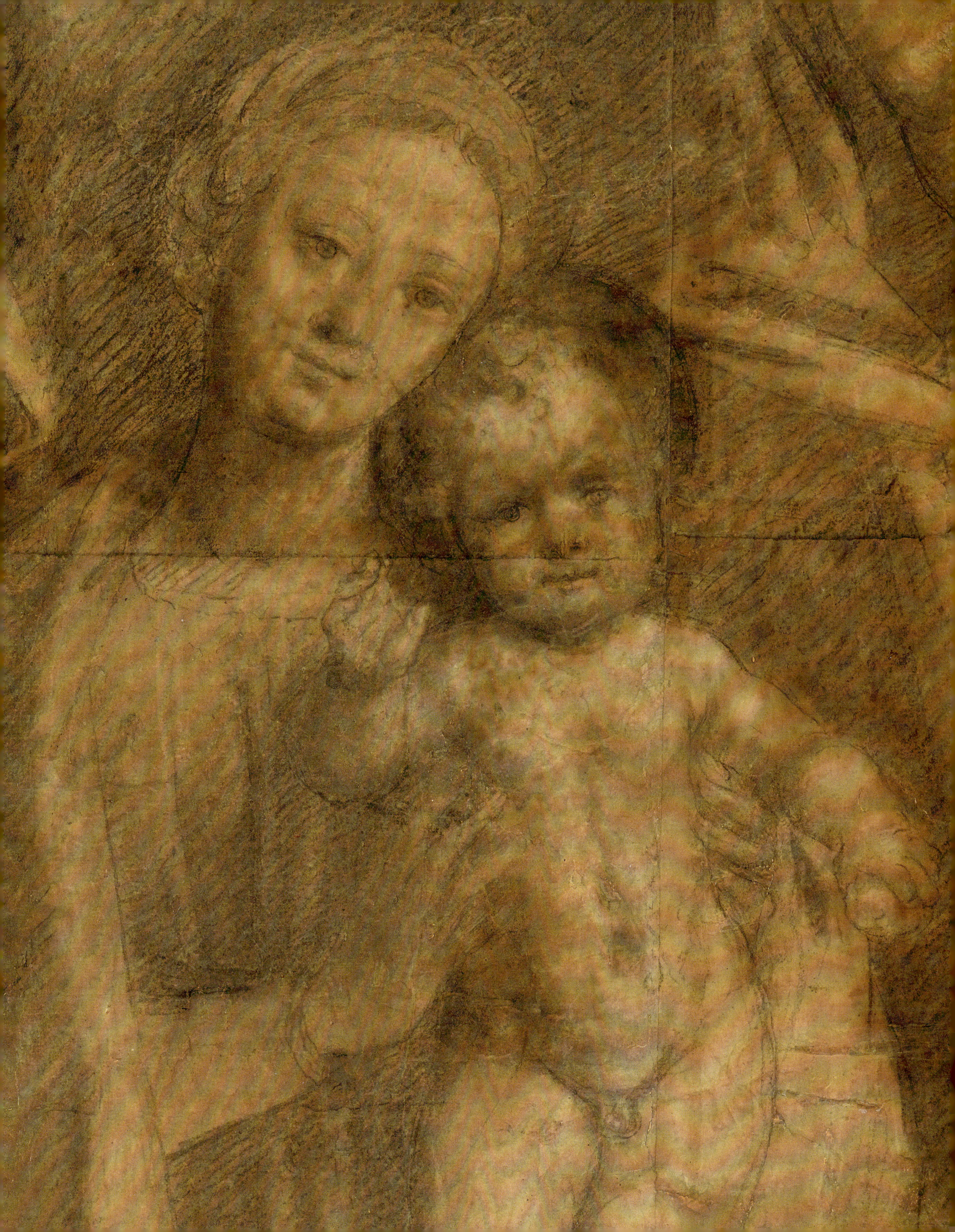

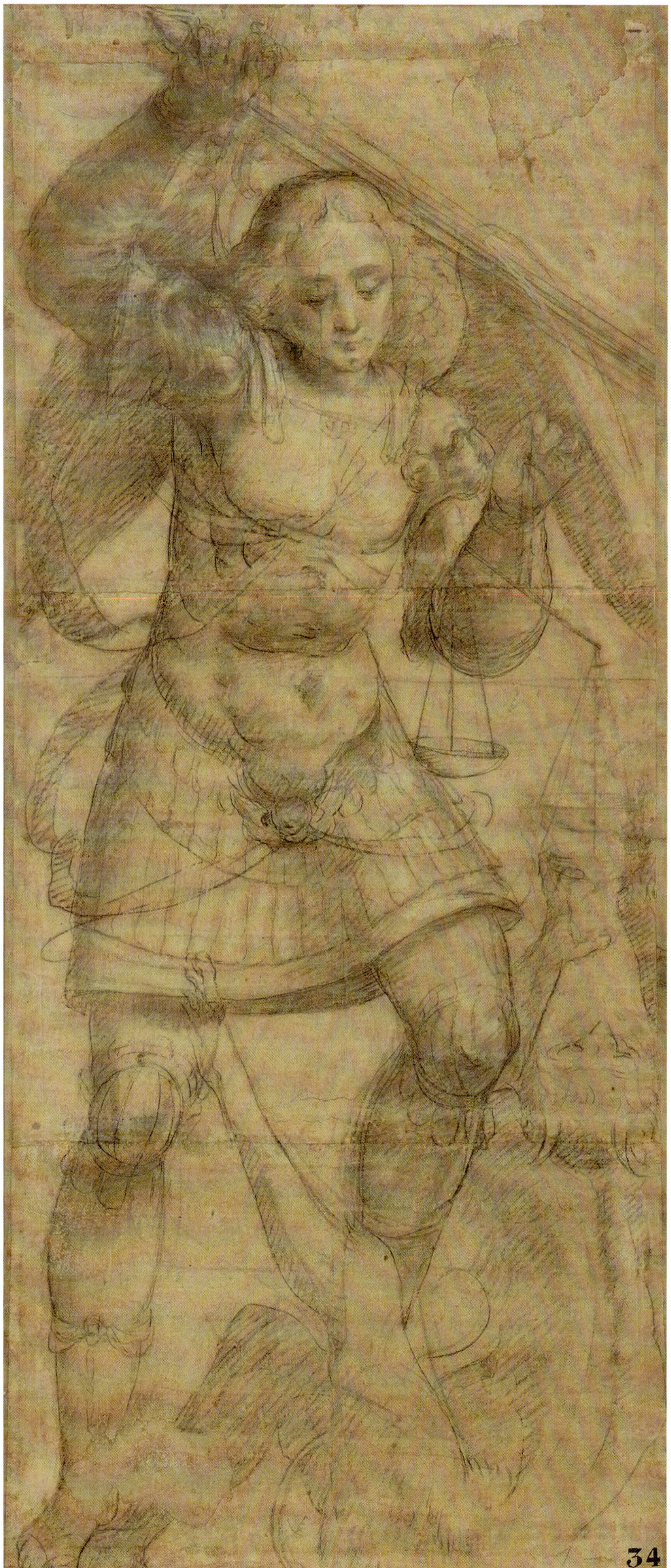

XXXV

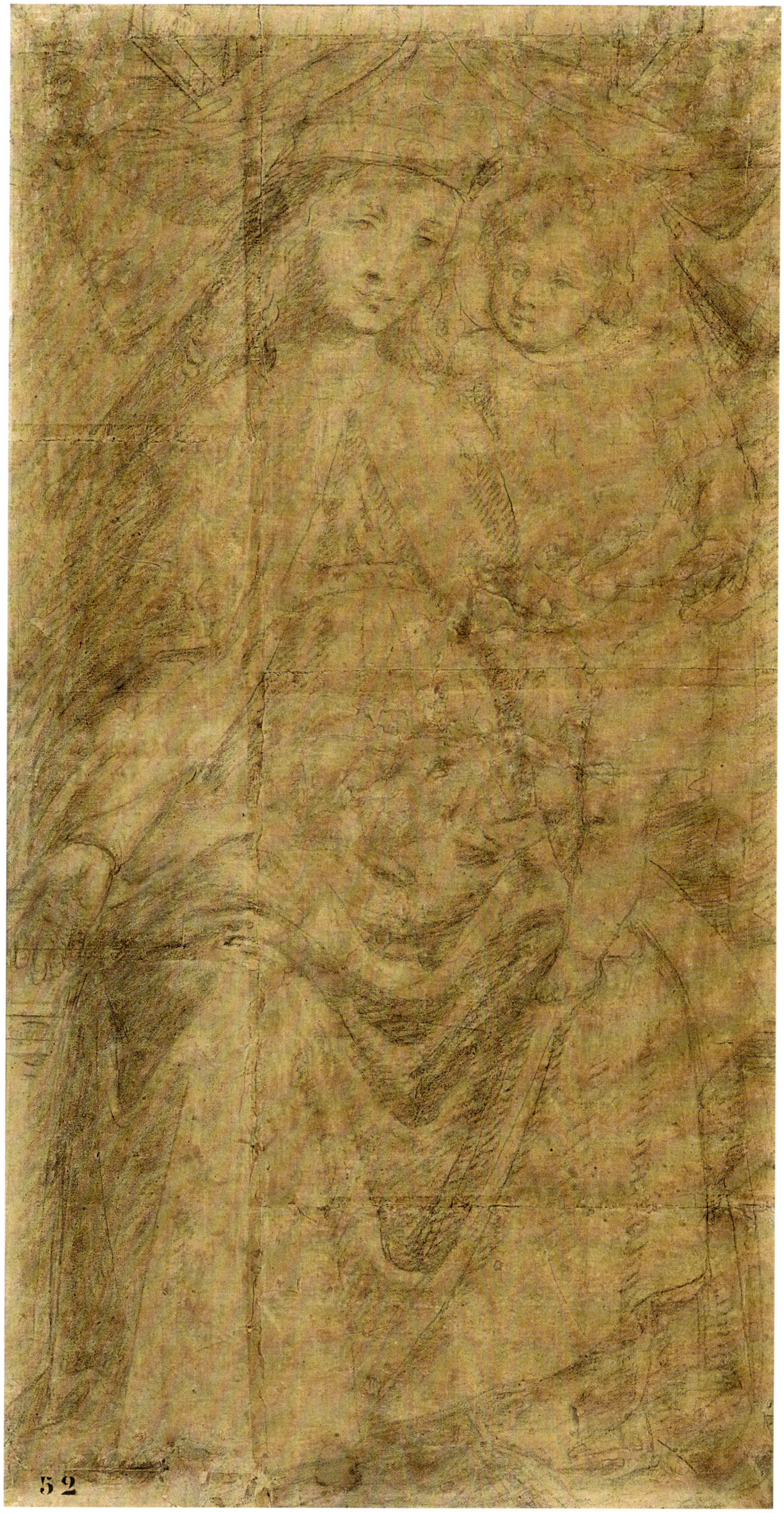

XXXVI

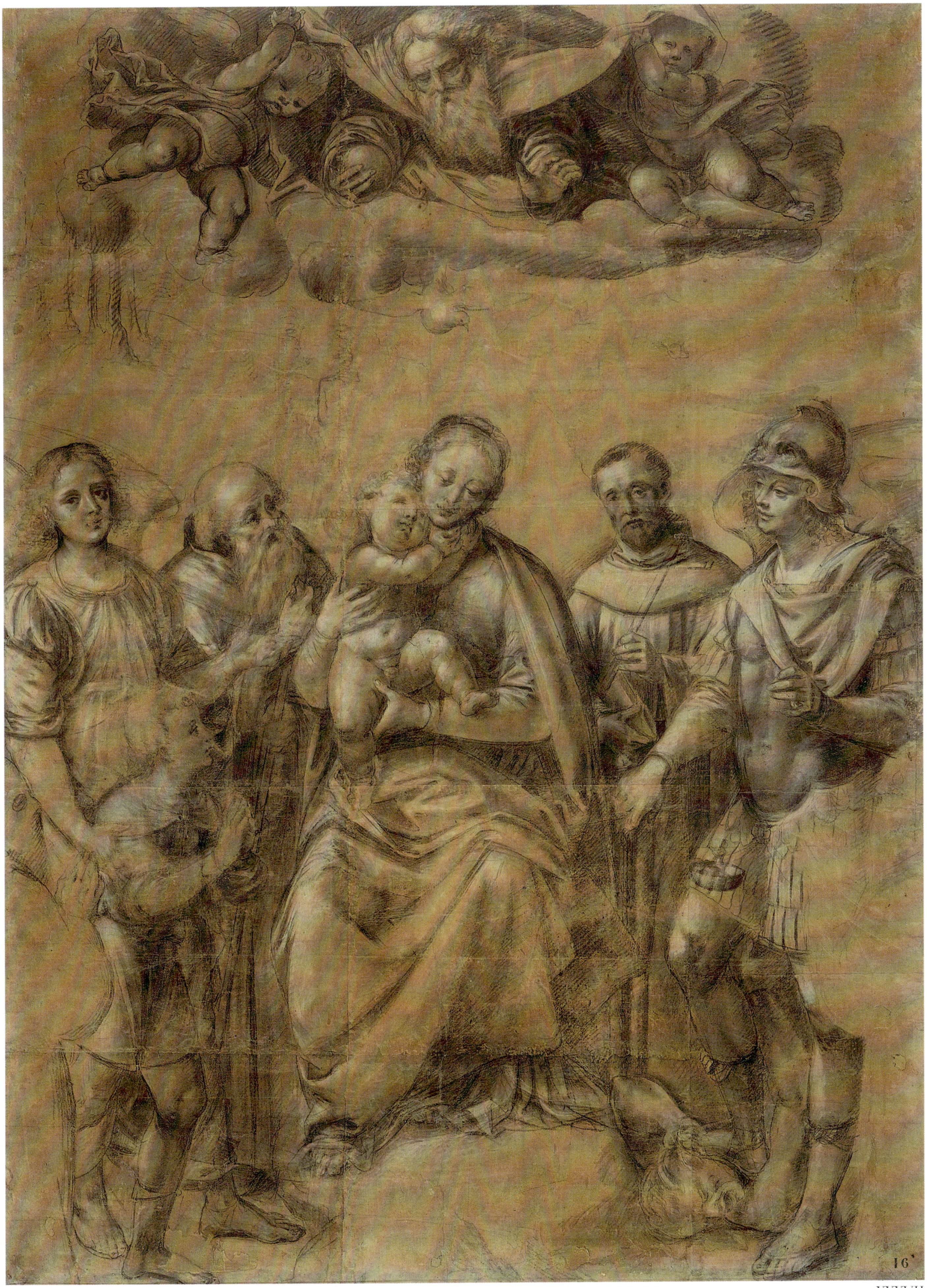

XXXVII

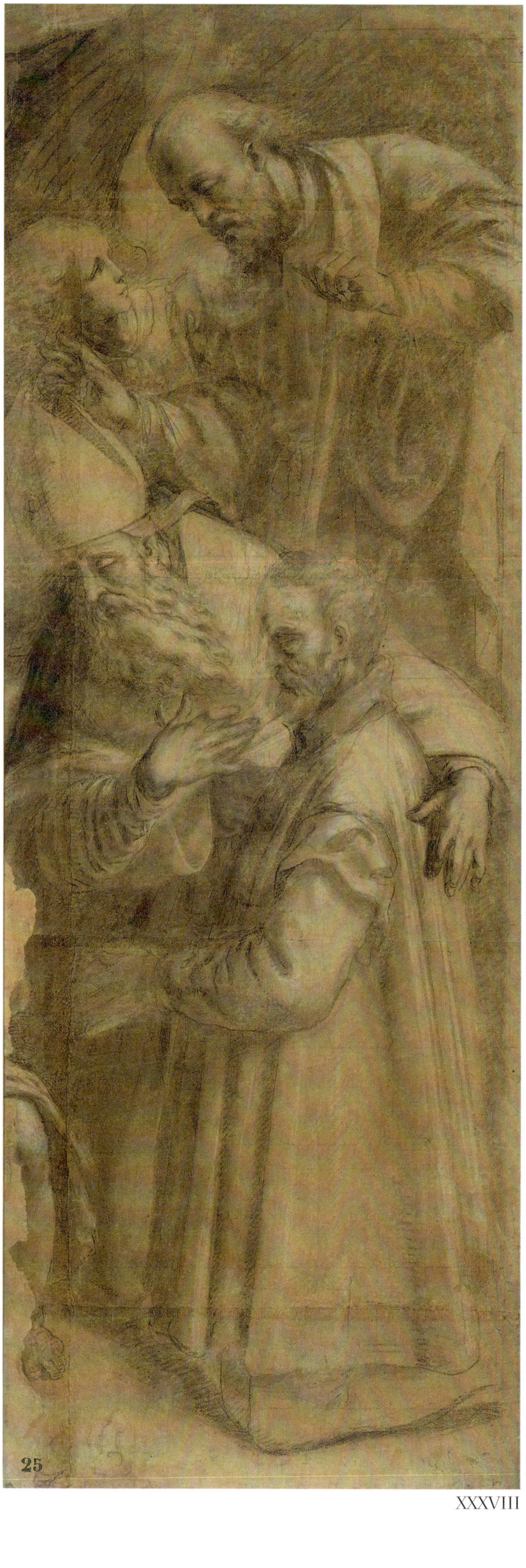

XXXVIII

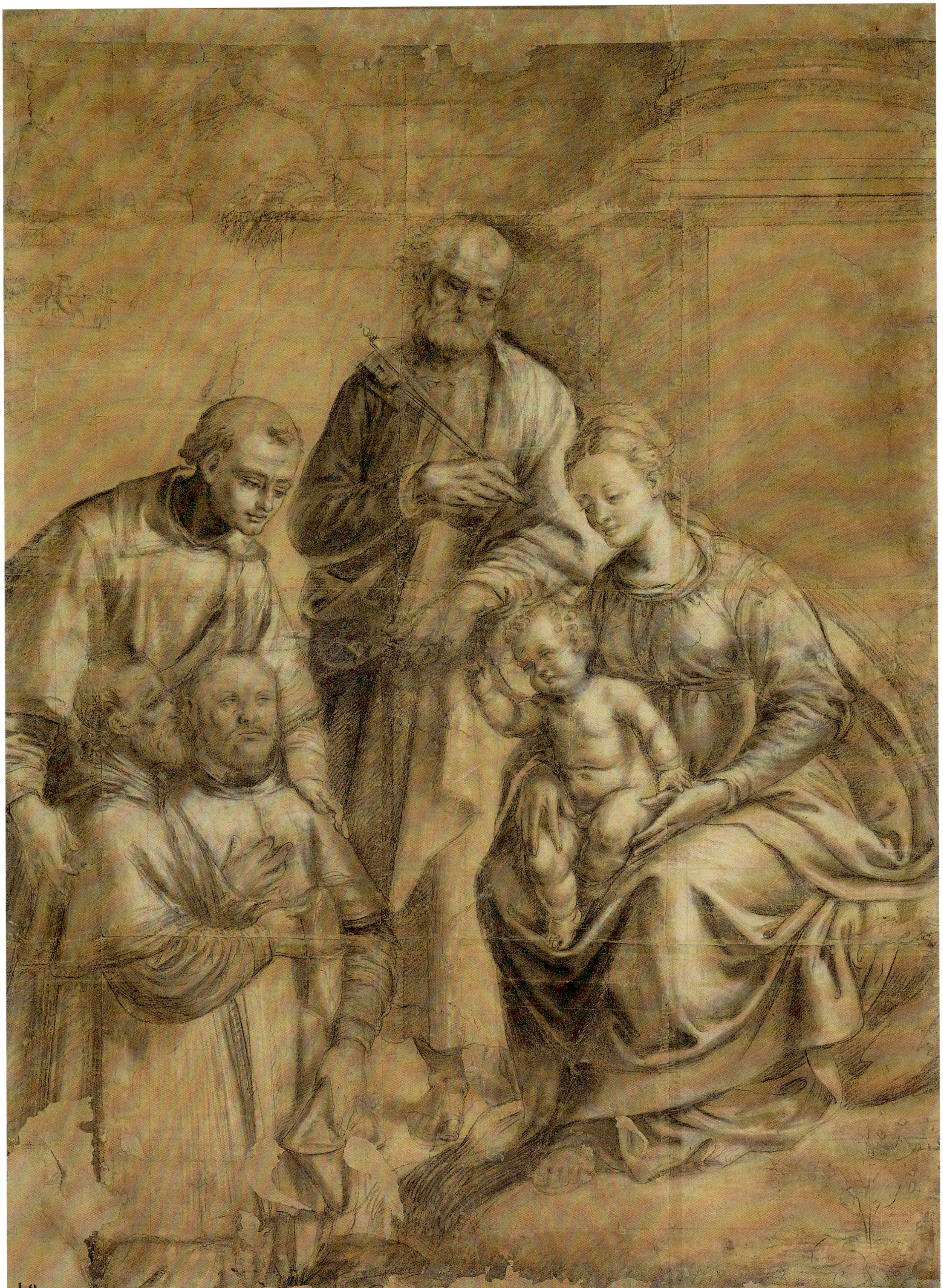

XXXIX

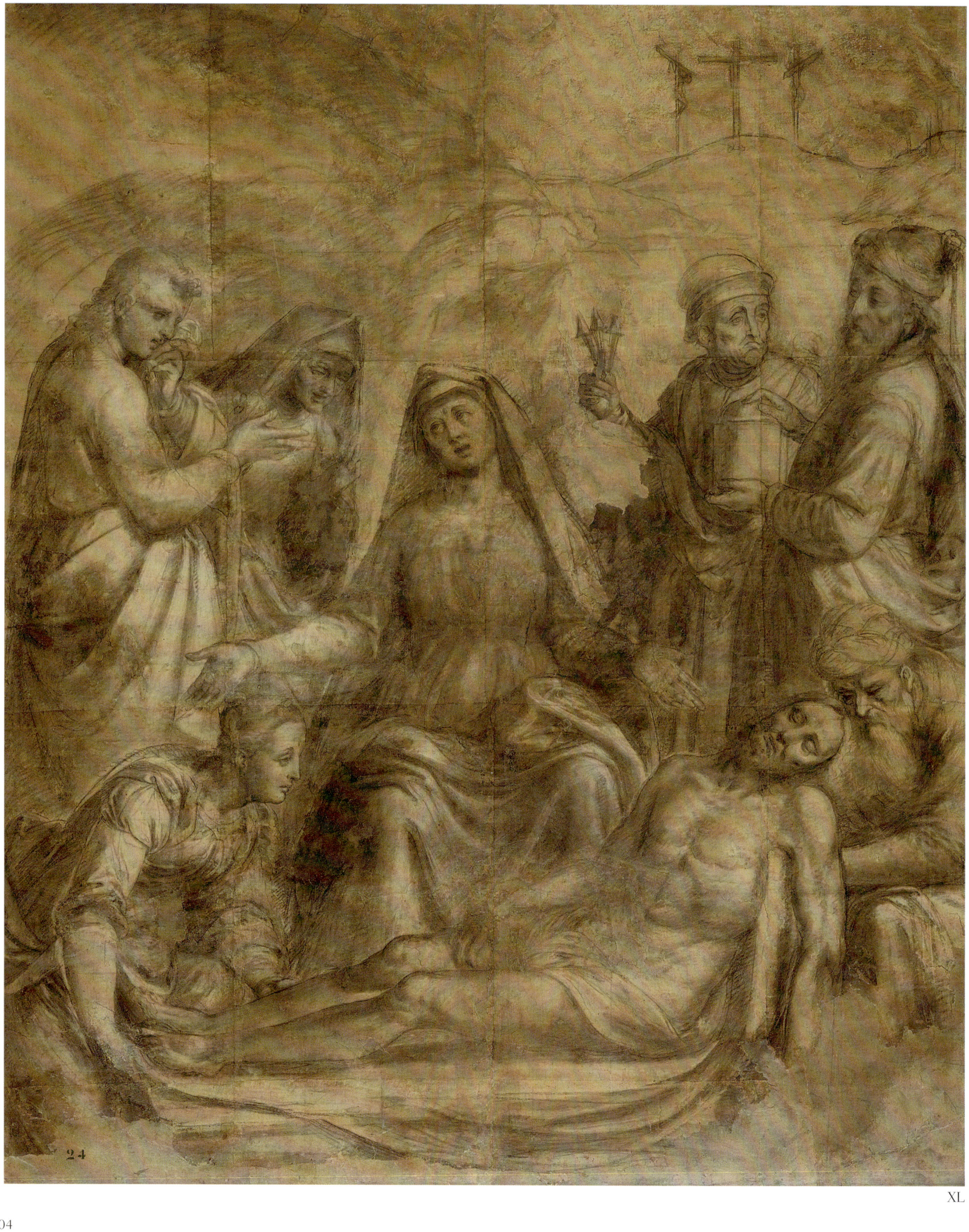

XL

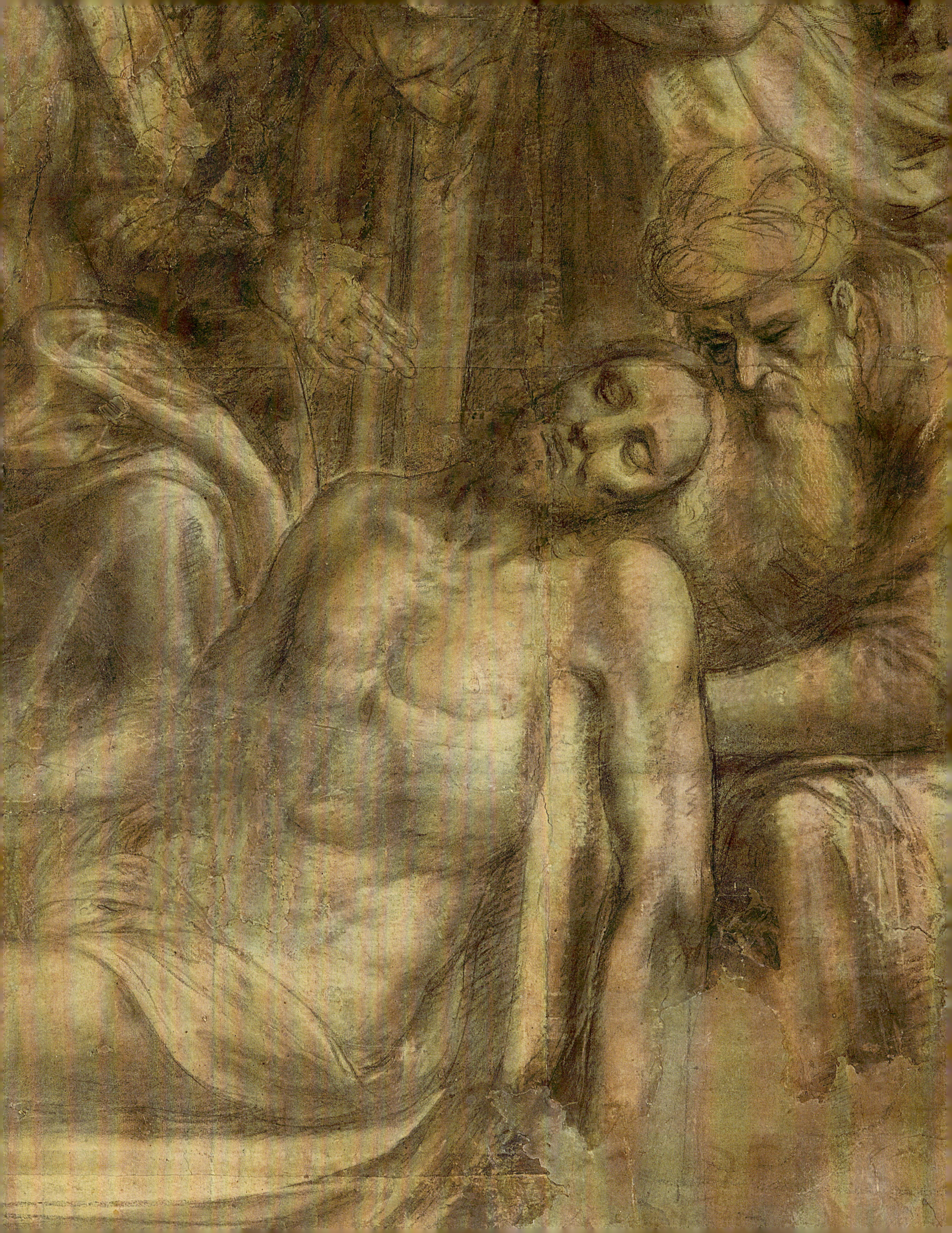

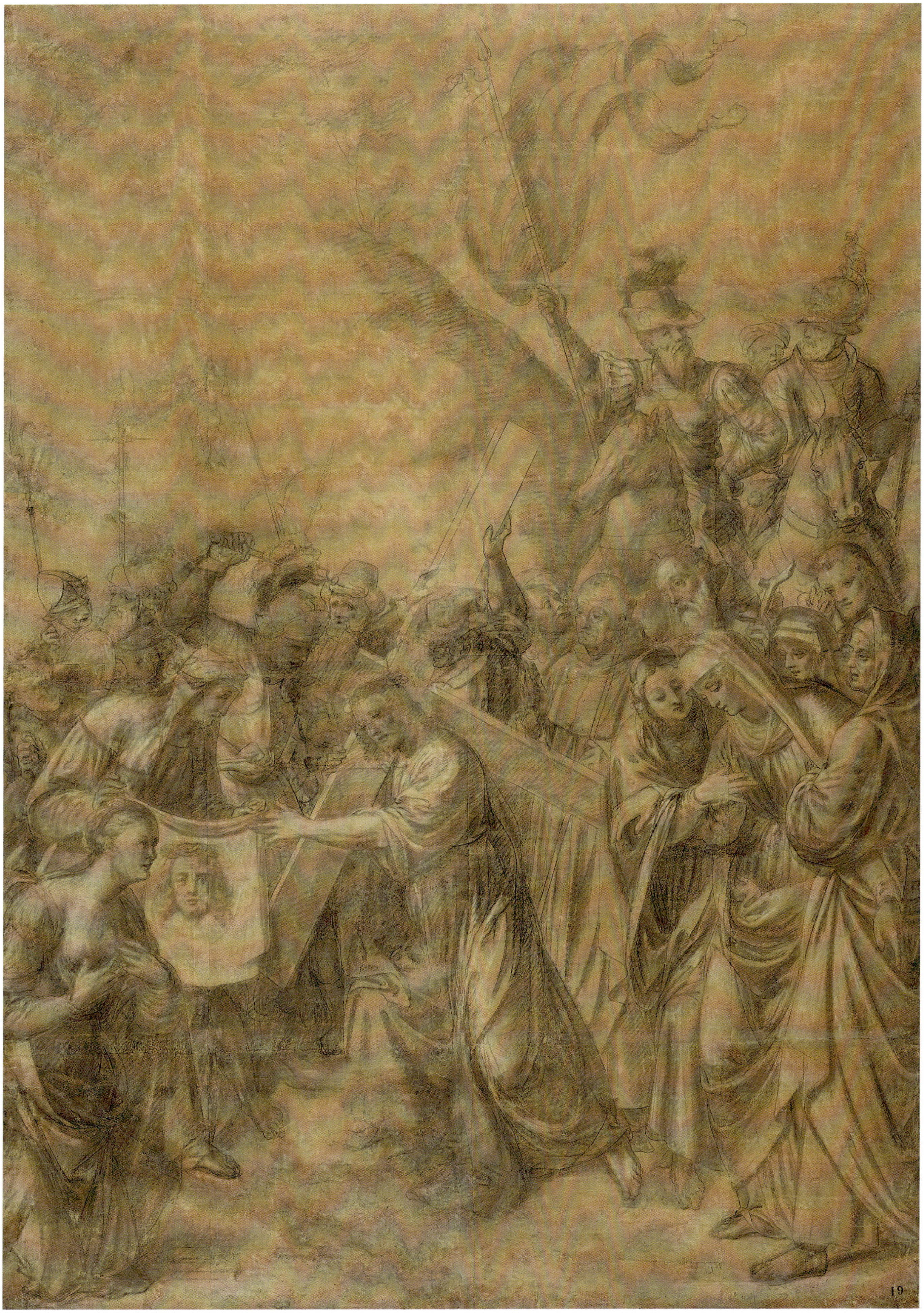

XLI

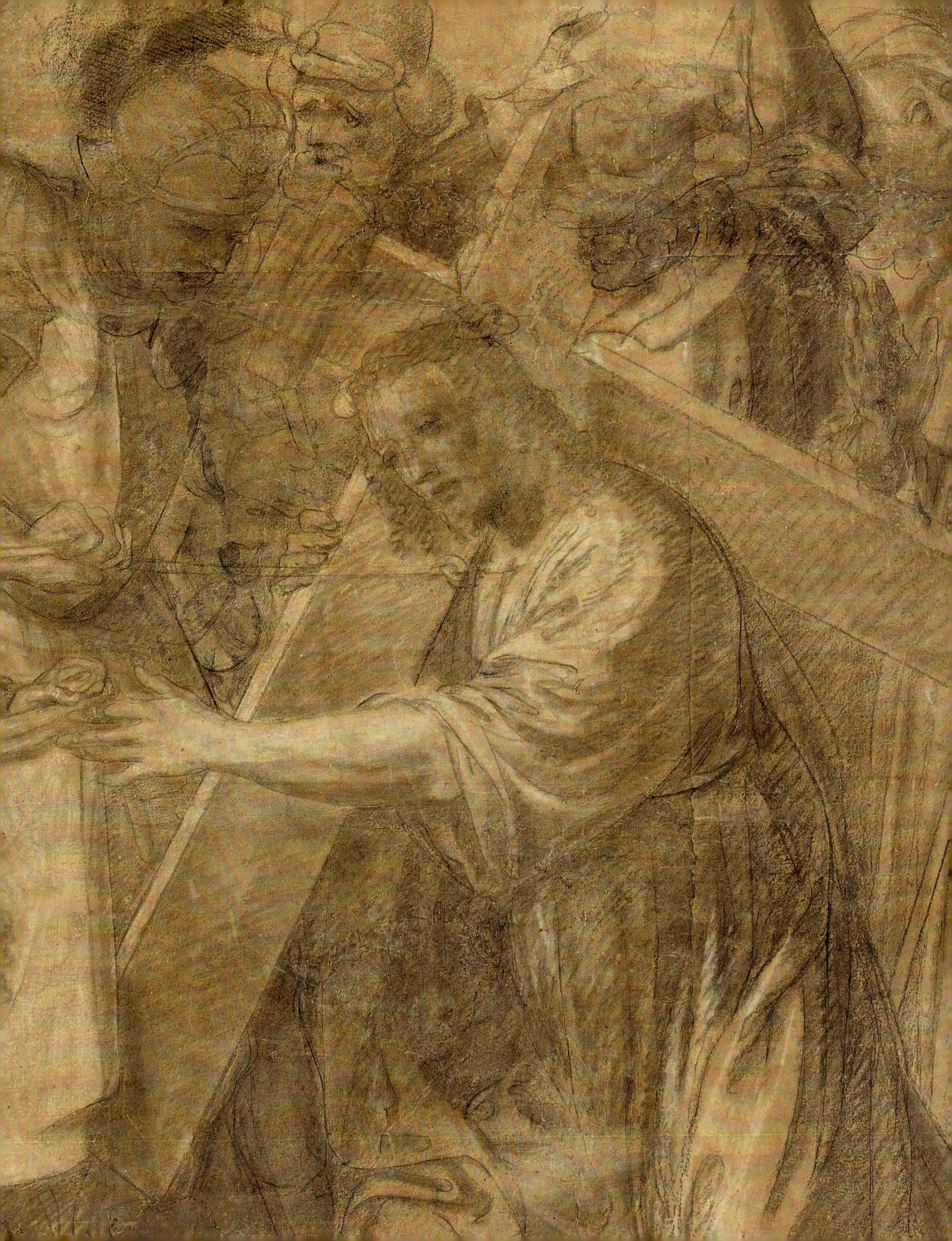

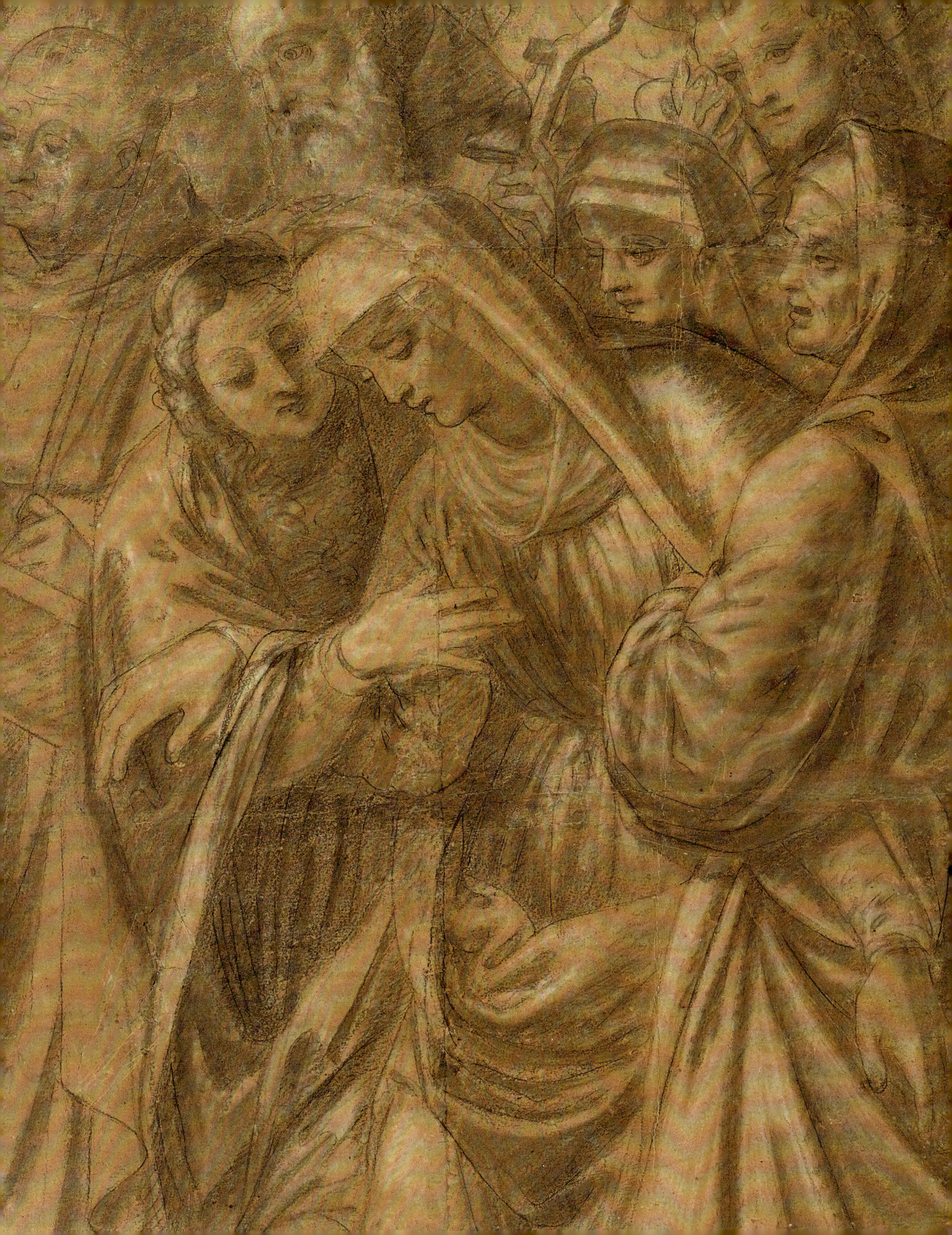

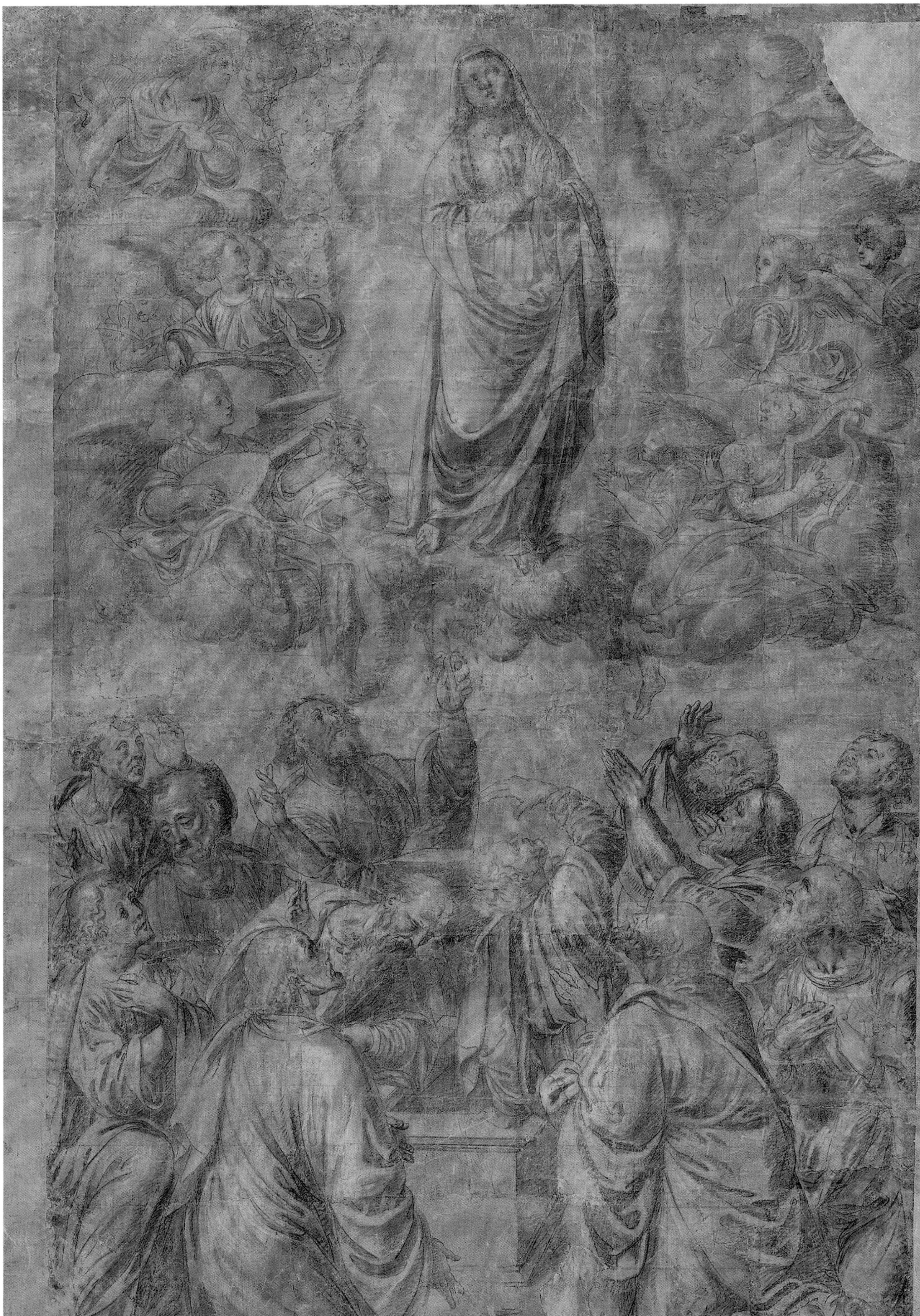

XLII

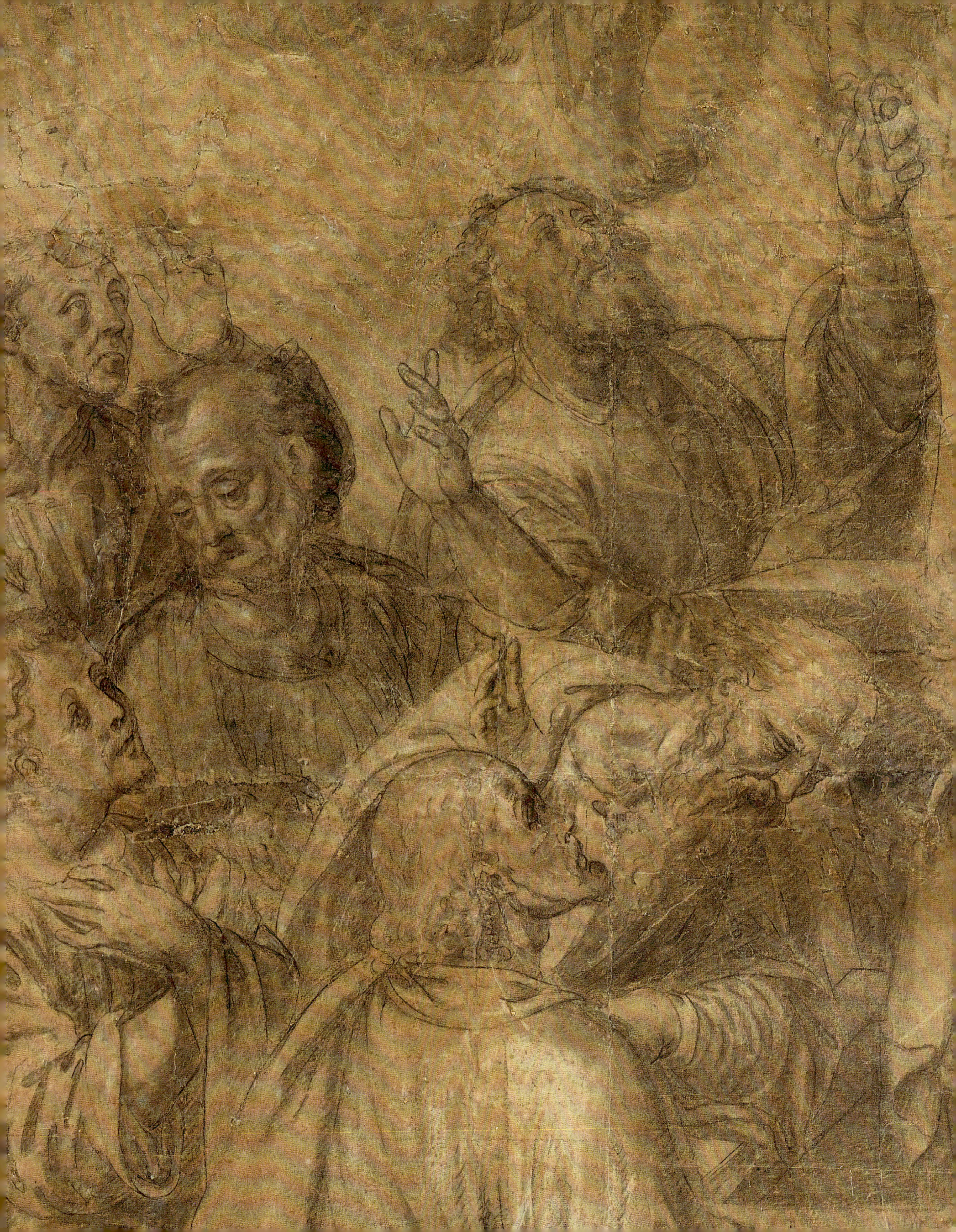

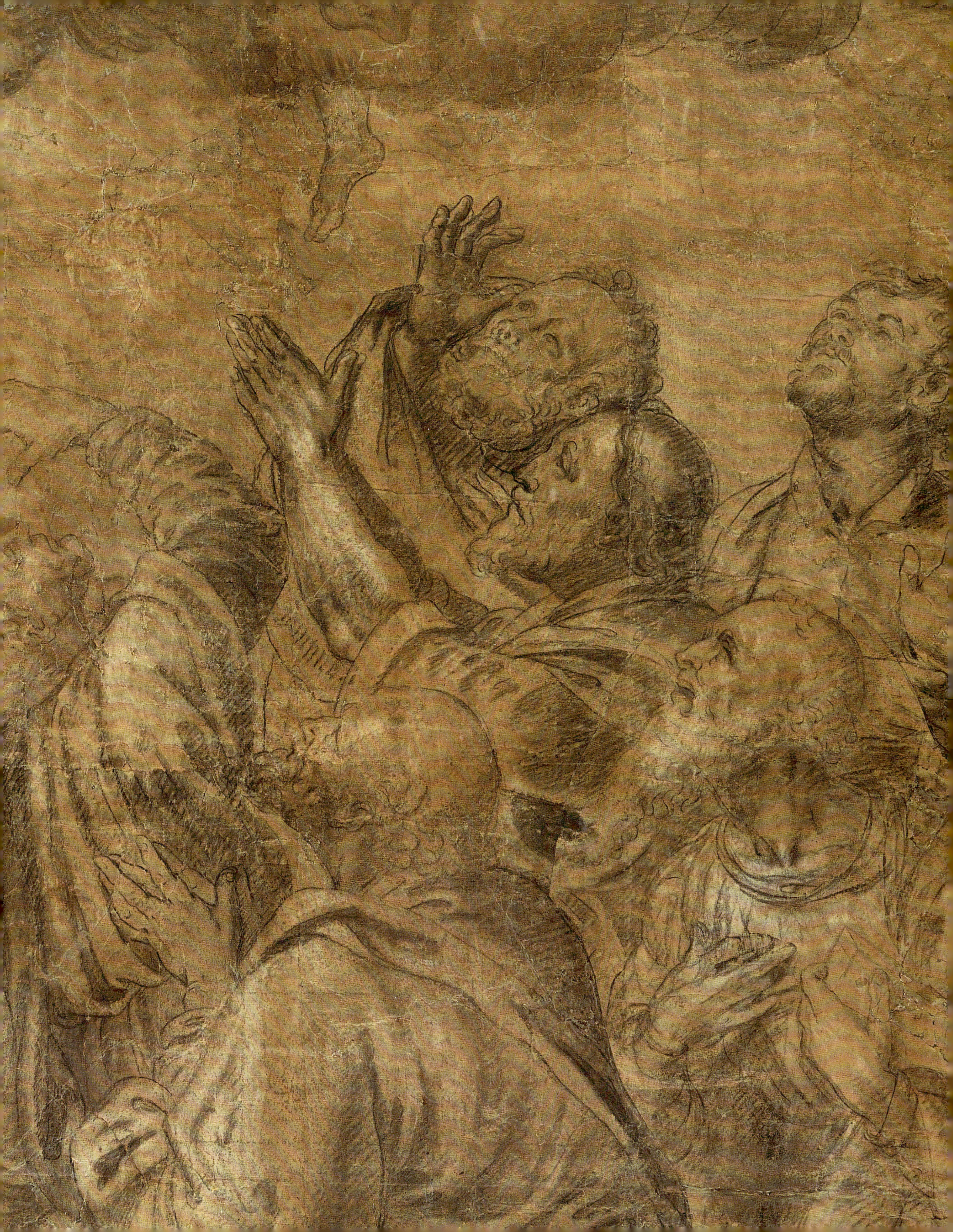

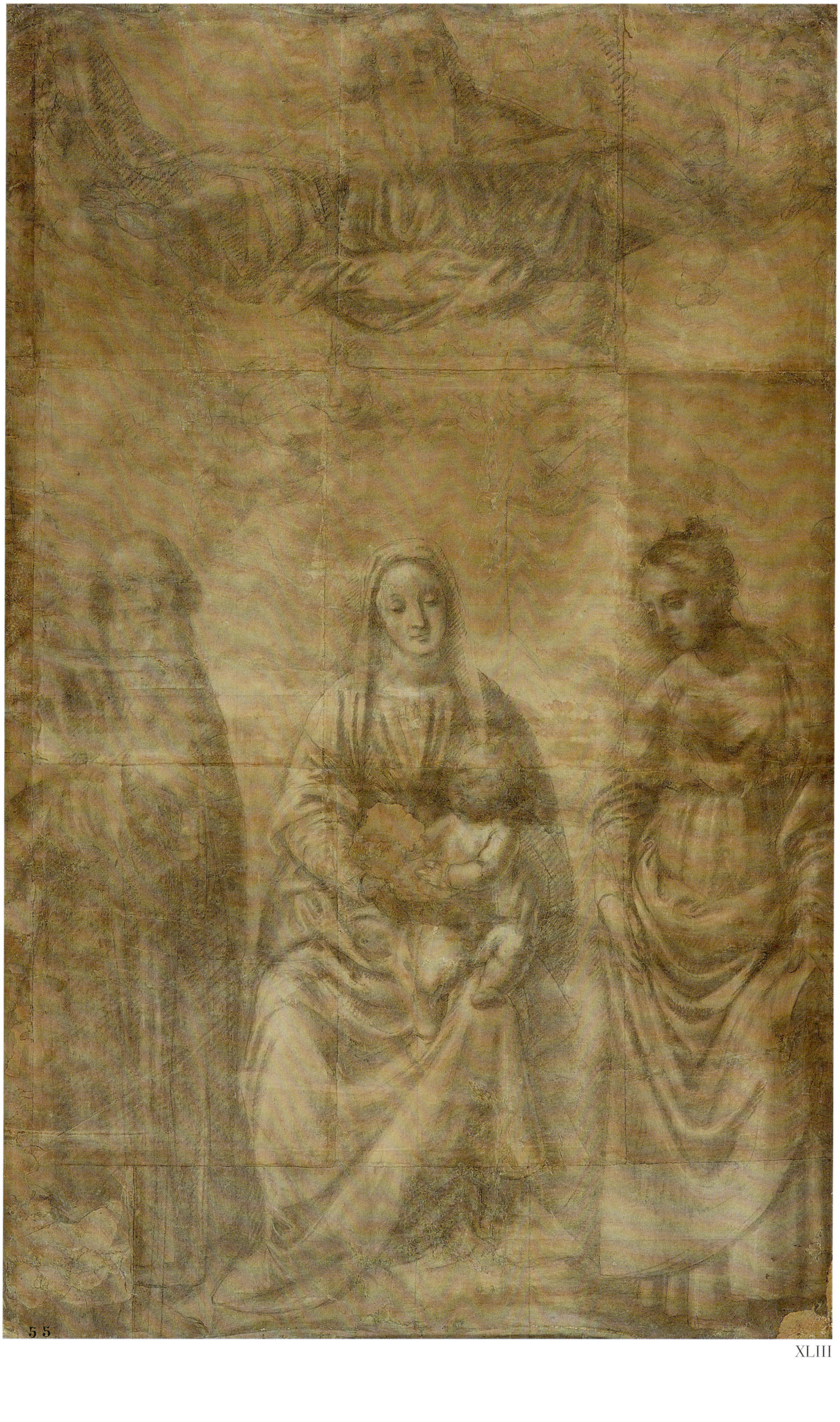

XLIII

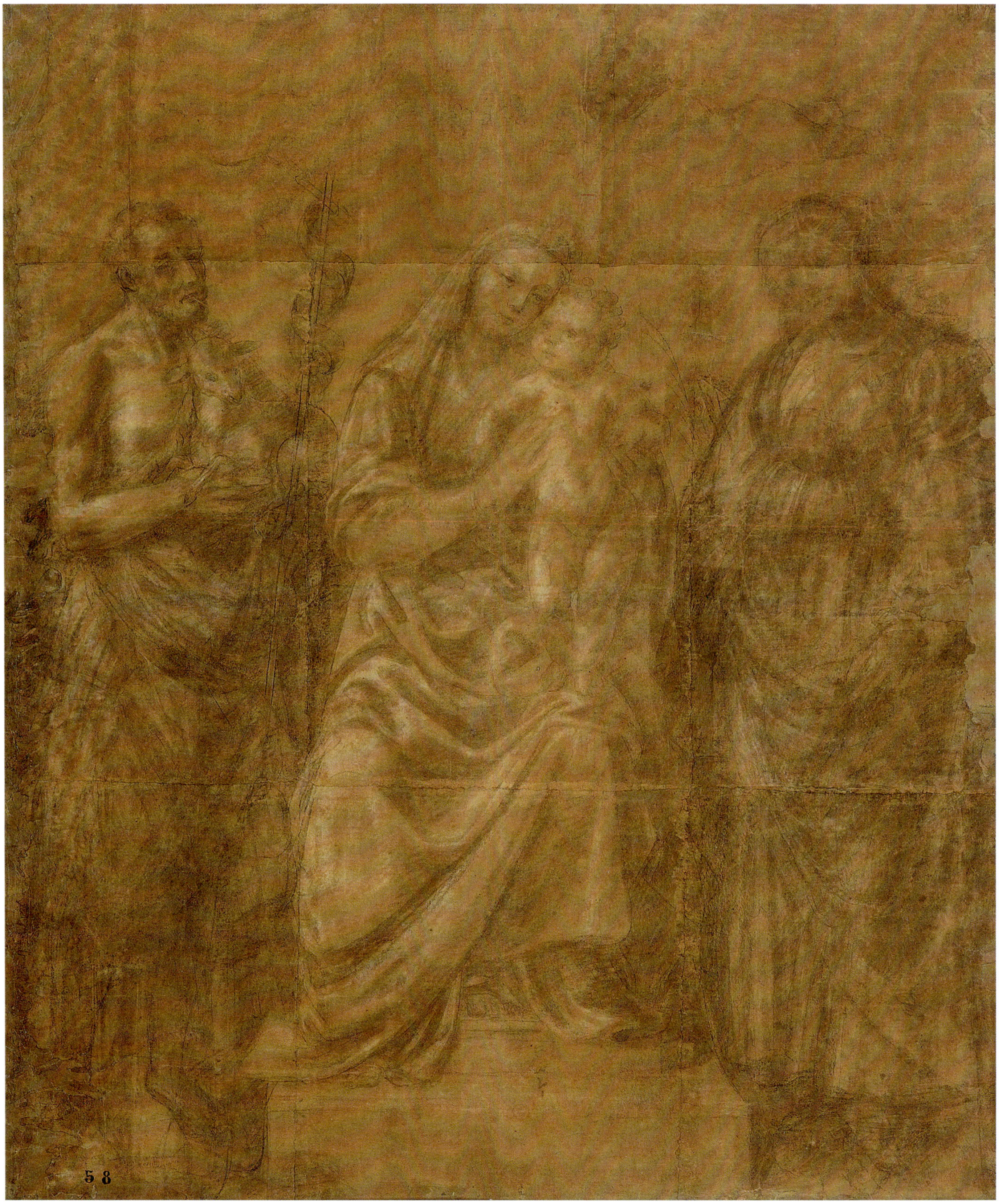

XLIV

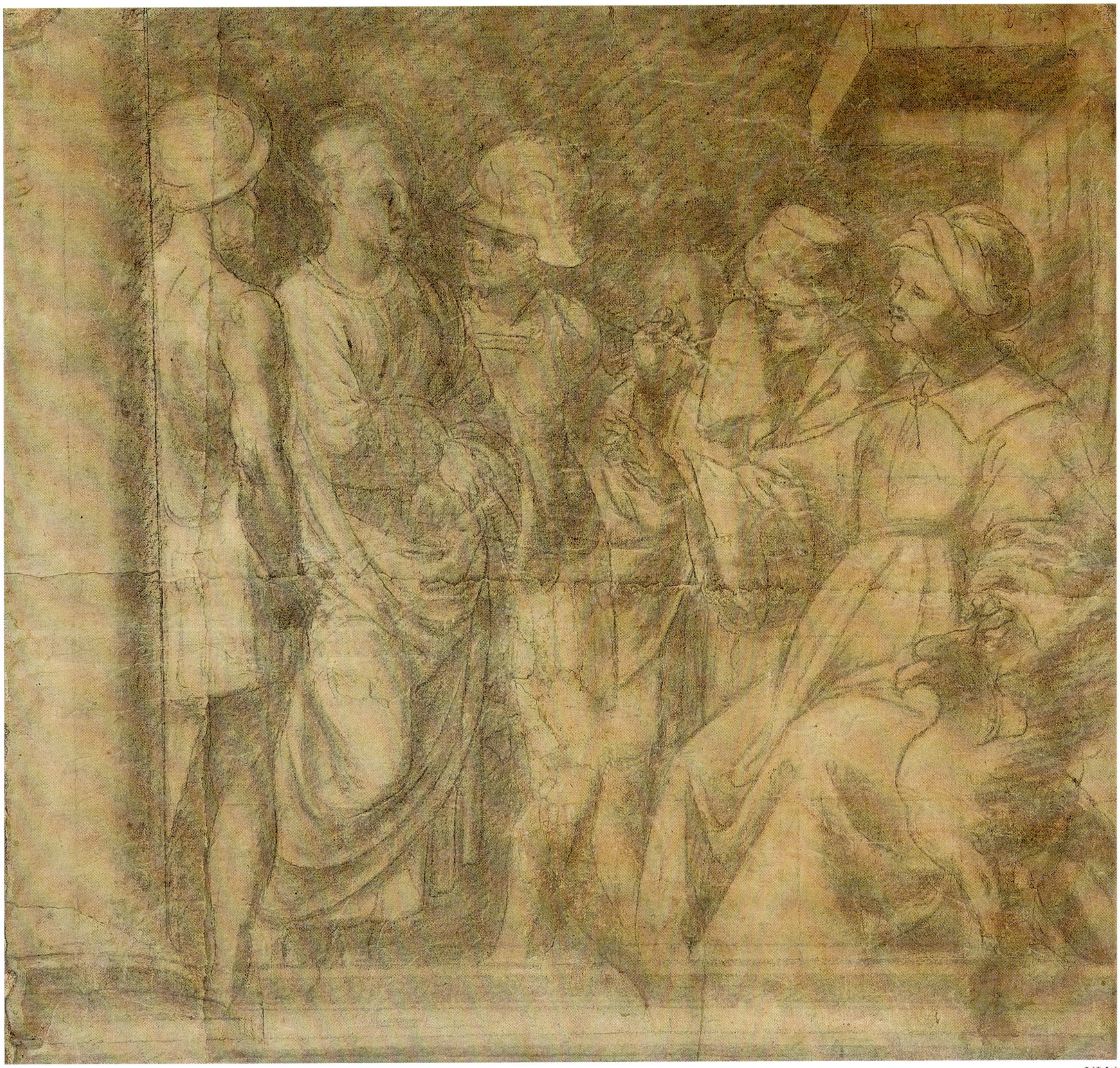

XLV

XLVI

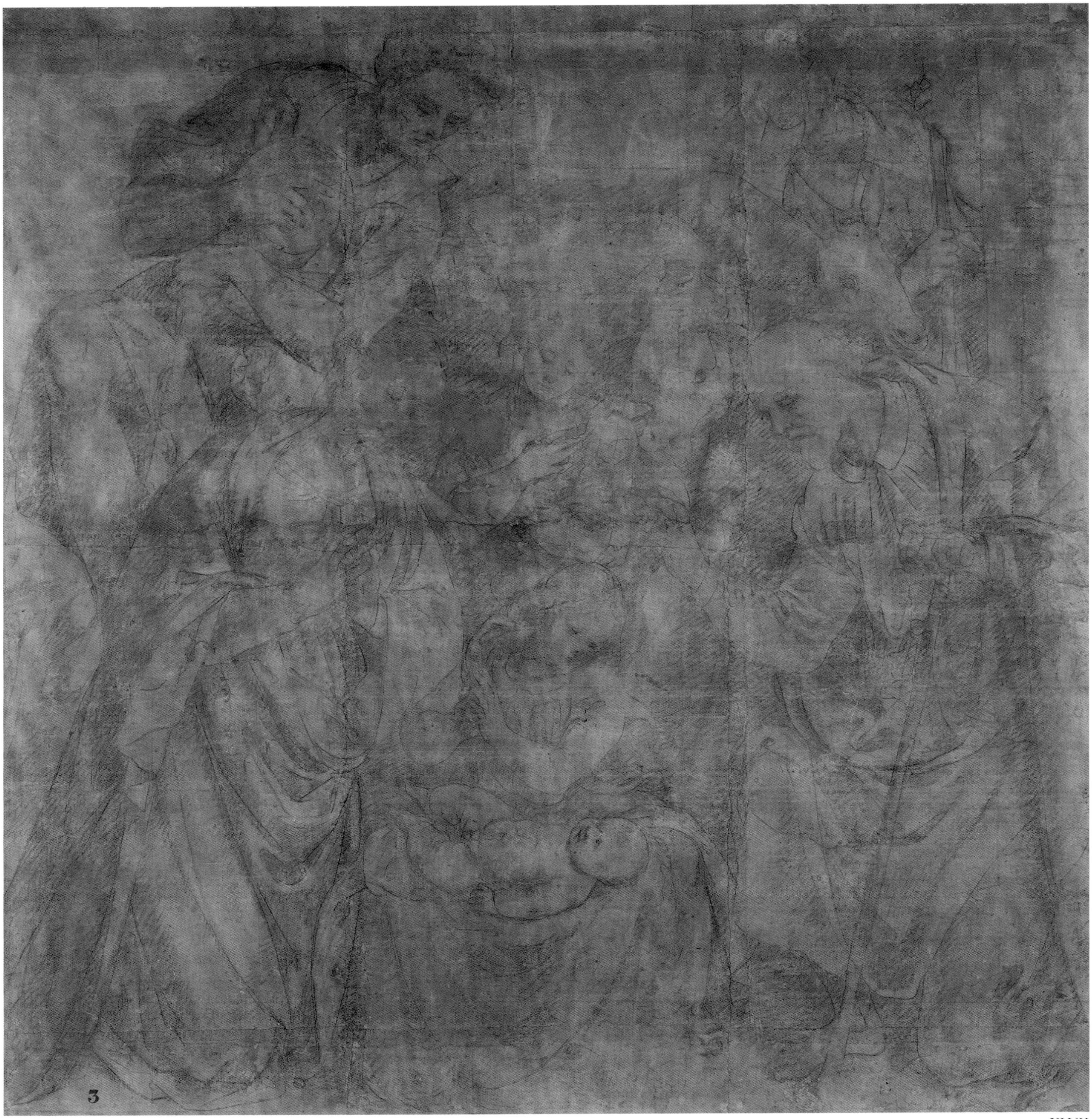

XLVII

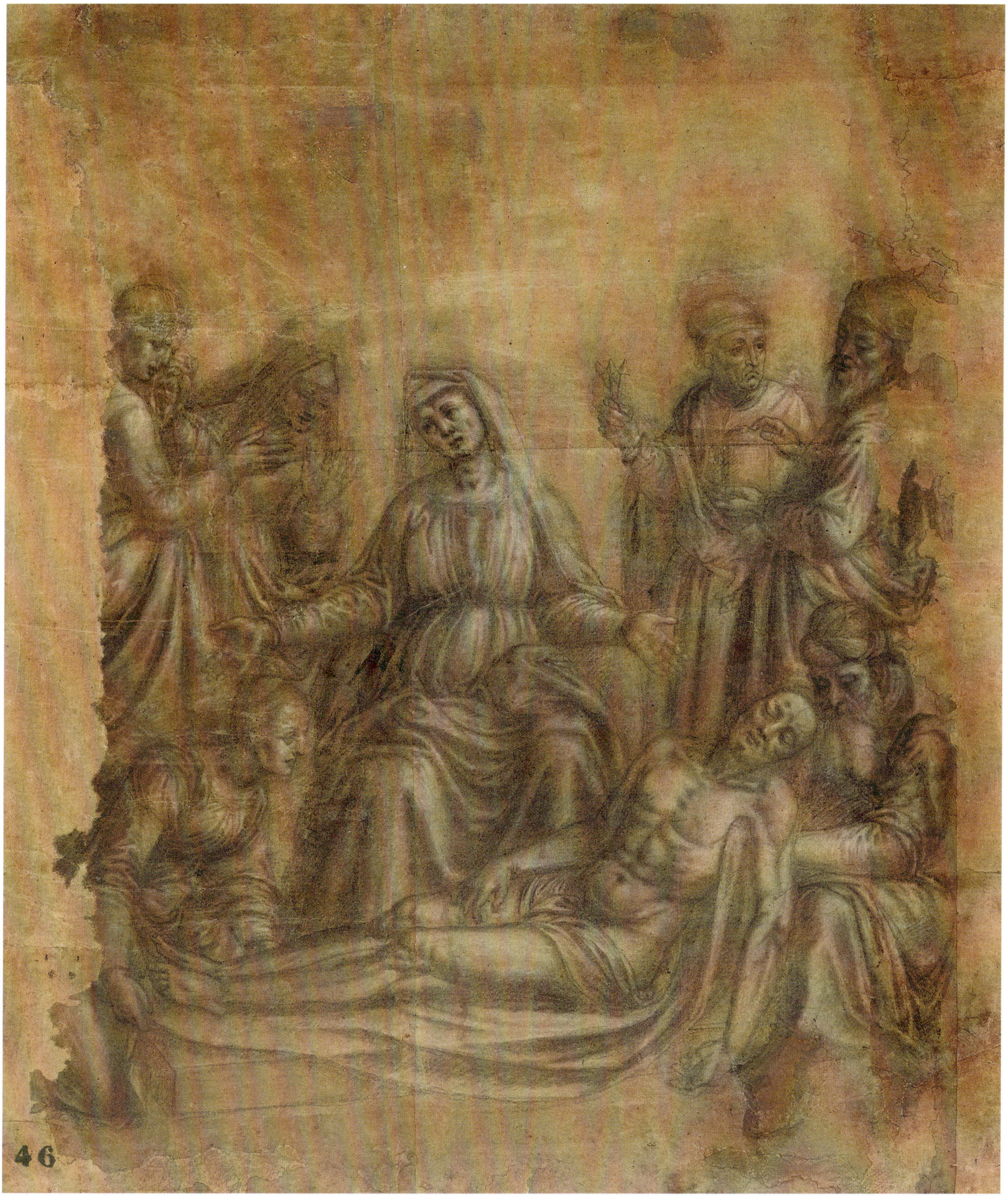

XLVIII

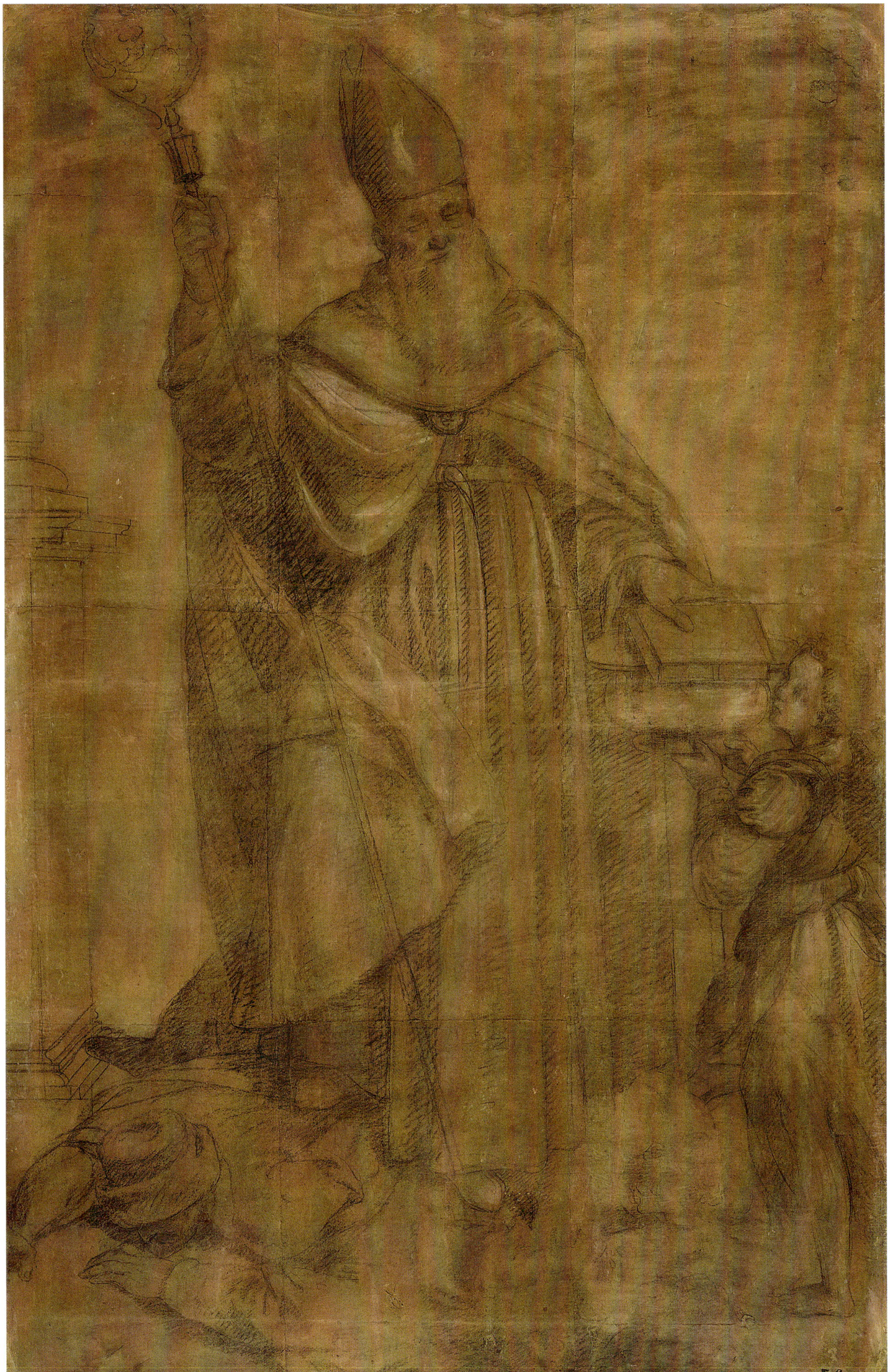

XLIX

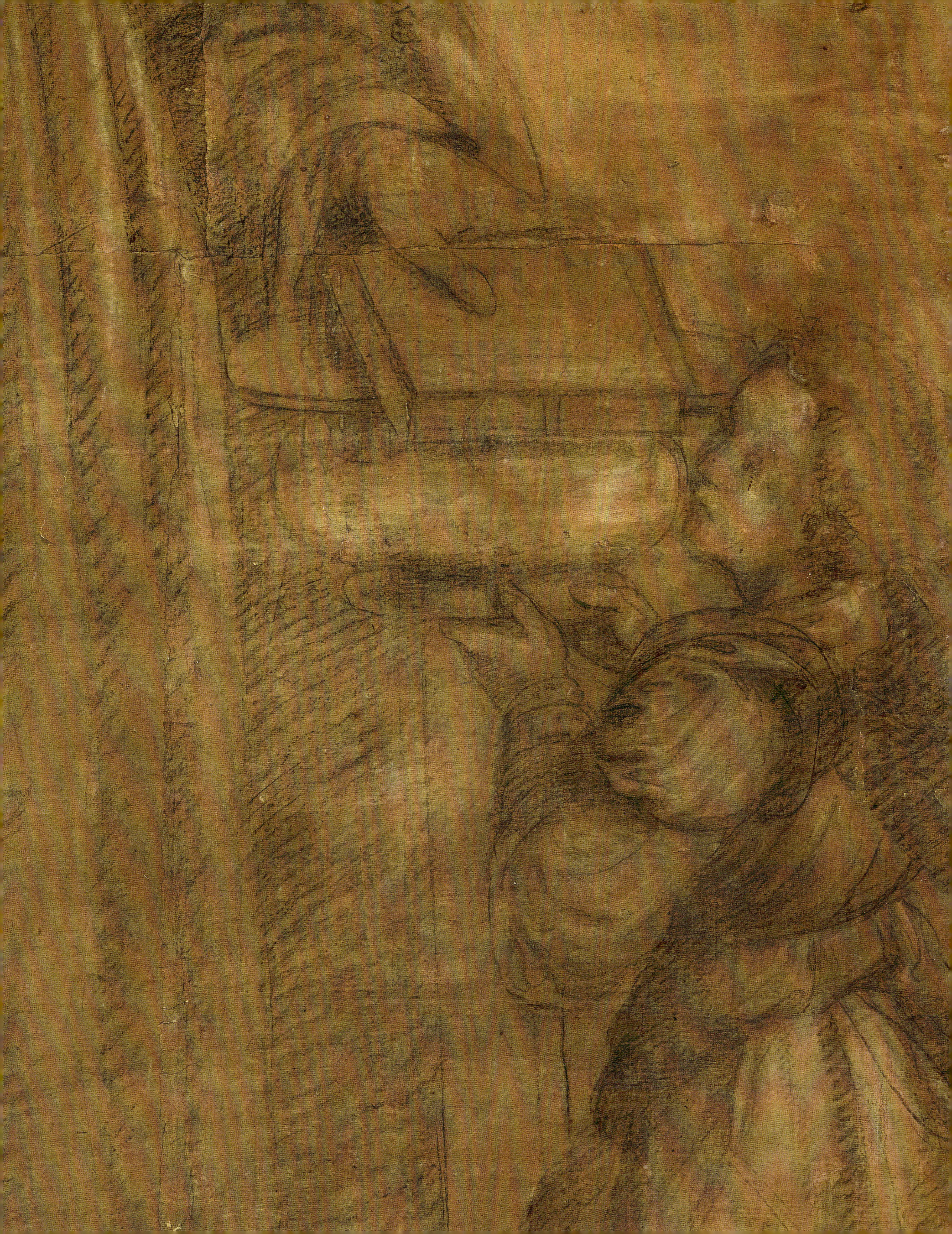

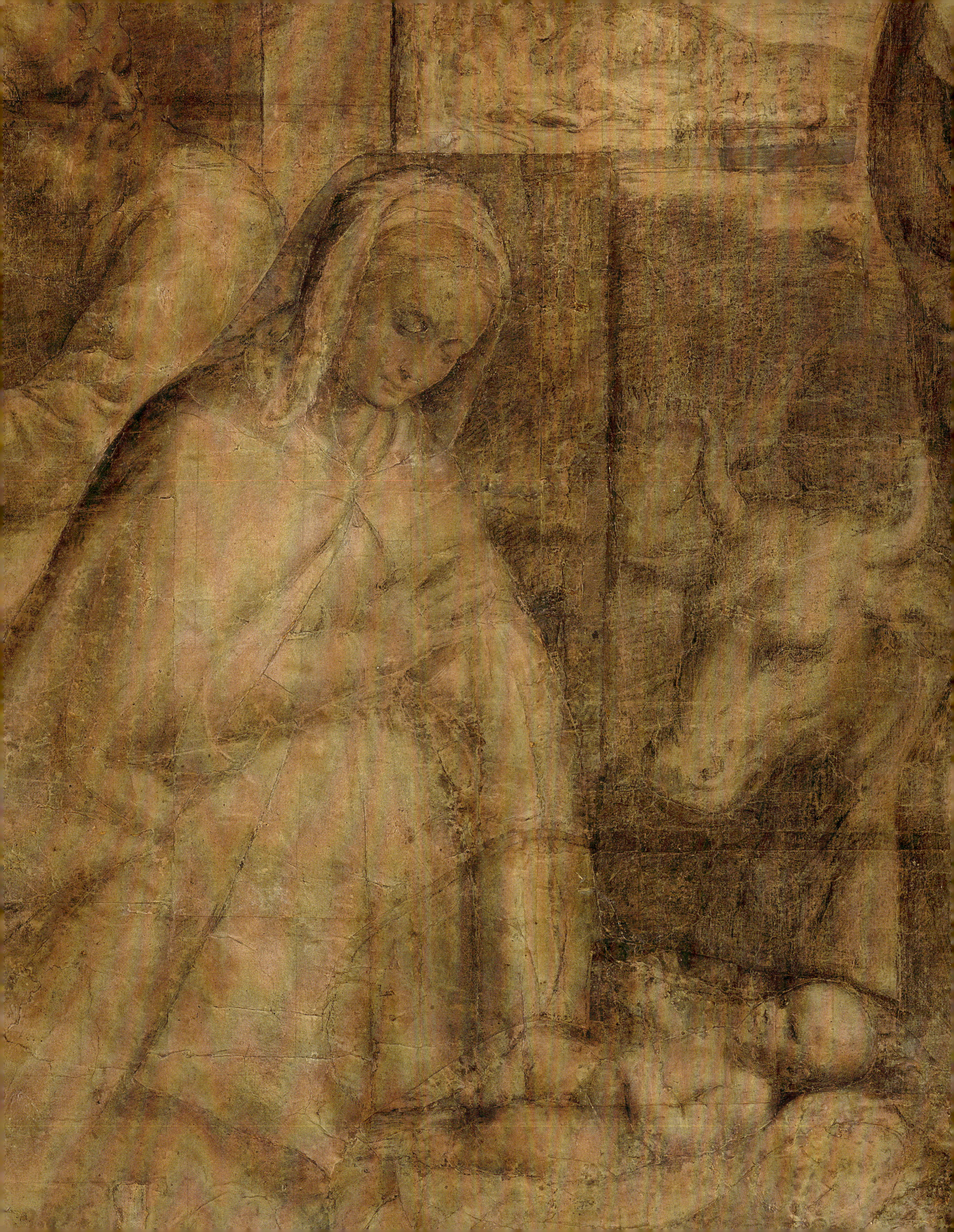

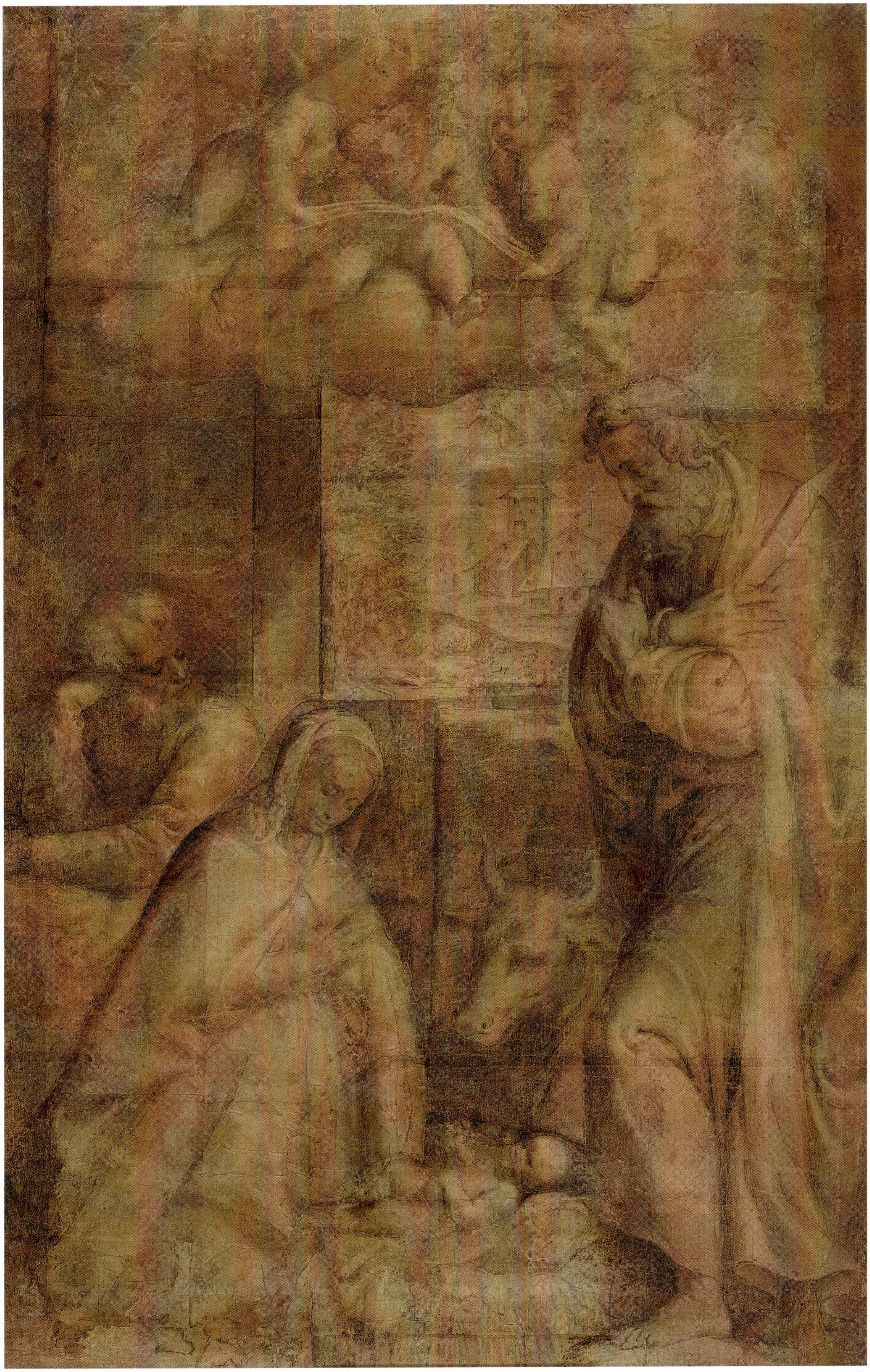

L

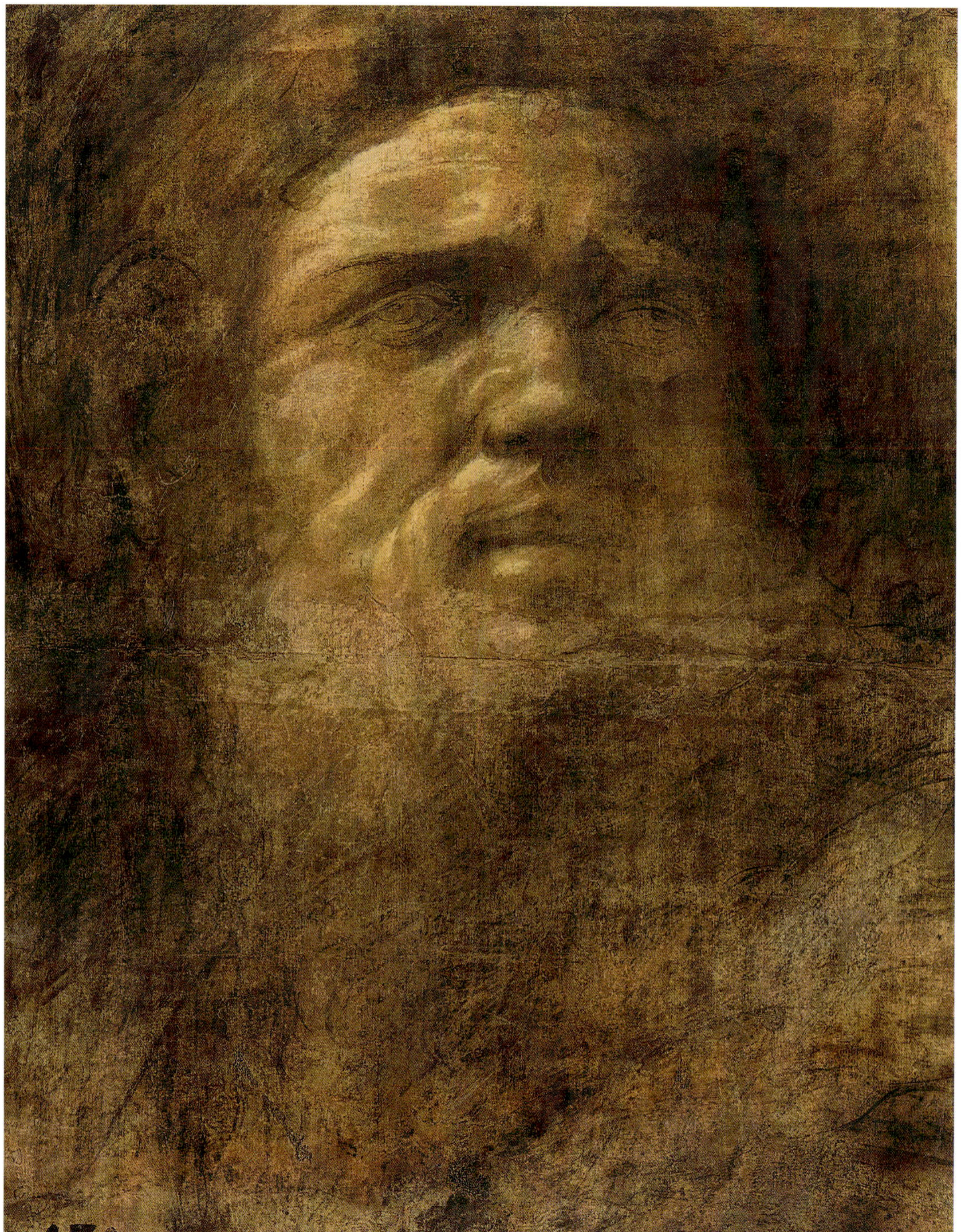

LI

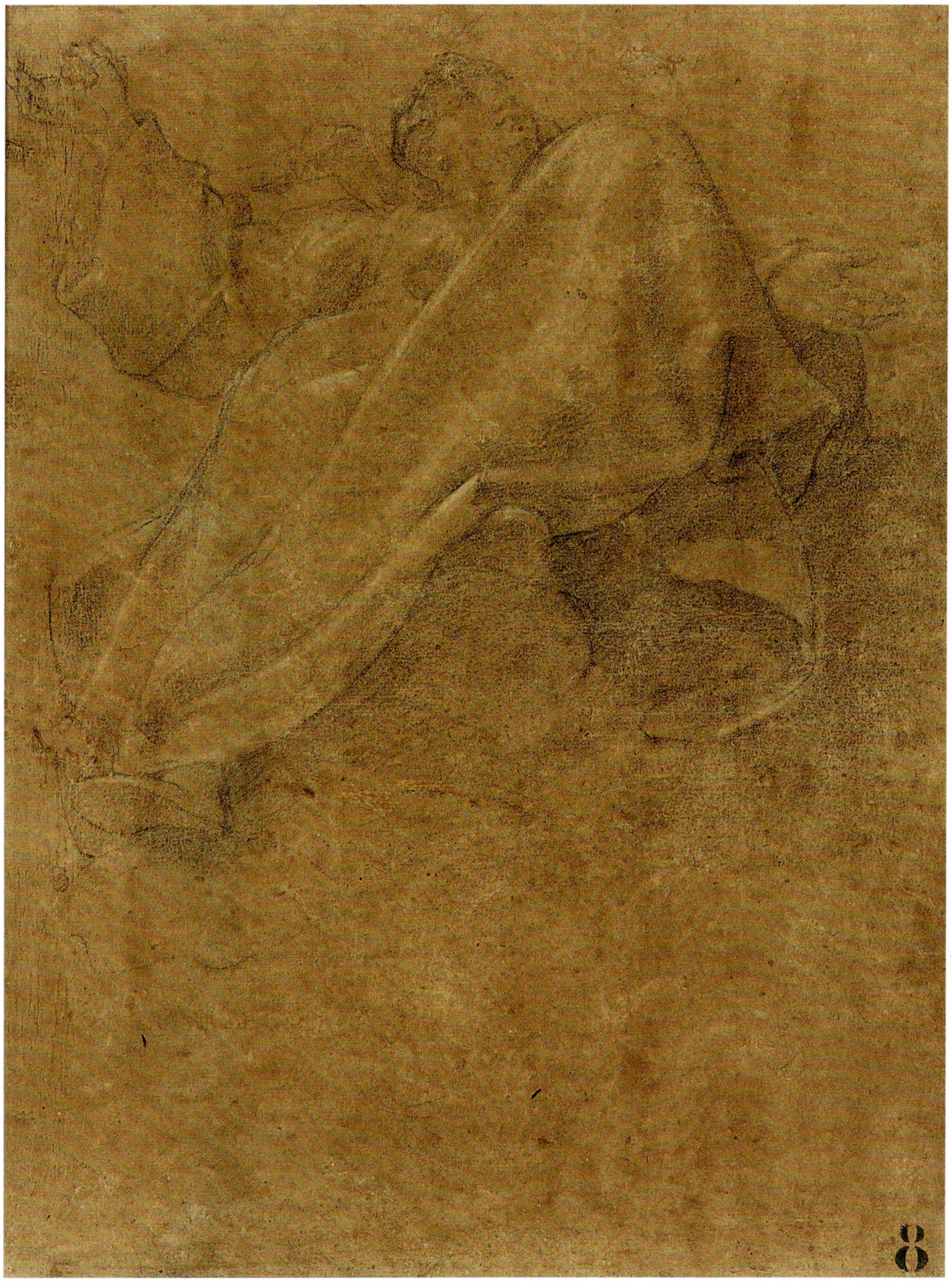

LII

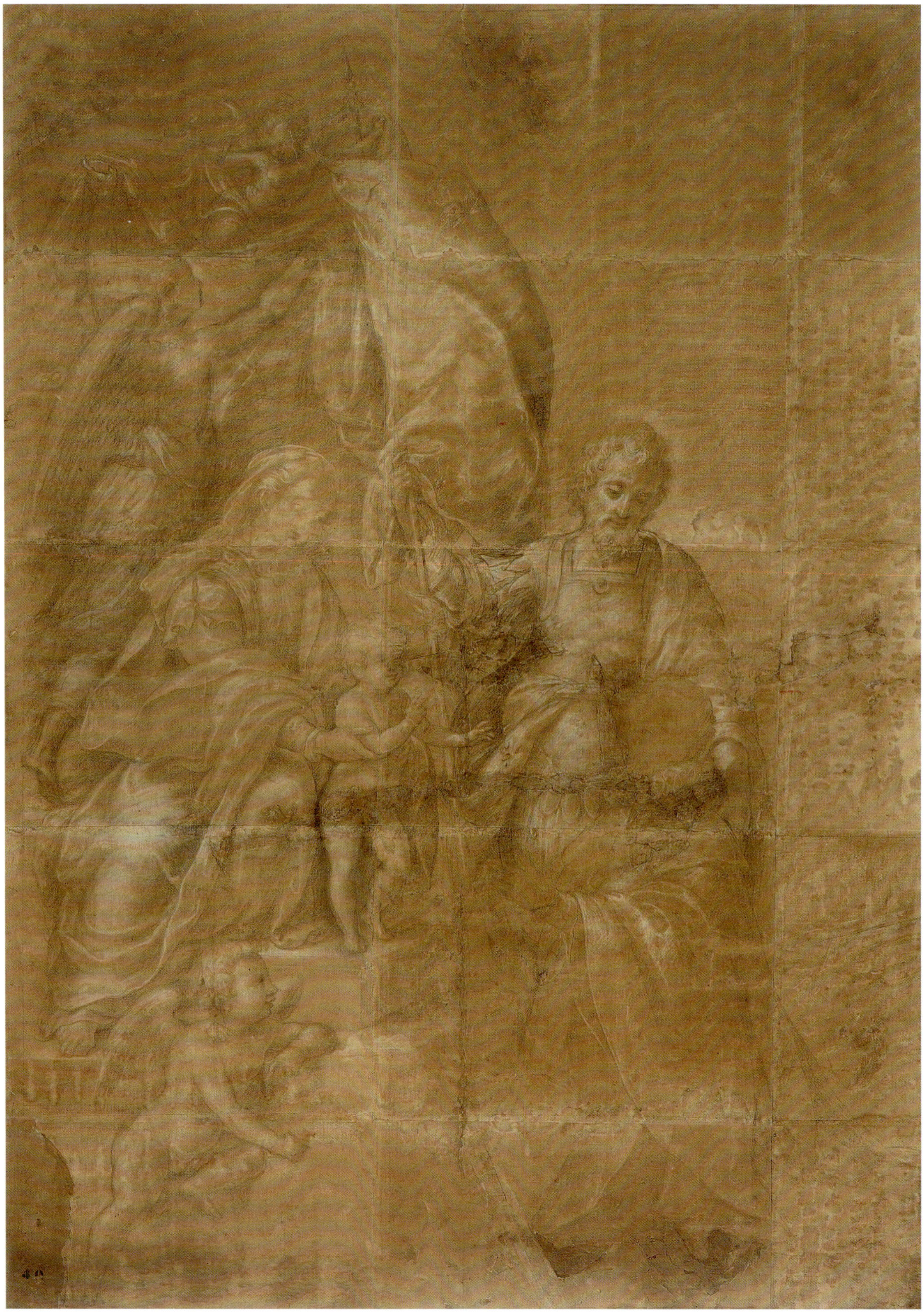

LIII

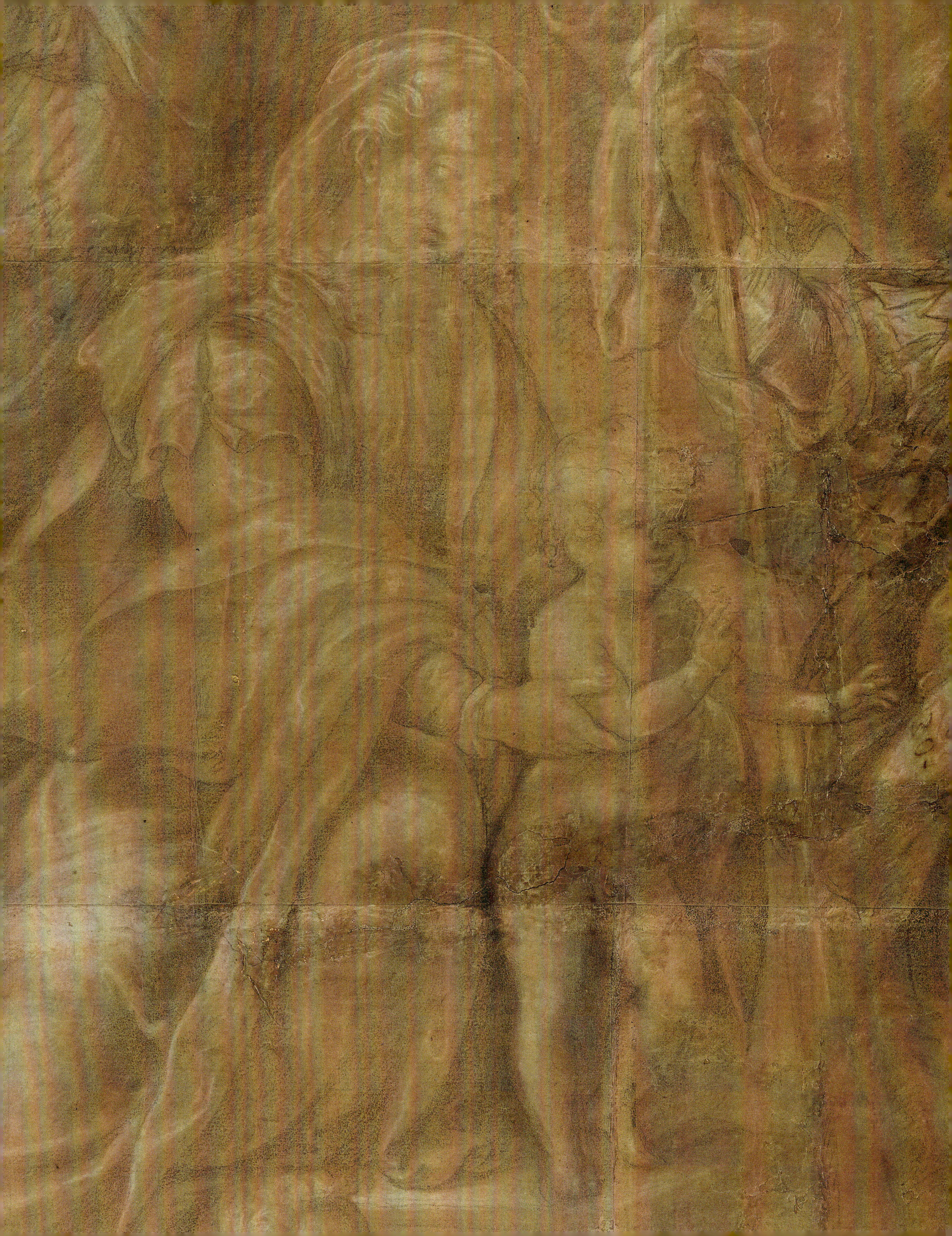

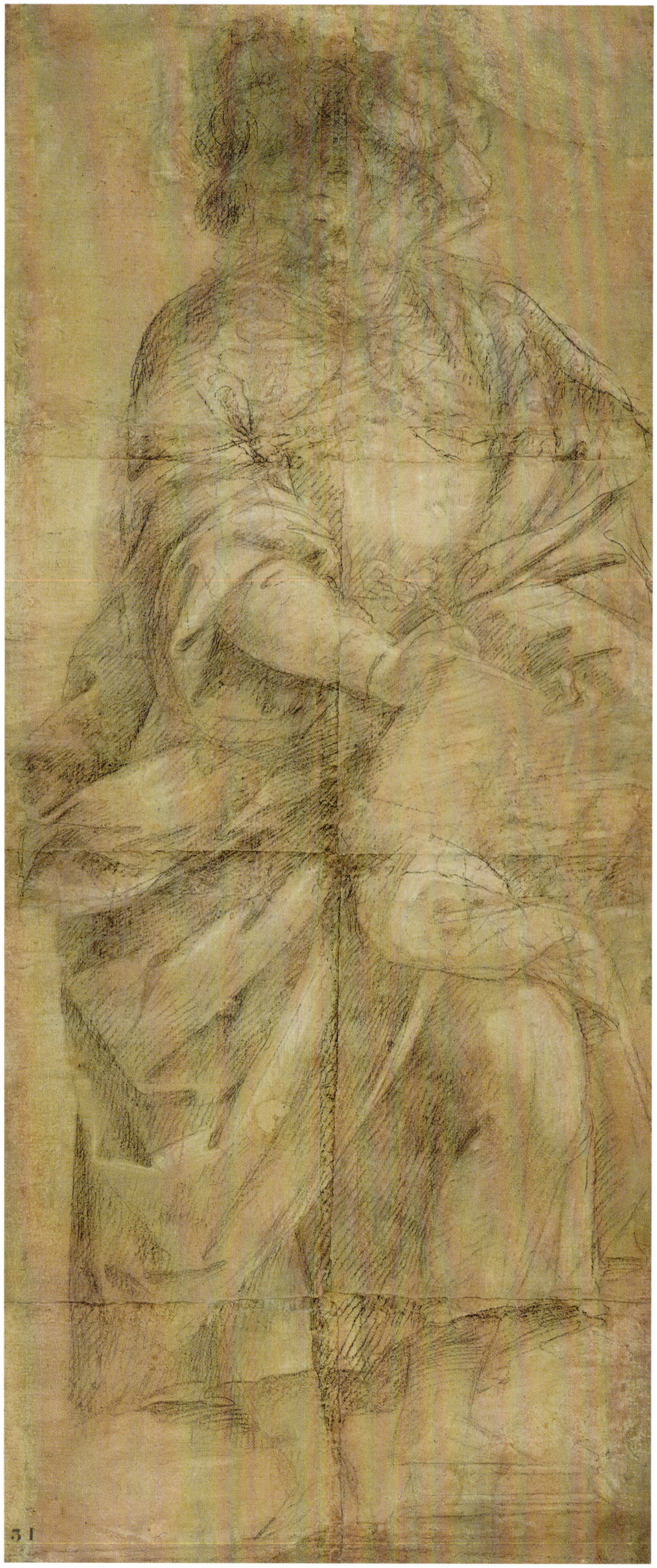

LIV

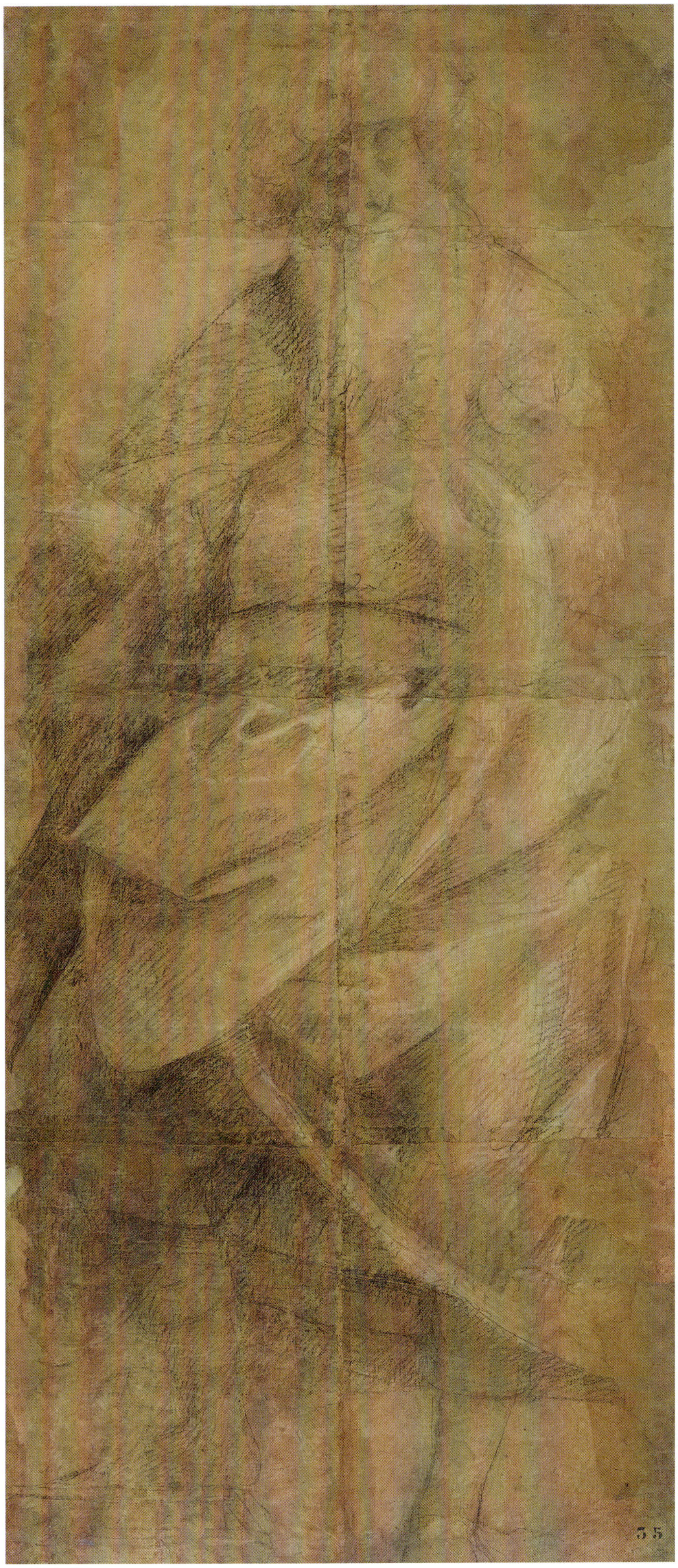

LV

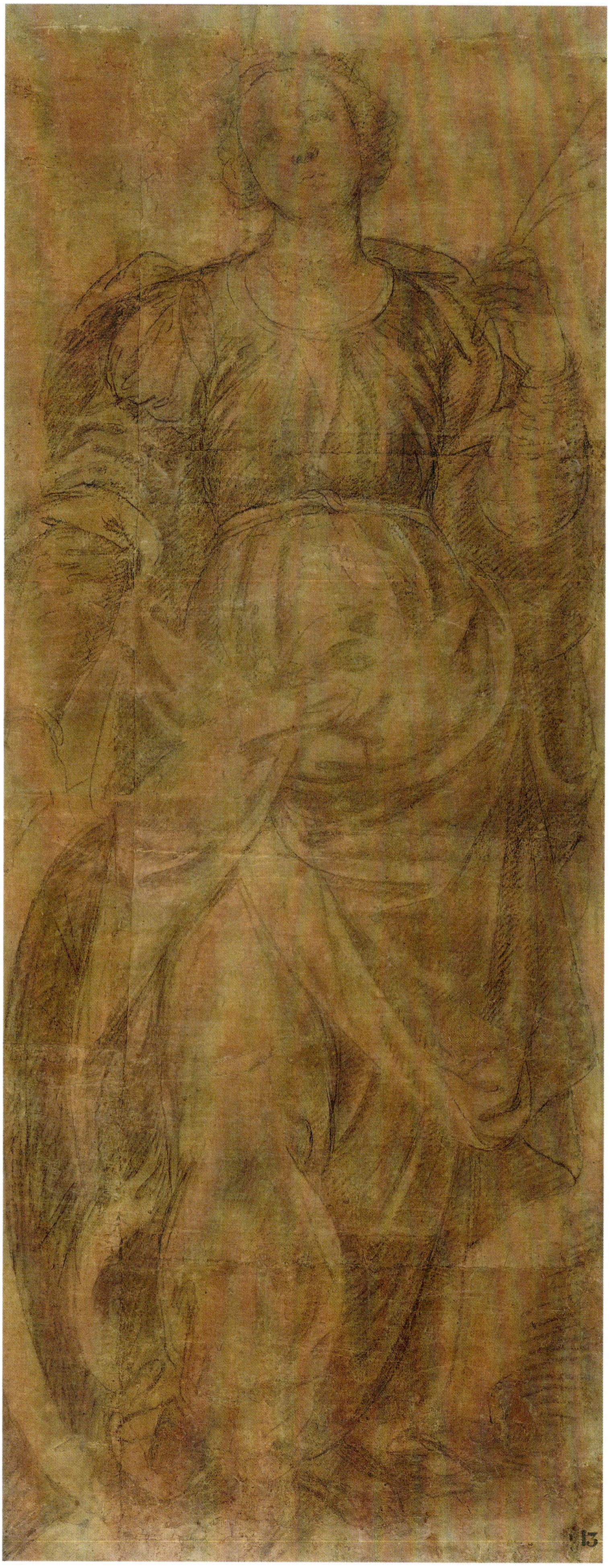

LVI

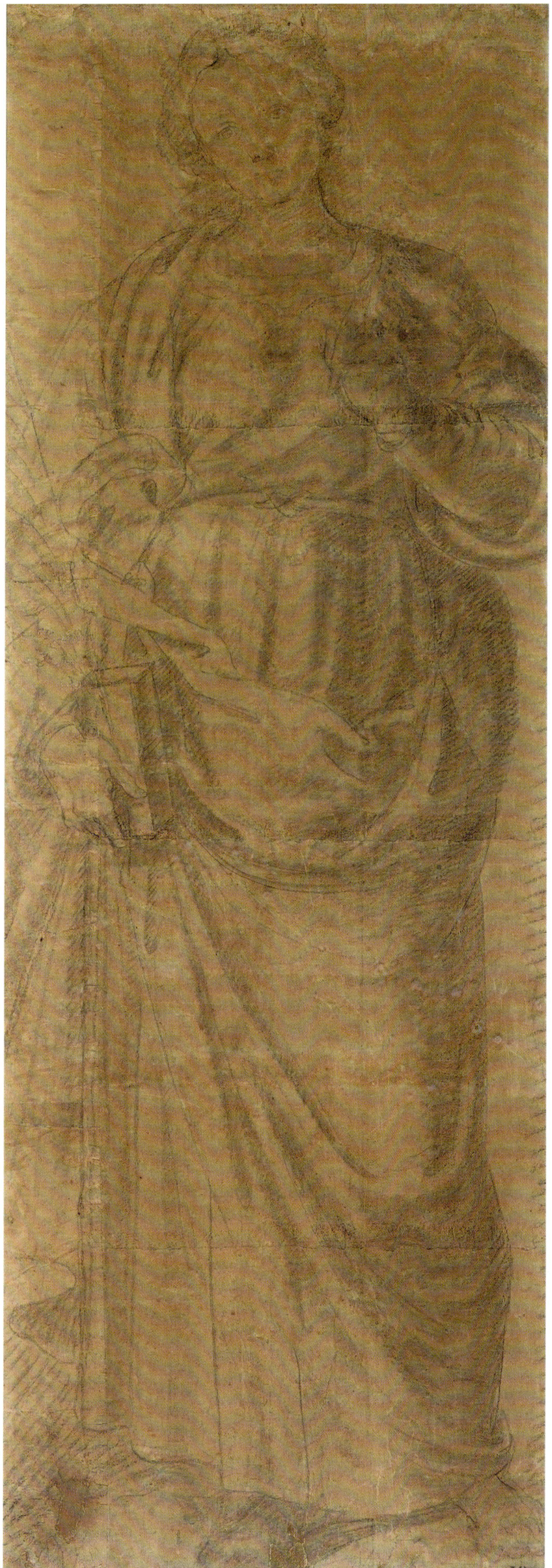

LVII

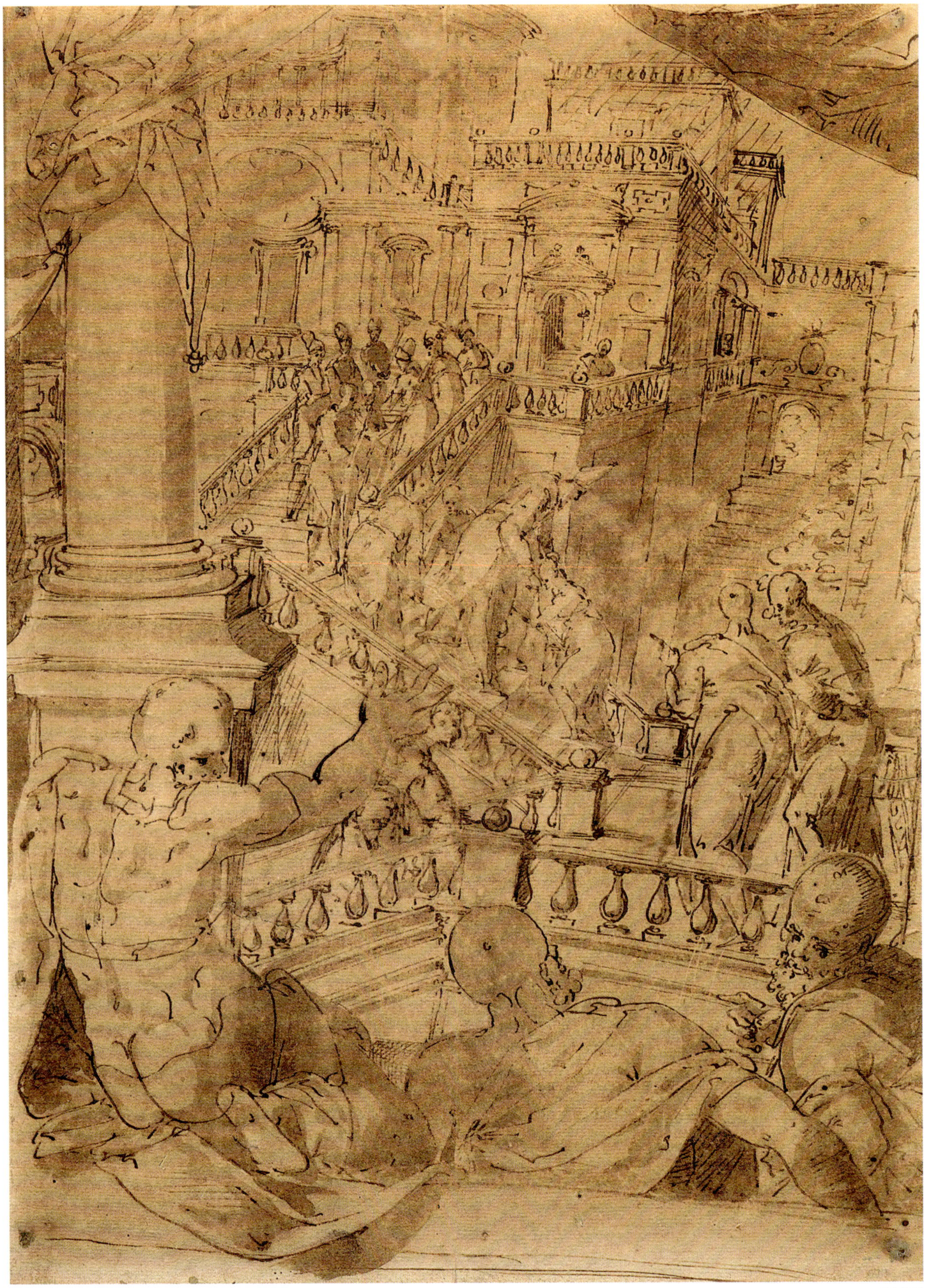

LVIII

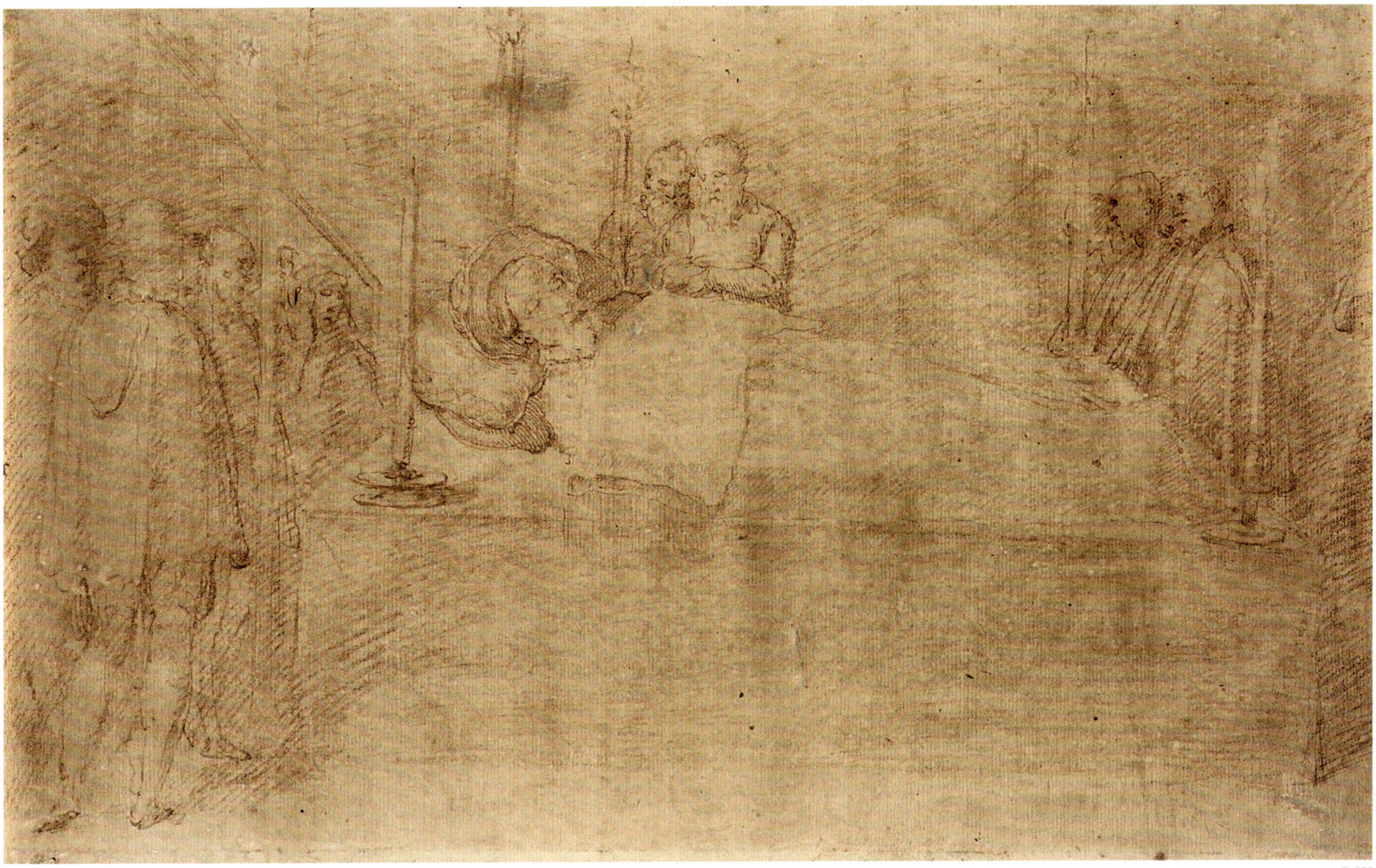

LIX

The Gaudentian Cartoons, a Vocation for Education

Enrico Zanellati

Sited in 1837 in the spaces of the Turin Academy of Fine Arts, the Pinacoteca Albertina was established for explicitly educational purposes, as evinced by the two major sections that it has housed since the outset: the painting collection of Archbishop Mossi di Morano, which contains more than two hundred works, and the collection of 16th-century cartoons donated by Charles Albert of Savoy, king of Sardinia-Piedmont. The stated wishes of the respective donors were that the collections should form an integral part of the artistic education of the students of the academy.

While it remains primarily geared towards those students, these days we like to define the Pinacoteca's educational vocation as being oriented towards a far larger target group, encompassing the whole of society. Specifically, there are now myriad opportunities to learn in more depth about the exceptional Renaissance cartoons conserved at the Albertina. The innovative technologies unveiled in 2019 in the Cartoon Room take their place alongside the endlessly fascinating tradition of our drawing and painting workshops, run by the CoopCulture educational team. Those selected as the best students at the Albertina academy are called upon to come up with workshop-based artistic activities for all age groups, from children right through to adults. What is revealed in the process is the world of the Renaissance studios and the use made there of preparatory cartoons. It is a story that is essentially "educational", as the very genesis of this extraordinary artistic legacy tells us.

A "cartoon" is a drawing on paper with very specific connotations. It is defined as such due to its large dimensions (*cartone* in Italian being an augmentative form of *carta*, "paper"), resulting from the glueing together of several sheets of paper. The drawing that takes shape on this extensive surface is not, then, a simple sketch; rather, on a cartoon, the artist traces out a preparatory study that is very close to how the finished work will be. As Giovan Battista Armenini wrote in his *On the True Precepts of the Art of Painting* in 1587, "it can be said that that is the work itself, aside from the colours", because in general the cartoon has the same dimensions that the painting will have on its final surface, which will be constituted by a wooden board, a canvas or a wall in the case of a fresco.

The drawing was traced out on the paper using a range of different tools and materials, including not only pencil and charcoal but also gesso, watercolour and white lead (which was applied using a brush in order to highlight, with its white colour, those parts of the drawing that had to be lightened up). But how did the transfer of the drawing from the cartoon to its definitive surface take place? In the 16th century, one of the most common methods was the so-called "pouncing" technique, which as far as frescoes were concerned led to the gradual abandonment of the sinopia, i.e. the preliminary drawing that the painter marked out on the wall before adding the paint. Having drawn the cartoon, before reaching the pouncing stage the artist would pierce the outlines with a needle. Charcoal powder would then be made to pass through those holes, thus marking the outlines of the figures on the wall or on the wood to be painted. The aforementioned Armenini recommended that the cartoon be perforated together with another sheet without a drawing on it, which would then be used for pouncing with charcoal powder; this technique made it possible to keep the first cartoon clean, safeguarding the drawing on it. Another process that facilitated the protection of the cartoon was to trace the contours with a blade: in the case of a fresco, the painter placed the cartoon against the wall and then traced the drawing with a pointed tool, thus leaving on the underlying plaster the imprint of the figures that would be frescoed. The operation for paintings on wood or canvas was different: in these cases, the reverse of the cartoon was covered by a layer of charcoal powder, and the pressure of the blade traced the outlines left the mark of the powder on the surface.

These techniques betray a desire to conserve the preparatory cartoons, often safeguarded in the studio along with cartoons based on finished works – i.e. with drawings produced subsequently to keep a record of a completed project. Handed down from the master to his pupils, these cartoons were considered a repository to be referred back to even many years later. In other words, they served as an internal working tool, useful to artists but for the most part neglected by the collectors of the time. As such, the limited number of cartoons that have come down to us is the result both of the natural deterioration of the paper used, and of this substantial disinterest on the part of early collectors. The fifty-nine 16th-century cartoons at the Pinacoteca Albertina are, for this reason, of the utmost interest, because they allow us to tip-toe our way into the studios of that time, discovering how artists were being trained shortly before the birth of the fine arts academies.

Our journey comes to an end with a curious fact that links the history of the cartoons to our modern day: the term "cartoon" was first used by the British magazine *Punch* in 1843, in reference to its satirical sketches. The first instance concerned caricatures of cartoons depicting murals due to be painted at the Houses of Parliament. That fateful "Cartoon n°1" triggered a far wider use of the term, whereby it no longer denoted simply the preparatory sketches made by artists but also modern animated cartoons, which are themselves testament to the fascination that, even in the contemporary world, drawings continue to exert over all of us.

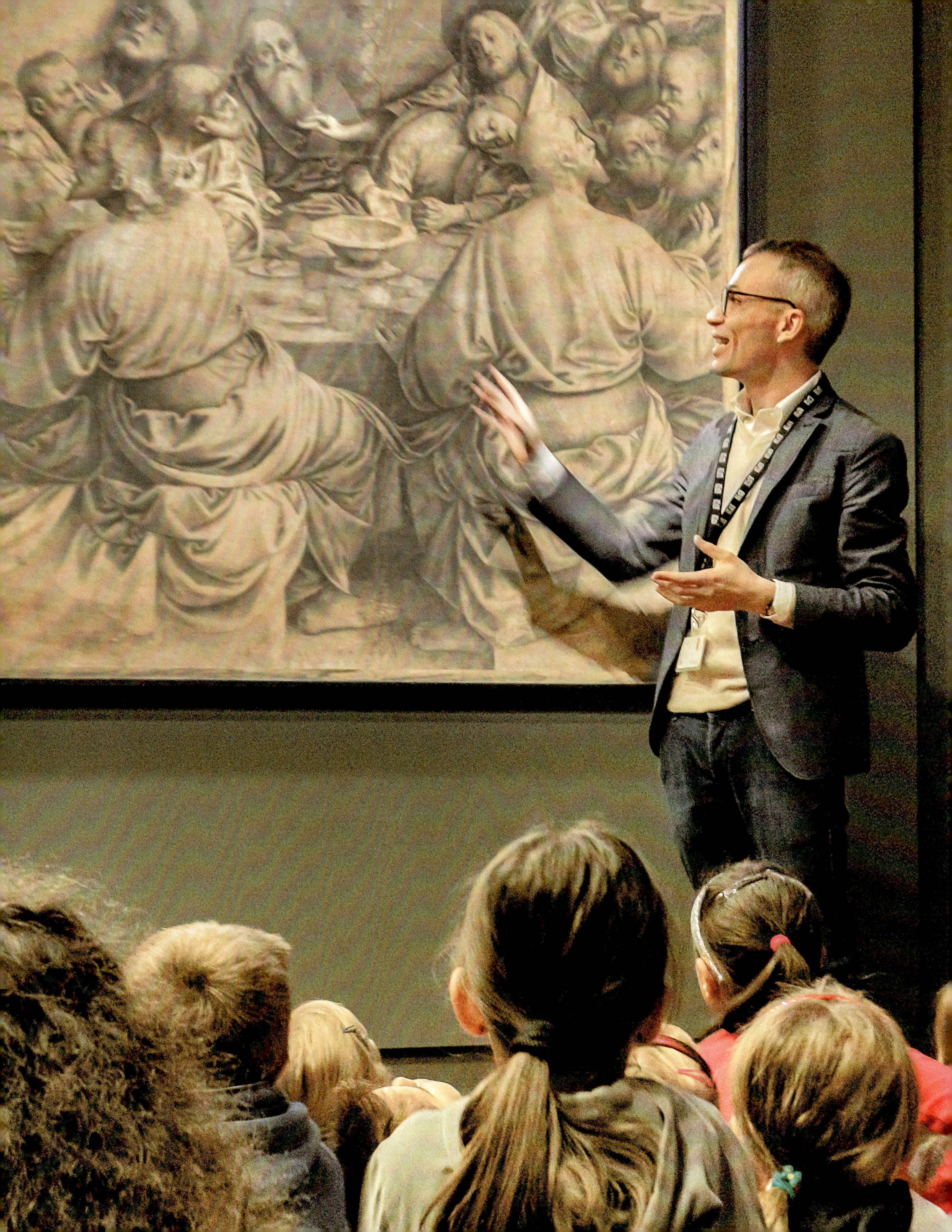

Under a New Light: The Displaying of the Cartoons Revamped in 2019

Diego Giachello and Michele Cirone, Officina delle Idee

Our starting point was a project to overhaul the lighting. By then, the room had already been playing host to the cartoons for some time, and they were arranged on the basis of a layout featuring a number of cutting-edge elements. The fibre-optic lights – at the time the best technology for controlling light flow on works of art – had been specifically designed for the space and were activated by a presence detector. In the absence of visitors to the space, everything remained in the dark, facilitating its conservation. Ultraviolet and infrared emissions were thus reduced to a minimum, in terms of both exposure and intensity, as a result of the technical properties of the sources used. For its part, thanks to sliding panels, the large wall that plays host to the entire collection was managed through the use of wall washers that distributed the light evenly. Here, too, these were devices embodying the state of the art at the time.

Since then, the technology had evolved considerably: it thus became necessary to update the existing luminaires, now surpassed by several generations of new products. As with the whole of the academy and a large part of the Pinacoteca itself, the room suffered from (fortunately only localised) areas of instability in the plasterwork of the ceilings, which had been installed using the materials available during the post-war reconstruction. They had by now deteriorated and were badly damaged due to numerous leaks from the pipework of the services. A major stabilisation operation was put in place, which also saw the false ceilings being removed and upgraded; their presence has now been limited to the bare minimum to support the track lights, while leaving the crawl space available for inspection – this being one of the components of the building that will be monitored on a regular basis and which now appears on the checklist, in accordance with the safety procedure that the Institute will undertake to implement in the future.

The new layout is not intended to overturn the good work done in the past. The arrangement of the works continues to respect the original set-up: on the walls there is a selection of cartoons while the entirety of the collection is laid out on the sliding panels. More than twenty years ago, ingenious and effective strategies were deployed for the ventilation of the paper. The painstakingly designed frames that were part of that solution have been retained and are now combined with a caption mounted into the wooden border and printed in a clear, easy-to-read typeface. The sliding panels are still functional, while the new lighting makes the most of the existing structure, which has simply been maintained.

The great innovation lies in the approach taken towards the visitor who, on entering the room, activates by means of a presence detector the illumination on the cartoons. Thanks to refined spotlights capable of shaping the light flow, the works appear – in the dark space – as suspended presences. Initially the sliding panels are not visible, they remain shrouded in darkness. In the centre of the wall, on a stand, there then appears another isolated cartoon – it is a trick, an illusion that encourages the viewer to move closer. What seems like a drawing separated from the rest is, in reality, a monitor suspended against a dark wall. While the selected cartoons are located behind and to the sides of the viewer, the entire collection remains in shadow behind the large screen that, until shortly before, looked like a cartoon but can now provide a wealth of information, available simply by touching it.

The screen activates new wall washers, which illuminate the whole wall and surprise the viewer, who ends up faced with the Pinacoteca's entire cartoon collection. Visitors will thus be struck by the ensemble, which seems to have come out of nowhere, finding themselves at the heart of the complete extant *oeuvre*: a total of fifty-nine preparatory drawings almost all relating to the paintings of Gaudenzio Ferrari and his school. In strict compliance with rigorous criteria of conservation, the new layout exploits the latest technologies to offer an approach that is engaging on an emotional level, enabling immersion into the significance and history of the works on show, but also on a technical level, thanks to precision illumination and to the opportunity to zoom in on every detail on the high-definition screen, which becomes a magnifying glass, a microscope, and a tool for gleaning an understanding of the entire story of Gaudenzio's cartoons.

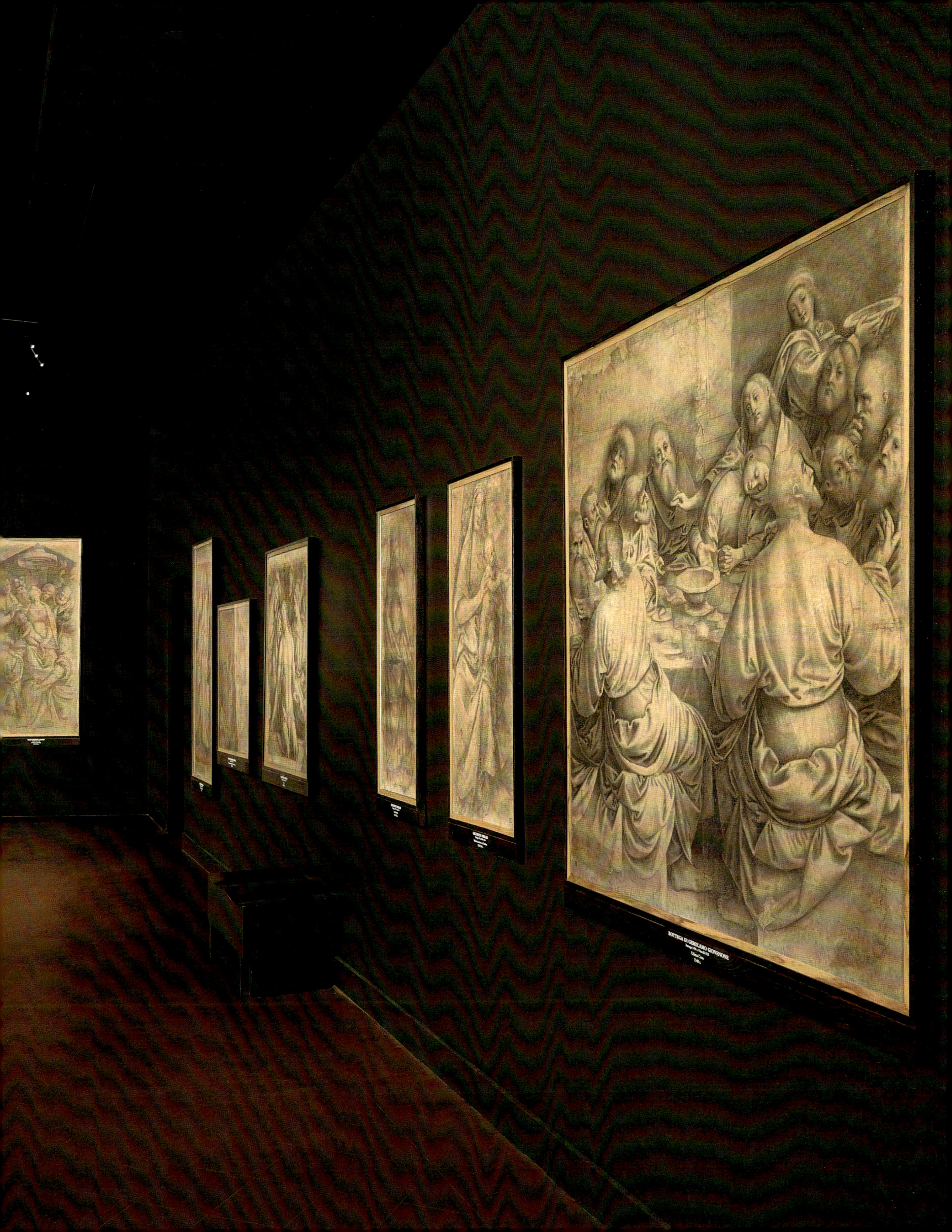

The 2019 overhaul, conceived and carried out by Officina delle Idee with Zumtobel (lighting systems) and Ribes Solutions (monitors and multimedia content), integrates seamlessly with the operation previously implemented by the Consulta per la Valorizzazione dei Beni Artistici e Culturali (Council for the Enhancement of the Artistic and Cultural Assets) of Turin in 1996. That initiative, instigated by the dean Carlo Giuliano, enabled the opening up to the public of the Pinacoteca Albertina and, thanks to the exemplary design by Studio Pagliero and Trucco, saw the room set aside for the cartoons being fitted with stylish sliding panels that succeed in conserving the fifty-nine Renaissance and Mannerist drawings as effectively as possible.

The 1996 and 2019 projects offered a new treasure trove and cast new light on an artistic legacy unlike any other – one that, having been restored in the 1970s, was showcased at the Salone dell'Accademia in 1982, on the occasion of the exhibition *Gaudenzio e la sua scuola. I cartoni cinquecenteschi dell'Accademia Albertina*.

Since 1982, other exhibitions have made it possible to compare the cartoons at the Albertina with the paintings to which they relate. In 1985, for example, a wealth of cartoons by Bernardino Lanino were displayed at the exhibition on him staged at the Museo Borgogna in Vercelli. In more recent years, from 2013 to 2014, on the initiative of the chairman Fiorenzo Alfieri and the dean Salvo Bitonti, and once again with the support of the Consulta, under the watchful eye of Angela Griseri and Mario Verdun high-profile Renaissance paintings have come face-to-face with the drawings in the Cartoon Room, as part of exhibition projects curated by Guido Curto, Anna Maria Bava, Massimiliano Caldera and Paola Nicita. Moreover, an interesting bridge between the cartoons at the Albertina and the Palazzo Madama collections was constructed in the period 2014–15, with the help of Enrica Pagella and Simone Baiocco, on the occasion of the exhibition *#Presepio. L'immagine della Natività dal medioevo all'arte contemporanea*.

In 2018, the Cartoon Room housed the first presentation in Turin of the *Adoration of the Child with Saints Francis of Assisi and Anthony of Padua*, acquired and restored by Banca Patrimoni Sella & C. and today exhibited at the Museo Borgogna in Vercelli. During the preparation of the catalogue for that exhibition, under the guidance of Daniela Magnetti and Filippo Timo, and thanks to the support of Banca Patrimoni Sella & C., the drawings were photographed once again, this time by Fabio Amerio, a lecturer in Photography at the Accademia Albertina di Belle Arti.

The history of the Renaissance cartoons at the Pinacoteca Albertina has also been charted by significant publications, few in number but extraordinarily valuable in terms of the richness of their content. The first photographic records date from 1895, and were produced by the renowned Anderson company. In 1930, to celebrate the wedding of Prince Umberto of Savoy and Maria-José of Belgium, Luigi Cesare Bollea's book – *La Reale Accademia Albertina delle Belle arti e la Real Casa di Savoia* – was published, and 1982 saw the appearance of the book associated with the aforementioned exhibition (*Gaudenzio Ferrari e la sua scuola. I cartoni cinquecenteschi dell'Accademia Albertina*), edited by Giovanni Romano, which remains to this day a touchstone of the history of 16th-century art. More recently, the catalogue was published of *Il Rinascimento di Gaudenzio Ferrari*, an exhibition curated by Giovanni Agosti and Jacopo Stoppa, staged in 2018 in Varallo, Vercelli and Novara, with the co-ordination of the Associazione Abbonamento Musei.

This history of research and positive exploitation echoes through the fifty-nine brief entries on the drawings, written in 2010 by Beatrice Zanelli and Erika Cristina, thanks to the research scholarships "Master of the Talents of Civil Society" supported by CRT Foundation and Goria Foundation (academic tutors Rosella Grassi and Guido Curto), and now updated with new content by Enrico Zanellati.

Catalogue of Works

I.
Gaudenzio Ferrari
Saint Agabius and Saint Paul
1514–16
charcoal, pencil and chalk on paper,
153.5 × 77.5 cm
inv. 302

In the list compiled by the Grand Chamberlain C. E. Alfieri di Sostegno at the time of Charles Albert of Savoy's donation, the cartoon was ascribed to Bernardino Lanino as number 2 in the inventory. The initial attribution to Gaudenzio Ferrari was made by N. Gabrielli (1933, pp. 154, 196) and was commonly accepted by the subsequent critics. The scholar proposed that the cartoon be considered in conjunction with the lower-right section, portraying Saint Paul and Saint Agabius, of the polyptych currently housed in the chapel of the Virgin at the church of San Gaudenzio in Novara. Gaudenzio Ferrari received the commission for the polyptych on 20 July 1514, and the payments were made over the following years up until 21 March 1521 (*Gaudenzio Ferrari e la sua scuola*, 1982, pp. 65–66). As highlighted by P. Gaglia (ibid., pp. 72–73), the pose and the dimensions of the figures in the cartoon and the painting coincide, albeit with some minor differences: in the cartoon, Saint Agabius is without his crosier, and his right hand is portrayed in two different overlaid solutions. In addition, the cartoon – drawn in its entirety by Gaudenzio – is of a higher quality than the painting, in which, alongside the master, there was probable input from Novara-born Sperindio Cagnoli, who was compensated for the execution of the altarpiece on 15 January 1518 and on 1 and 21 March 1521, as stated by P. Venturoli (in *Le arti del disegno all'Accademia Albertina*, 1995, pp. 40–41) who proposed a date of 1514 for the cartoon, immediately after the aforementioned contract of 20 July of that year. The same conclusion was reached by S. Bruzzese in *Il Rinascimento di Gaudenzio Ferrari*, 2018, pp. 244–46 and A. Cottino in *La Pinacoteca dell'Accademia Albertina*, 2019, p. 38.

II.
Gaudenzio Ferrari
Saint Gaudentius
1519–20
charcoal, pencil and chalk on paper,
122 × 55.5 cm
inv. 32bis

In the list compiled by the Grand Chamberlain C. E. Alfieri di Sostegno at the time of Charles Albert of Savoy's donation, the cartoon was ascribed to Bernardino Lanino as number 32bis in the inventory. The cartoon was attributed to Gaudenzio Ferrari by P. Gaglia (in *Gaudenzio Ferrari e la sua scuola*, 1982, pp. 74–75) who drew parallels between it and the lower left section, portraying Saint Gaudentius, of the polyptych by Gaudenzio Ferrari in the church of San Gaudenzio in Varallo Sesia. No extant document enables the precise dating of the polyptych. However, the stylistic analysis conducted by Gaglia makes it possible to date its execution to around the time of the polyptych of Novara Cathedral, which was begun in 1514 and completed in 1521 (*Gaudenzio Ferrari e la sua scuola*, 1982, pp. 65–66); R. Sacchi proposed a date of the end of the second decade (1996, p. 576). There are several differences between the cartoon and the painting: in the former, the cape is closed by a large clasp on the chest and a more elaborate system of folds is collected on the left hand of the saint, whose garment falls to the ground with more simplified folds. The cartoon is the only one in the series not to be cited in the N. Gabrielli inventory.

III.
Gaudenzio Ferrari
Pietà
c. 1535
charcoal, pencil and chalk on paper,
108.5 × 99 cm
inv. 323

In the list compiled by the Grand Chamberlain C. E. Alfieri di Sostegno at the time of Charles Albert of Savoy's donation, the cartoon was ascribed to Gaudenzio Ferrari as number 23 in the inventory. This attribution was accepted by all of the subsequent critics. In the same list, the cartoon was considered in relation to a Gaudenzio Ferrari painting at that time located in the second sacristy of Novara Cathedral but today no longer traceable. P. Gaglia (in *Gaudenzio Ferrari e la sua scuola*, 1982, pp. 76–78) proposed that the painting in question was in fact the *Pietà* by Gaudenzio Ferrari, sited in the National Museum of Budapest, previously linked to our cartoon by A. Bertini (in *Mostra di Gaudenzio Ferrari*, 1956, p. 117) and by G. Testori (1956, ibid., p. 105). Compared to this painting, the cartoon does not differ significantly, aside from the slight revisioning of Christ's right hand. Various dates have been proposed for our cartoon: the years 1528–30, immediately prior to Gaudenzio's sojourn in Vercelli (Bertini, 1956, p. 117; Mallé, 1969, p. 48; Viale, 1969, p. 65); the early years of the fourth decade, when the frescoes of San Cristoforo in Vercelli (completed in 1534) were under way (Gaglia in *Gaudenzio Ferrari e la sua scuola*, 1982, pp. 76–78); the years immediately after the frescoes in the cupola of Santa Maria dei Miracoli in Saronno (1535–36); or between 1536 and 1537 (Romano in *Opere scelte della Pinacoteca*, 1993, pp. 42–43). G. Renzi saw an homage by Gaudenzio Ferrari to Bramantino in the hand concealed by the cloth (in *Il Rinascimento di Gaudenzio Ferrari*, 2018, pp. 410–14) and A. Cottino recognised echoes of Leonardo in the expression of the figures and in the subdued, constructive use of chiaroscuro (in *La Pinacoteca dell'Accademia Albertina*, 2019, p. 38).

IV.
Gaudenzio Ferrari
Saint Anthony of Padua
1530–34
charcoal, watercolour and chalk
on paper, 124 × 60 cm
inv. 306

In the list compiled by the Grand Chamberlain C. E. Alfieri di Sostegno at the time of Charles Albert of Savoy's donation, the cartoon was ascribed to Bernardino Lanino as number 6 in the inventory. This attribution was discounted by N. Gabrielli who, considering it to be the work of Gaudenzio's studio, recognised typical hallmarks of Gerolamo

Giovenone (Gabrielli, 1933, pp. 156, 196). The cartoon was attributed for the first time to Gaudenzio Ferrari by M. di Macco (in *Gaudenzio Ferrari e la sua scuola*, 1982, pp. 78–80), who also identified Saint Anthony of Padua as the person portrayed. It has not, however, been possible to identify the painting to which the cartoon refers; the fact that the image is inscribed in an arched sanguine frame, accompanied by the text "lato dritto" (right side), renders possible the hypothesis that the cartoon may relate to a polyptych showing Saint Anthony of Padua to the right of the central image. The stylistic characteristics allow it to be dated to the early years of the fourth decade, as proposed by Di Macco in the aforementioned study.

V.
Gaudenzio Ferrari
Virgin Enthroned and Child
1539–46
charcoal, pencil and chalk on paper,
124 × 63 cm
inv. 317

In the list compiled by the Grand Chamberlain C. E. Alfieri di Sostegno at the time of Charles Albert of Savoy's donation, the cartoon was ascribed to Bernardino Lanino as number 17 in the inventory. The first attribution to Gaudenzio Ferrari came from N. Gabrielli (1933, pp. 154, 197), but was not universally accepted, given that A. Bertini preferred to locate it in the ambit of the Gaudentian school (Bertini, 1956, p. 41), whereas L. Mallé (1971, p. 205) attributed it to the area of Gerolamo Giovenone. For his part, P. Gaglia saw in it the clear stylistic traits of Gaudenzio's Milanese period – i.e. the final phase of the artist's career, dating from 1539 to 1546 (in *Gaudenzio Ferrari e la sua scuola*, 1982, pp. 84–86). Refuting Viale's idea that the cartoon was a possible model for the Gaudenzio Ferrari painting at the Pinacoteca di Brera (Viale, 1969), a work stylistically datable to around 1520, Gaglia posited that the cartoon may have constituted a return, twenty years on, to the solutions deployed in the Brera painting, without however being in a position to identify the painting that may have served as the template.

VI.
Gaudenzio Ferrari
Virgin and Child
1530–35
charcoal, watercolour, white lead, earth pigments and chalk on paper,
104.3 × 63 cm
inv. 304

In the list compiled by the Grand Chamberlain C. E. Alfieri di Sostegno at the time of Charles Albert of Savoy's donation, the cartoon was ascribed to Gaudenzio Ferrari as number 4 in the inventory. The same attribution is also found in the inventory of 1933 (Gabrielli, 1933, pp. 154, 196). M. di Macco highlighted how the last sheet at the bottom is stylistically divergent from the rest of the cartoon, betraying soft undertones more easily associable with Lanino (in *Gaudenzio Ferrari e la sua scuola*, 1982, pp. 80–83). The scholar proposed that the cartoon matches no. 701 of the works located in the "Room up above that of the celestial signs. Cartoons drawn in chiaroscuro", as described by the painter Antonio della Cornia in the inventory of the ducal collections compiled in 1635: "The Virgin and Child who has a crown in his hands, full figures. By Gaudenzio. Beautiful" (Baudi di Vesme, 1897, p. 62). Although it is clear, due to the widespread traces of perforation caused by the pouncing technique, that the cartoon was used in the creation of a work, it has not as yet been possible to identify the painting to which it corresponds. The success of this Gaudentian invention is evinced by a drawing located in the Uffizi in Florence (drawing no. 1924F), claimed by Di Macco in the aforementioned text to have been an exercise carried out by Gaudenzio in the workshop of Gerolamo Giovenone in the early 1540s.

VII.
Gaudenzio Ferrari
Angel Holding Two Heraldic Shields
c. 1540
black pencil, charcoal, traces of chalk and red pencil on paper, 96 × 54 cm
inv. 337

In the list compiled by the Grand Chamberlain C. E. Alfieri di Sostegno at the time of Charles Albert of Savoy's donation, the cartoon appeared as number 37 in the inventory, but without an attribution. Stated as being by Gaudenzio Ferrari in the inventories of 1832, 1856 and 1933 (Gabrielli, 1933, pp. 155, 197), the cartoon was cautiously ascribed to Gaudenzio by L. C. Bollea (1932, p. 452) and by A. Bertini (1956, pp. 86–88), who considered it, though, to have been almost entirely re-done. Both V. Viale (1969, p. 186) and C. Debiaggi (1977, p. 91) claimed that it may date from Gaudenzio's time in Vercelli, between 1530 and 1535; Debiaggi associated it with the contract, stipulated by the painter with Troilo Avogadro di Collobiano on 2 December 1530, for the fresco decoration, complete with coats of arms, of the chapel of Saint Anthony in the church of San Marco in Vercelli. The stylistic analysis conducted by P. Gaglia (in *Gaudenzio Ferrari e la sua scuola*, 1982, pp. 86–88) emphasised how the monumentality and solemnity of the figure can be traced back to similar solutions deployed by Gaudenzio Ferrari in the early works of his Milanese period, proposing a date of later than 1540. The scholar noted how in the cartoon the definition of the drawing is weaker and more rigid than usually found in Gaudenzio's output, positing that it may have been carried out in partnership with Giovan Battista della Cerva, who was active in the same period alongside Gaudenzio in the church of Sant'Ambrogio in Milan, where he produced figures of angels relatively similar to that depicted in our cartoon. Viewing the work as having been created solely by Gaudenzio, Romano (in *Opere scelte della Pinacoteca*, 1993, pp. 44–45) proposed that it related to a contract of 12 March 1540 that saw Gaudenzio undertake to decorate the chapel of the Gallarati brothers at the church of Sant'Angelo in Milan (a church already destroyed by the 16th century) and specifically to decorate the ceiling "cum figuris octo angellorum". For E. Maggio, too (in *Il Rinascimento di Gaudenzio Ferrari*, 2018, pp. 492–94), the link between the cartoon and the decoration of the Gallarati chapel remained a fascinating idea. The likelihood is weakened, though, if we imagine that the eight lost angels may have been similar to those – rendered with greater agility and liveliness – painted by Gaudenzio in the eight segments of the ceiling of the chapel of Santa Corona in the church of Santa Maria delle Grazie.

VIII.
Workshop of Gaudenzio Ferrari
Virgin Worshipping the Child Being Held by Angels
charcoal, chalk and pencil on paper,
85 × 98.5 cm
inv. 344

In the list compiled by the Grand Chamberlain C. E. Alfieri di Sostegno at the time of Charles Albert of Savoy's donation, the cartoon was ascribed to Gaudenzio Ferrari as number 44 in the inventory. The attribution reappeared in N. Gabrielli (1933, pp. 155, 197), who associated it with the upper central panel of the polyptych produced by Gaudenzio Ferrari between 1514 and 1521 for the church of San Gaudenzio in Novara. P. Gaglia (in *Gaudenzio Ferrari e la sua scuola*, 1982, pp. 88–90) highlighted how the cartoon betrays significant stylistic differences with respect to the Novara painting, since – aside from the dimensions not matching – it is characterised by a dryness in the strokes that was unusual for Gaudenzio; however, the scholar also noted how the composition could nevertheless be attributed to Ferrari both for the innovative nature of the concept and for its frequent repetitions within the Gaudentian ambit. These considerations led Gaglia to propose that the original drawing for the Novarese Adoration, which was used as a model of reference numerous times by the workshop, may have been lost, or damaged due to its frequent use by the pupils, necessitating the production of a new drawing, completed at an unknown time, by an anonymous artist who had trained in Gaudenzio's workshop.

IX.
Gerolamo Giovenone
Virgin and Child
1530–31
charcoal and pencil on paper,
103.6 × 52.4 cm
inv. 336

As emerges from the 1832 inventory, this cartoon – the only one in the series – remained for some time in the possession of "Sig.r Cavaliere Pietro Datta", who in 1852 (date of a new inventory) is recorded as having already returned it. In the list compiled by the Grand Chamberlain C. E. Alfieri di Sostegno at the time of Charles Albert of Savoy's donation, the cartoon was ascribed to Gaudenzio Ferrari as number 36 in the inventory (Bollea, 1936, Appendix 4). We also find this attribution in the inventory compiled by N. Gabrielli, who associated it with the central panel in the triptych of the Gattinara Virgin of the Rosary, a work by Gerolamo Giovenone (Gabrielli, 1933, pp. 155, 197). The first attribution to Gerolamo Giovenone appeared in G. Romano (1970, p. 21) in the wake of the association with the Giovenone Gattinara painting already proposed by Gabrielli. M. di Macco (in *Gaudenzio Ferrari e la sua scuola*, 1982, pp. 100–03) stated that the model of reference for the Piedmontese painter was Gaudenzio Ferrari, and proposed a comparison with a drawing, attributed to Gaudenzio by Romano and datable to 1529, in the National Gallery in Dublin. The scholar observed that the Gattinara painting, so heavily indebted to the aforementioned Gaudentian invention, betrays in the drapery that covers the Virgin's legs the same solutions adopted by Giovenone himself in the painting depicting Saint Agatha in the parish church of Santhià, datable to 1531. S. Baiocco arrived at the same conclusions vis-à-vis the dating of the painting and the cartoon, in a critical interpretation written after the restoration of the Gattinara triptych (Baiocco, 2003, pp. 11, 17–19).

X.
Gerolamo Giovenone
Saint Protasius
1527–35
charcoal and pencil on paper,
123.4 × 57.2 cm
inv. 321

In the list compiled by the Grand Chamberlain C. E. Alfieri di Sostegno at the time of Charles Albert of Savoy's donation, the cartoon was ascribed to Gaudenzio Ferrari as number 21 in the inventory, an attribution only partially accepted by N. Gabrielli, who considered it to have been produced by Gaudenzio's workshop (Gabrielli, 1933, pp. 157, 197). Subsequently, G. Romano (1970, p. 21) associated it with the painting at the Auckland Art Gallery depicting Saint Protasius, which at the time was deemed to have been the work of Bernardino Lanino. The scholar proposed an attribution to Gerolamo Giovenone, later validated by L. Mallé (1971, p. 206), who proposed that it be dated to Giovenone's late period, around the time of the frescoes in the church of San Giuliano in Vercelli. S. Ghisotti (in *Gaudenzio Ferrari e la sua scuola*, 1982, pp. 104–07) connected the Auckland painting and its companion piece, portraying Saint Gervasius (held by the same museum), to the document of 29 December 1527 (ibid., pp. 96–97) which saw Giovenone undertake to produce a triptych for the chapel of the Congregation of Saint Ambrosius in the church of San Francesco in Vercelli – a work for which final payment was not made until 23 November 1535. The triptych was to depict Saint Gervasius and Saint Protasius on the side panels, with Saint Ambrosius in the central panel, which is currently to be found on the right-hand wall of the sixth altar of the left aisle of the church of San Francesco in Vercelli. Ghisotti put forward the idea that the Saint Protasius, to which the cartoon refers and which constituted the left section of the triptych, was the later of the two paintings to be worked on by Giovenone, due to the marked Gaudentian influence visible in the saint's reclining head. The Pinacoteca of the Accademia Albertina also holds the cartoon depicting Saint Gervasius (inv. 339).

XI.
Gerolamo Giovenone
Saint Gervasius
1527–35
charcoal and pencil on paper,
127.9 × 55.5 cm
inv. 339

In the list compiled by the Grand Chamberlain C. E. Alfieri di Sostegno at the time of Charles Albert of Savoy's donation, the cartoon was ascribed to Bernardino Lanino as number 39 in the inventory (Bollea, 1936, Appendix 4), an attribution refuted by N. Gabrielli, who deemed it to have been produced in Gaudenzio's workshop (Gabrielli, 1933, pp. 157, 197). Subsequently, G. Romano (1970, p. 21) associated it with the painting in the Auckland Art Gallery, depicting Saint Gervasius, at the time considered to be a work by Bernardino Lanino. The scholar proposed an attribution to Gerolamo Giovenone, later confirmed by L. Mallé (1971, p. 206), who posited that the work was a product of Giovenone's late period, around the time of the frescoes in the church of San Giuliano in Vercelli. S. Ghisotti (in *Gaudenzio Ferrari e la sua scuola*, 1982, pp. 104–07) linked the Auckland painting and its companion piece, portraying Saint Protasius (held by the same museum), to the document of 29 December 1527 (ibid., pp. 96–97) which saw Giovenone undertake to produce a triptych for the chapel of the Congregation of Saint Ambrosius in the church of San Francesco in Vercelli – a work for which final payment was not made until 23 November 1535. The triptych was to depict Saint Gervasius and Saint Protasius on the side panels, with Saint Ambrosius in the central panel, which is currently to be found on the right-hand wall of the sixth altar of the left aisle of the church of San Francesco in Vercelli. Ghisotti put forward the idea that the Saint Gervasius, to which the cartoon refers and which constituted the right section of the triptych, was the earlier of the two paintings to be worked on by Giovenone, due to its more archaic appearance, betraying a lesser influence of the Gaudentian model. The Pinacoteca of the Accademia Albertina also holds the cartoon depicting Saint Protasius (inv. 321).

XII.
Gerolamo Giovenone
Virgin and Child with Saints Laurence, John the Baptist, Sebastian and Francis
1534–38
charcoal, chalk and watercolour
on paper, 110 × 120 cm
inv. 357

In the list compiled by the Grand Chamberlain C. E. Alfieri di Sostegno at the time of the donation, the cartoon was ascribed to Gaudenzio Ferrari as number 57 in the inventory, an attribution that we also find in the inventories of 1856 and 1933 (Gabrielli, 1933, pp. 156, 198). Subsequently, the cartoon was traced back to the Giovenonian ambit by A. Griseri (in *Mostra di Gaudenzio Ferrari*, 1956, pp. 83, 139), while also linking it to Giovanni Battista Giovenone; an initial attribution to Gerolamo was proposed by G. Romano (1970, p. 21) and was confirmed by the subsequent critics. The painting to which the cartoon relates has not been identified. M. di Macco (in *Gaudenzio Ferrari e la sua scuola*, 1982, pp. 108–10) stressed the cartoon's substantial Gaudentian component, offering a date of the second half of the fourth decade. The scholar highlighted how in this period Gerolamo Giovenone, who had remained in Vercelli as the only documented heir of the older generation, reflected in great detail on the frescoes painted by Gaudenzio at the church of San Cristoforo between 1530 and 1534. In this re-reading of the Gaudentian model, the painter would have been flanked by the young Lanino, to whom he was very close. According to Romano (in 1986, p. 59), the Virgin and Child with saints produced by Lanino in 1534 for the church of Sant'Eusebio in Ternengo, now in the Galleria Sabauda, constitutes the precedent for our cartoon, of which the academic proposes as the *terminus ante quem* 1538 – the date of execution, by Gerolamo Giovenone at the behest of the Frichignono family, of the altarpiece for Biella Cathedral (originally sited in the church of San Domenico); a work that "paid clear tribute to the altarpiece of Ternengo, of which it is a free replica" (Astrua, D'Agostino in *Bernardino Lanino e il Cinquecento a Vercelli*, 1986, p. 80). With reference to the poor state of conservation, in 1932 L. C. Bollea informed us that the cartoon had been "reduced to serving as a fireguard and only two years ago was I able to return it to its original format and put it in a frame and under glass" (Bollea, 1932, p. 466).

XIII.
Gerolamo Giovenone (?)
Saint John the Evangelist
1550–55
charcoal, pencil, white lead and chalk
on paper, 125.3 × 60 cm
inv. 349

In the list compiled by the Grand Chamberlain C. E. Alfieri di Sostegno at the time of the donation, the cartoon was ascribed to Gaudenzio Ferrari as number 49 in the inventory, an attribution only partially accepted by N. Gabrielli, who deemed it to be the work of Gaudenzio's workshop (Gabrielli, 1933, pp. 158, 197). Subsequently, the cartoon was ascribed to Bernardino Lanino by A. Gallino (1964, p. 73), whereas G. Romano (1970, pp. 20–21) attributed it to Giovenone's workshop "at the time of the transfer of the consignments from Gerolamo to Giuseppe the Younger" around the middle of the century, when Gerolamo's models were still valid reference points for his son Giuseppe and his nephew Giovanni Battista. For his part, L. Mallé (1971, pp. 193, 206), perceiving a Milanese character, proposed its attribution to Giuseppe Giovenone the Elder, with the work arising from an idea of Gerolamo's with influences from late-period Gaudenzio. All of these attributions are discussed by S. Ghisotti (in *Gaudenzio Ferrari e la sua scuola*, 1982, pp. 111–13) who, clarifying how the cartoon is a new take on the John the Evangelist painted by Gerolamo in the very early 1530s as part of the triptych of the Gattinara Virgin of the Rosary, supported the attribution put forward by Romano to the workshop of Gerolamo around the middle of the century. The scholar highlights the cultural affinity that binds the cartoon to the painting produced by Bernardino Lanino for the church of Santi Pietro e Paolo in Oleggio (Quazza in *Bernardino Lanino e il Cinquecento a Vercelli*, 1986, p. 260), highlighting the hypothesis of exchanges and reciprocal influences between the workshops of the two painters. S. Baiocco reached the same conclusions in a critical text on the Gattinara triptych and on the relationship between the workshops of Giovenone and Gaudenzio, first, and later between those of Giovenone and Lanino (Baiocco, 2003, pp. 17–18).

XIV.
Workshop of Gerolamo Giovenone
and Bernardino Lanino
Saint John the Baptist
1550–55
charcoal, chalk and earth pigments
on paper, 126.8 × 58.4 cm
inv. 332

In the list compiled by the Grand Chamberlain C. E. Alfieri di Sostegno at the time of Charles Albert of Savoy's donation, the cartoon was ascribed to Bernardino Lanino as number 32 – an attribution discounted in the 1933 inventory, where it was assigned to the workshop of Gaudenzio Ferrari (Gabrielli, 1933, pp. 158, 197). The first attribution to the workshop of Gerolamo Giovenone came from G. Romano (1970, pp. 20–21) and was accepted by the subsequent critics, starting with L. Mallé (1971, pp. 193, 206), who detected in it the influence of the late Gaudenzio and a marked Milanese accent. While not casting doubt over the attribution proposed by Romano and Mallé, S. Ghisotti (in *Gaudenzio Ferrari e la sua scuola*, 1982, pp. 114–15) underlined the influence exerted on the artist responsible for the cartoon by Gaudenzio in his late Milanese period, and by his pupils and collaborators – an influence evident above all in the saint's muscular build, "the result of an anatomical study by now almost overtly Mannerist". Stressing the documented link between the workshop of Gerolamo Giovenone and that of Bernardino Lanino, Ghisotti foregrounded how the solutions developed in the cartoon later returned in two different works by Lanino depicting Saint John the Baptist: in the altarpiece at the church of Santi Pietro e Paolo in Oleggio, where the chest and arm of the saint are identical, as is the position of the lamb, and in the polyptych in the parish church of Campiglia Cervo, which features the same method of rendering the left leg.

XV.
Workshop of Gerolamo Giovenone
(Gerolamo Giovenone and Bernardino
Lanino?)
Adoration of the Child
1550–55
charcoal and chalk on paper,
126 × 122 cm
inv. 330

In the list compiled by the Grand Chamberlain C. E. Alfieri di Sostegno at the time of Charles Albert of Savoy's donation, the cartoon was cited as number 30 in the inventory, but without attribution. S. Ghisotti (in *Gaudenzio Ferrari e la sua scuola*, 1982, pp. 116–19) proposed identifying it as cartoon no. 704 in the inventory of the ducal collections compiled in 1635 by Antonio della Cornia and described in the following terms: "Another larger Nativity, with Christ raised up behind the Angel, figure 7; not very finished. By Gaudenzio. Imperfect" (Baudi di Vesme, 1897, p. 62). The inscription "Gaudenzio Ferrari da Valduggia" written in 19th-century cursive characters at the lower right was probably added after the Charles Albertine inventory. N. Gabrielli (1933, pp. 155, 197) proposed the attribution to Gaudenzio, discounted by A. Griseri (1956, p. 136) in favour of Pier Francesco Lanino. Ghisotti highlighted how the cartoon is a re-casting, by the workshop of Gerolamo Giovenone around the sixth decade, of solutions developed by Gaudenzio on the theme of the Nativity. She observed how the Nativities painted by Gaudenzio in the polyptych at the collegiate church of Santa Maria in Arona (1511) or in the polyptych at the church of San Gaudenzio in Novara (1514–21) became prototypes for all of the variations on the theme produced over the subsequent decades by the workshops of Gerolamo Giovenone and Bernardino Lanino, united by a relationship of intense exchanges evinced by the cartoon. The latter reveals debts towards both Lanino's fresco, depicting the Adoration of the Child, in the church of Santa Caterina in Vercelli, for the general composition and the iconography (the inverted mirror image of Saint Joseph is identical), and towards the Adoration of the Child by Giovenone in the Museo Leone in Vercelli (which came from the sacristy of the church of San Cristoforo) for the shepherd visible on the right. In 2018, another painting was presented with strong links to the cartoon. This was the *Adoration of the Child with Saints Francis of Assisi and Anthony of Padua*, now owned by Banca Patrimoni Sella & C. and exhibited to the public at the Museo Borgogna in Vercelli. Comparing it with the painting, M. Caldera (in *Gerolamo Giovenone. Un capolavoro ritrovato*, 2018, pp. 27–33) states that the cartoon can be attributed to Gerolamo Giovenone and to Lanino for the captivating qualitative tension, now clouded by reworking and damage.

XVI.
Workshop of Gerolamo Giovenone (?)
Last Supper
c. 1540
charcoal, pencil, chalk and watercolour
on paper, 149 × 142.5 cm
inv. 311

In the list compiled by the Grand Chamberlain C. E. Alfieri di Sostegno at the time of the donation, the cartoon was attributed to Gaudenzio Ferrari as number 11 in the inventory and was associated with the Last Supper in the church of Santa Maria della Passione in Milan (Bollea, 1936, Appendix 4). The attribution to Gaudenzio was subsequently endorsed by R. Carità (1955, p. 242), whereas in the 1933 inventory N. Gabrielli considered it to be a product of the workshop (Gabrielli, 1933, pp. 157, 196). The cartoon was later ascribed to Boniforte Oldoni by A. Griseri (1956, pp. 78, 128–29) and by L. Mallé (1969, pp. 27–28, 88, 220); the first attribution to the workshop of Gerolamo Giovenone appeared in G. Romano (1970, p. 68) and was then supported by Mallé (1971, p. 206) and by all the subsequent scholars (Dalmasso, Gaglia, Poli, 1982, p. 178). M. Dell'Omo Rossini (in *Gaudenzio Ferrari e la sua scuola*, 1982, pp. 120–22) flagged up how the cartoon should not be considered the model for the Last Supper in Novara Cathedral, painted by Sperindio Cagnoli to a drawing produced by Gaudenzio no later than 1525, but rather as deriving from it, exhibiting Giovenonian qualities together with a marked Laninian influence, evident above all in the figures of Saint John and the servant and in the general realism with which the various characters are rendered. These properties lead us to consider the cartoon as the work of the late Giovenonian circle, dating from around 1540. The exhibition *Il Rinascimento di Gaudenzio Ferrari*, curated by Giovanni Agosti and Jacopo Stoppa, also compared the cartoon with the painting in Novara Cathedral (C. Battezzati in *Il Rinascimento di Gaudenzio Ferrari*, 2018, pp. 258–65).

XVII.
Giovanni Battista Giovenone (?)
Saint Dorothy Presents a Devotee
c. 1547
charcoal, white lead, chalk and
watercolour on paper, 123.2 × 62.4 cm
inv. 351

In the list compiled by the Grand Chamberlain C. E. Alfieri di Sostegno at the time of Charles Albert of Savoy's donation, the cartoon was ascribed to Gaudenzio Ferrari as number 51 in the inventory. That attribution reappeared in N. Gabrielli (1933, pp. 156, 197), who posited that it was the model for the right section of the triptych by Gaudenzio's workshop that was previously owned by Gallo and is now in a private Turinese collection. The attribution of the cartoon to Gaudenzio was accepted by most of the subsequent critics, who offered up various dates: around 1515 (Viale, 1969, p. 28), 1522–23 (Mallé, 1969, pp. 190–91) and 1531–33 (Grassi, 1941, p. 196). The first attribution to Giovanni Battista Giovenone was made by G. Romano (1970, p. 21) and was accepted by S. Ghisotti (in *Gaudenzio Ferrari e la sua scuola*, 1982, pp. 126–28) who highlighted how the established relationship between the cartoon and the painting in the aforementioned polyptych should be overturned: the polyptych was probably produced around 1540 in Gaudenzio's workshop, with considerable input from a collaborator hailing from Novara or Milan, while the cartoon, deriving from the late models of Gerolamo Giovenone and influenced by the style of Bernardino Lanino in the 1540s, was certainly produced by a painter from Vercelli. Ghisotti stresses the affinities that bind the cartoon to the painting created in 1547 by Giovanni Battista Giovenone, located in Vercelli in the Museo Borgogna, a copy of the Mystical Wedding of Saint Catherine by Gaudenzio Ferrari in Novara Cathedral. The cartoon, too, is a return, made in the same period, to a Gaudentian model: the aforementioned polyptych in the private Turinese collection.

XVIII.
Bernardino Lanino
Virgin and Child Crowned by Two Putti
c. 1534–39
charcoal, chalk and pencil on paper,
152 × 105.5 cm
inv. 312

In the list compiled by the Grand Chamberlain C. E. Alfieri di Sostegno at the time of Charles Albert of Savoy's donation, the cartoon was ascribed to Bernardino Lanino as number 12 in the inventory. The attribution has never been cast into doubt by the critics. Although the identity of the painting for which the cartoon constitutes the preparatory model is not known, it has been proposed that it dates from the painter's earliest recorded output (Romano, 1970, p. 21), a group of works containing paintings such as: the Virgin and Child with saints of 1534 in the

Galleria Sabauda in Turin; the Virgin and Child with saints and angels in the Museo Borgogna in Vercelli; the fresco depicting St Roch and sourced from the church of San Tommaso in Vercelli; and the Virgin and Child with saints in the parish church of Borgosesia of 1539. C. Mossetti (in *Gaudenzio Ferrari e la sua scuola*, 1982, pp. 140–42; and in *Bernardino Lanino*, 1985, pp. 45–47) noted the affinities that, with minimal variations, bind the figures of the Virgin and Child of this last-mentioned painting to those of the cartoon, to be associated also with the Virgin and Child at the Rijksmuseum in Amsterdam, due to a collaboration on the part of Lanino with the workshop of Gerolamo Giovenone. The scholar proposes a date later than the painting in the Galleria Sabauda of 1534, but prior to the Borgosesia painting of 1539, where we can discern an initial "adaptation of the Laninian idiom" and the painter "demonstrates a personal elaboration of the lesson of Gaudenzio". Up above it is possible to see traces of cut-outs at the edges in accordance with a typical 18th-century mixtilinear outline, which imply the use of the cartoon as an overdoor (F. Mazzini, *in Gaudenzio Ferrari e la sua scuola*, 1982, p. 54).

XIX.
Bernardino Lanino
Adoration of the Magi
c. 1539–43
charcoal, chalk and pencil on paper, 168 × 78.5 cm
inv. 314

In the list compiled by the Grand Chamberlain C. E. Alfieri di Sostegno at the time of Charles Albert of Savoy's donation, the cartoon appeared as number 14 in the inventory, but without attribution (Bollea, 1936, Appendix 4). In the 1856 inventory, it was ascribed to Gaudenzio Ferrari, an attribution endorsed by E. Halsey (1904, p. 128) but then discounted by N. Gabrielli in favour of Bernardino Lanino (Gabrielli, 1933, pp. 163, 197); subsequently, A. Griseri associated it with Lanino's sons, positing a date of around 1580 (Griseri, 1956, p. 143). C. Mossetti once again attributed it to Bernardino Lanino due to the compactness of the volumes and the sweetness of the expressions, assigning to it a period between the Virgin and Child with saints of the parish church of Borgosesia of 1539 and the Assumption in the church of San Sebastiano in Biella of 1543. The dating, proposed on a stylistic basis, falls in years in which "Lanino has already chosen his own autonomous mode with respect to the strict Gaudentian influence of the immediately preceding years, while maintaining references to the typologies of the master" (in *Gaudenzio Ferrari e la sua scuola*, 1982, pp. 143–45; and in *Bernardino Lanino*, 1985, pp. 51–53). The close dialogue with Gerolamo Giovenone's workshop is brought to light by the comparison between our cartoon and the Mystical Wedding of Saint Catherine in the parish church of San Germano Vercellese, a copy by Giovenone, a work that features similar compositional solutions in the figures of the Virgin and Child. The painting derived from the cartoon has not been traced; it can, however, be posited, as Mossetti does, that the painting in question is an Adoration of the Magi in the parish church of Pettinengo, the copy of an original by Lanino.

XX.
Bernardino Lanino
Christ of the Precious Blood, Saints and Devotees
1543–46
charcoal, chalk, white lead and pencil on paper, 196 × 130.5 cm
inv. 309

In the list compiled by the Grand Chamberlain C. E. Alfieri di Sostegno at the time of Charles Albert of Savoy's donation, the cartoon was ascribed to Bernardino Lanino as number 9 in the inventory. Later, it was subject to various attributions, associated with the name assigned from time to time to the author of the altarpiece of the Precious Blood in the church of San Giovanni Battista in Bellagio, clearly derived from the cartoon. This was initially ascribed to Gaudenzio Ferrari and dated to the years 1525–30 (Halsey, 1904, pp. 89, 135; Berenson, 1932, p. 163), then to Gaudenzio's workshop (Gabrielli, 1933, pp. 156, 196; Bollea, 1936, p. 490); then to Bernardino Lanino's sons, dated to around 1580 (Griseri, 1956, pp. 84, 143; Griseri, 1958, pp. 85–86); and lastly to the first phase of Giuseppe Giovenone the Younger (Romano, 1964, p. 76). C. Mossetti (in *Gaudenzio Ferrari e la sua scuola*, 1982, pp. 146–49; and in *Bernardino Lanino*, 1985, pp. 74–77) separated the two artworks, highlighting the higher quality of the cartoon with respect to the painting. The former was ascribed to Bernardino Lanino and dated slightly later than the Assumption in the church of San Sebastiano in Biella of 1543, but prior to the works produced by the painter in Saronno and in Milan between 1546 and 1550, and Mossetti also flagged up the debts towards Gaudenzio's Milanese paintings from 1540 to 1545. The scholar, however, attributed the Bellagio altarpiece to another painter who was up to speed with the Gaudentian models, but more associated with those of Gerolamo Giovenone, cautiously putting forward in this regard the name of Giuseppe Giovenone the Elder.

XXI.
Bernardino Lanino
Virgin and Child, Two Saints and Devotees
c. 1545
charcoal, pencil, watercolour and chalk on paper, 130 × 105 cm
inv. 328

In the list compiled by the Grand Chamberlain C. E. Alfieri di Sostegno at the time of Charles Albert of Savoy's donation, the cartoon was ascribed to Bernardino Lanino as number 28 in the inventory. This attribution was never cast into doubt by the subsequent critics. A. Griseri (1956, pp. 81, 141–42; 1958, pp. 74–75) judged the cartoon to be stylistically similar to the Virgin and Child with saints and donors at the Museum of Art in New Raleigh, dated 1552, and to the paintings depicting Saint Clare and Saint Francis at the Accademia Albertina in Turin (nos. 252 and 254), proposing a date of around 1550. G. Galante Garrone (in *Gaudenzio Ferrari e la sua scuola*, 1982, pp. 149–51) considered the cartoon to be "at the centre of an intricate network of relationships that Lanino had with the workshops of the late Gerolamo Giovenone and the Oldoni", recognising the analogies that associate him with two other cartoons at the Pinacoteca Albertina: inv. 357 by Gerolamo Giovenone, and inv. 305, attributed to Boniforte Oldoni (now lost, but recorded thanks to an 1895 photograph). Through a series of cross-references between works produced by the three workshops, the scholar arrived at a date of around the second half of the fifth decade; a date subsequently revised to the middle of the fifth decade (in *Bernardino Lanino*, 1985, pp. 71–73).

XXII.
Bernardino Lanino
Lamentation over the Dead Christ
c. 1546–53
charcoal, pencil and chalk on paper, 180 × 116.5 cm
inv. 327

In the list compiled by the Grand Chamberlain C. E. Alfieri di Sostegno at the time of Charles Albert of Savoy's donation, the cartoon was ascribed to Gaudenzio Ferrari as number 27 in the inventory. This attribution reappeared in the inventories of 1856 and 1933 (Gabrielli, 1933, pp. 155, 197). Ascribed to Bernardino Lanino by A. Griseri (1956, p. 134; 1958, p. 85), and once again to Gaudenzio by V. Viale (1969, p. 52), the cartoon was definitively attributed to Lanino by G. Galante Garrone (*Opere d'arte*, 1976). C. Mossetti (in *Gaudenzio Ferrari e la sua scuola*, 1982, pp. 152–54; and in *Bernardino Lanino*, 1985, pp. 78–80) drew attention to how the cartoon constitutes "a moment of reflection on the theme of the Lamentation over the dead Christ, which Lanino offered up time and again throughout the fifth and sixth decade", reinterpreting the iconographic model embodied by Gaudenzio's Lamentation, now in the Galleria Sabauda (no. 51), and "constituting its moment of dissemination amongst the painters of the Gaudentian school, at least until the end of the century". The cartoon was faithfully re-cast by Giuseppe Giovenone the Younger in the Lamentation at the Museo Borgogna in Vercelli (Viale, 1969, p. 52), produced by the middle of the seventh decade. The rapid circulation of drawings amongst the Gaudentian artists led to them not only adopting variants in the composition but also, on occasion, intervening on the cartoon itself at the time of its reutilisation. According to Mossetti, Giovenone was responsible for the ongoing anatomical fascination with Christ's body. The scholar proposed a date for the cartoon of between 1546 and 1553, the period of the execution of the frescoes for the chapel of Novara Cathedral – the Laninian works that betray the closest stylistic affinities.

XXIII.
Bernardino Lanino
Wedding of the Virgin
c. 1553–56
charcoal, pencil, watercolour, chalk and white lead on paper, 123.5 × 57.5 cm
inv. 333

In the list compiled by the Grand Chamberlain C. E. Alfieri di Sostegno at the time of Charles Albert of Savoy's donation, the cartoon was ascribed to Gaudenzio Ferrari as number 33 in the inventory – an attribution that reappears in the inventories of 1856 and 1933 (Gabrielli, 1933, pp. 155, 197). L. Mallé (1969, pp. 221–22) observed that the cartoon did not correspond to the known Weddings by Gaudenzio, positing the existence of a different model dating from the final phase of the artist's output. The first attribution to Bernardino Lanino was made by G. Galante Garrone (in *Gaudenzio Ferrari e la sua scuola*, 1982, pp. 155–58) who highlighted in the cartoon "the psychologies and the smooth enveloping of the drapery typically found in Lanino's advanced phase of heart-rending Leonardism", noting stylistic similarities with Mortara's 1553 Adoration of the Magi, the Last Supper in the church of San Nazzaro in Milan and the 1554 Baptism in the Baptistery in Busto Arsizio (originally in the church of San Giovanni in Conca in Milan). The expert postulated for the cartoon a date somewhere between the second half of the sixth and the start of the seventh decade. In a second essay on the subject (in *Bernardino Lanino*, 1985, pp. 85–87) she narrowed it down to "a date that cannot be much later than the middle of the sixth decade", close to the time of the Novara frescoes, which were completed in 1553. In all likelihood, the cartoon should be considered in relation to inv. 338 at the Accademia Albertina, portraying the Adoration of the Shepherds: both have similar dimensions and stylistic characteristics.

XXIV.
Bernardino Lanino
Adoration of the Shepherds
c. 1553–56
charcoal, pencil, watercolour, chalk and white lead on paper, 125 × 58 cm
inv. 338

In the list compiled by the Grand Chamberlain C. E. Alfieri di Sostegno at the time of Charles Albert of Savoy's donation, the cartoon was ascribed to Gaudenzio Ferrari as number 38 in the inventory. It is an attribution that we also find in the inventories of 1856 (where the cartoon was cited as an Adoration of the Magi) and of 1933, where it was matched with the fresco attributed to Bernardino Lanino, now in the Museo Borgogna in Vercelli, having been removed from the Gattinara home in Vercelli (Gabrielli, 1933, pp. 155, 197). V. Viale (1969, p. 54) attributed to Lanino both the cartoon and the fresco, which he dated to the fifth or sixth decade of the century. Yet the cartoon and the fresco may have been produced by different artists at different times, as indicated by G. Galante Garrone (in *Gaudenzio Ferrari e la sua scuola*, 1982, pp. 155–58) who, considering the latter to be a "late and awkward work of the studio" datable to around 1600, noted in the first "the psychologies and the smooth enveloping of the drapery typically found in Lanino's advanced phase of heart-rending Leonardism", flagging up stylistic affinities with Mortara's 1553 Adoration of the Magi, the Last Supper in the church of San Nazzaro in Milan and the 1554 Baptism in the Baptistery in Busto Arsizio (which came from the church of San Giovanni in Conca in Milan). The scholar proposed for the cartoon a date of between the second half of the sixth and the beginning of the seventh decade. In a second essay on the subject (in *Bernardino Lanino*, 1985, pp. 85–87) she narrowed it down to "a date that cannot be much later than the middle of the sixth decade", close to the time of the Novara frescoes, which were completed in 1553. In all likelihood, the cartoon should be considered in relation to inv. 333 at the Accademia Albertina, portraying the Wedding of the Virgin: both have similar dimensions and stylistic characteristics.

XXV.
Bernardino Lanino (?)
Virgin and Child with Saint Anne
c. 1539–43
charcoal, pencil, watercolour and white lead on paper, 127 × 86 cm
inv. 348

In the list compiled by the Grand Chamberlain C. E. Alfieri di Sostegno at the time of Charles Albert of Savoy's donation, the cartoon was hesitantly ascribed to Bernardino Lanino as number 48 in the inventory. In the 1631 inventory of the works held at the Castello di Torino (Campori, 1870, p. 98), there is an entry for a "cartoon of the Virgin and Child with Saint Anne, by Leonardo da Vinci". It is not our cartoon, which was cited for the first time in the inventory of the ducal collections compiled by Antonio della Cornia in 1635. In that year, a full three cartoons with the same subject were mentioned: no. 698, "Saint Anne, and the Virgin holding the Child, who embraces the head of the lamb, full figures. By Leonardo da Vinci. Very rare work", which corresponds to that described in 1631; no. 699, "The same. By Gaudentio, copied exquisitely"; and no. 218, a copy by Francesco Cairo "from the Cartoon by Leonardo. Mediocre" (Baudi di Vesme, 1897, p. 62). All trace of the first and third has been lost, whereas the second (no. 699) matches our cartoon, already ascribed to Bernardino in the inventories of 1832 and 1856. The 17th-century attribution to Gaudenzio was endorsed by A. Baudi Di Vesme (1897, p. 62) and by G. Rodolfo (1927, pp. 2–3), whereas N. Gabrielli ascribed it to Leonardo's workshop (1933, pp. 164–65, 197). It appeared at the 1939 exhibition on Leonardo da Vinci with the indication "Sixteenth-century Lombard master" (*Mostra di Leonardo*, 1939, p. 32). The 19th-century attribution of the cartoon to Bernardino Lanino, scarcely legible due to a major restoration carried out in 1846 by Giovanni Volpato (Bollea, 1932, pp. 466–74, 494–501; Gabrielli, 1933, pp. 164–65), was supported by G. Galante Garrone (in *Gaudenzio Ferrari e la sua scuola*, 1982, pp. 159–61; and in *Bernardino Lanino*, 1985, pp. 68–70), who places the work close to the Lanino painting on the same subject, held at the Pinacoteca di Brera in Milan, but the differences in the drapery prevent the cartoon from being identified as a preparatory study for the panel. Indeed, that panel reinterprets Leonardo's painting in the Louvre (already attested early on as being at Casale Monferrato, where it remained until 1629) and dates to the early 1540s due to the stylistic affinities with Lanino's 1543 altarpiece for Francesco Strata (National Gallery, London): "in both, the modelling is compact, still echoing the Borgosesia altarpiece of 1539" (*Gaudenzio Ferrari e la sua scuola*, 1982, p. 161). A. Musiari (in *Leonardo da Vinci. Disegnare il futuro*, 2019, pp. 407–09) claims as a Da Vincian hypotext the anonymous "Resta-Esterházy" cartoon that, although lost in Budapest during the Second World War, is known thanks to high-quality black-and-white photographs. A probable copy of one of Leonardo's cartoons for the *Virgin and Child with Saint Anne*, produced by a pupil during the Milanese period (1508–13), the "Resta-Esterházy" therefore is connected with Lanino's journey through the Da Vincian models, which inspired variants "among which we should include the drawing held at the Albertina" (ibid., p. 408).

XXVI.
Workshop of Bernardino Lanino (?)
Christ Led to Calvary
c. 1546–53
charcoal, watercolour, white lead and pencil on paper, 87 × 101 cm
inv. 343

In the list compiled by the Grand Chamberlain C. E. Alfieri di Sostegno at the time of Charles Albert of Savoy's donation, the cartoon was ascribed to Gaudenzio Ferrari as number 43 in the inventory. This attribution was then supported by G. Colombo (1881, p. 244), whereas N. Gabrielli considered it to be a work by Gaudenzio's workshop (1933, pp. 157, 197). It should be highlighted that in the 1856 inventory the cartoon was stated to be by Lanino. G. Galante Garrone (in *Gaudenzio Ferrari e la sua scuola*, 1982, pp. 162–65) considered it "closely associated with Lanino's works of the fifth decade", proposing a date "within the years of the Milanese and specifically Novarese output of the painter, documented between 1546 and 1553".

XXVII.
Pietro Francesco or Gerolamo Lanino
Vision of Death, Judgement and Hell
c. 1580–89
watercolour and white lead on paper, 85 × 72.2 cm
inv. 345

In the list compiled by the Grand Chamberlain C. E. Alfieri di Sostegno at the time of Charles Albert of Savoy's donation, the cartoon was ascribed to Gaudenzio Ferrari as number 45 in the inventory. L. C. Bollea (1932, p. 463) postulated that it be matched with the "chiaroscuro drawing of the resurrection of the dead", cited in the 1631 inventory (Campori, 1870, p. 91), but the hypothesis does not stand up to scrutiny, as G. Galante Garrone demonstrated (in *Gaudenzio Ferrari e la sua scuola*, 1982, pp. 171–72). The attribution to Gaudenzio was validated by G. Colombo (1881, p. 245) and by N. Gabrielli (1933, pp. 156, 197). The first attribution, albeit cautious, to the sons of Bernardino Lanino appeared in the aforementioned essay by Galante Garrone, who noted the stylistic affinity between the cartoon and two drawings in the Biblioteca Reale, nos. 15955 and 14659, dating respectively from the beginning and the end of the ninth decade and associated with works of Pietro Francesco and Gerolamo Lanino. The scholar did not specify to which of the two brothers the cartoon may be attributed, highlighting nevertheless the "rapid and confident artistry (particularly in the central group) with clear and simplified chiaroscuro divisions, almost like a woodcut, played out on two sepia tones, raised by touches of white lead".

XXVIII.
Giuseppe Giovenone the Younger
Angels Bearing in Glory the Instruments of the Passion
c. 1550
charcoal and chalk on paper,
80.5 × 125 cm
inv. 342

In the list compiled by the Grand Chamberlain C. E. Alfieri di Sostegno at the time of Charles Albert of Savoy's donation, the cartoon was ascribed to Bernardino Lanino as number 42 in the inventory. Subsequently, E. Halsey (1904, p. 124) ascribed it tentatively to Gaudenzio, whereas N. Gabrielli (1933, pp. 163, 197), supporting the attribution to Lanino, associated it – alongside cartoon inv. 326 at the Accademia Albertina (portraying the Resurrection of Christ with two bishop-saints) – with painting no. 54 of the Galleria Sabauda in Torino, having as its subject the Resurrection of Christ, two bishop-saints and, above, the angels with the instruments of the Passion. Studying the aforementioned painting at the Sabauda, attributed to Giuseppe Giovenone the Younger, A. Griseri (1956, pp. 139–40; 1958, p. 85) ascribed to this painter also the two cartoons at the Albertina, which since then have been generally considered the work of Giuseppe Giovenone the Younger. P. Astrua (in *Gaudenzio Ferrari e la sua scuola*, 1982, pp. 194–97) drew attention to the way in which the angels differ from the Gaudentian models, "preferring more composed movements, more in keeping with their role as witnesses to sacred events, behaviour more aligned with Lanino's angels", in particular the musician angel in Lanino's altarpiece in Borgosesia, dating from 1539, which is very similar to the angel visible in the top right of the cartoon. The scholar underlined a constant characteristic that emerges by comparing the cartoons and paintings of Giuseppe Giovenone the Younger: the discrepancy between the quality visible in the former and the "plain translation of the effort of visionary conception into reductive, trivialised prose" that can be detected in the latter. These differences can be explained by postulating the substantial input of the workshop in the execution in paint of the models drawn by the master himself. The cartoon can be dated on the basis of the aforementioned relationship with cartoon inv. 326, which may be attributed, through stylistic comparisons, to the middle of the century (Dalmasso, Gaglia, Poli, 1982, p. 183).

XXIX.
Giuseppe Giovenone the Younger
Resurrection of Christ and Two Bishop Saints
c. 1550
charcoal, chalk, watercolour, white lead, bister and pencil on paper,
176 × 143.5 cm
inv. 326

In the list compiled by the Grand Chamberlain C. E. Alfieri di Sostegno at the time of Charles Albert of Savoy's donation, the cartoon was ascribed to Gaudenzio Ferrari as number 26 in the inventory. This attribution was then confirmed by G. Colombo (1881, p. 244), E. Halsey (1904, p. 223) and N. Gabrielli (1933, pp. 155, 197). Gabrielli associated it, together with cartoon inv. 342 at the Accademia Albertina (depicting the angels with the instruments of the Passion), with painting no. 54 of the Galleria Sabauda in Turin, having as its subject the Resurrection of Christ, two bishop-saints and, above, the angels with the instruments of the Passion. A. Griseri (1956, pp. 139–40; 1958, p. 85), studying the aforementioned painting at the Sabauda attributed to Giuseppe Giovenone the Younger, also assigned to this painter the two cartoons at the Albertina, which since then have generally been ascribed to him. P. Astrua (in *Gaudenzio Ferrari e la sua scuola*, 1982, pp. 194–97), discerning in the cartoon "the highly personal style of Giuseppe the Younger", noted the emergence of the "reference to the powerful approach of the late-period Gaudenzio"; particularly in relation to the figure of Christ, he established a connection with Gaudenzio's Risen Christ at the National Gallery in London, datable to around 1540. Astrua identified Bernardino Lanino as the possible go-between who allowed Giuseppe the Younger to stay abreast of Gaudenzio's progress in Milan and of the latest developments in Milanese painting. The complex network of references to works by Gaudenzio and Lanino at the end of the fourth and the beginning of the fifth decade spotlighted by the scholar, together with the similarities between the emphasised anatomies of the two warriors who shield their faces and a number of figures frescoed by Lanino at the church of San Nazzaro in Milan around 1548, may enable the cartoon to be dated to around the middle of the century, as proposed by P. Gaglia (in Dalmasso, Gaglia, Poli, 1982). Astrua flagged up the qualitative difference between the cartoon and the painting in the Galleria Sabauda, described as a "plain translation of the effort of visionary conception into reductive, trivialised prose"; this discrepancy can be explained by the substantial input of the workshop into the painting.

XXX.
Giuseppe Giovenone the Younger
Saint Nicholas of Bari
c. 1555
charcoal, chalk and pencil on paper,
119 × 54 cm
inv. 350bis

In the list compiled by the Grand Chamberlain C. E. Alfieri di Sostegno at the time of Charles Albert of Savoy's donation, the cartoon was ascribed to Gaudenzio Ferrari as number 50bis in the inventory. This initial attribution was accepted by E. Halsey (1904, p. 124) and N. Gabrielli (1933, pp. 156, 197). Indeed, Gabrielli associated it, alongside cartoon inv. 350 in the Accademia Albertina (depicting Saint Nicholas), with the triptych of the church of Sant'Eusebio in Moncrivello, portraying Saint Nicholas and Saint Eusebius in the lateral panels, with the Resurrection of Christ in the central section. The cartoon was once again assigned to Gaudenzio by A. Griseri (1958, p. 85), whereas the first attribution to Giuseppe Giovenone the Younger was made by G. Galante Garrone (*Opere d'arte*, 1976, p. 33), an opinion later seconded by P. Astrua (in *Gaudenzio Ferrari e la sua scuola*, 1982, pp. 198–202). Astrua, underscoring the "refined archaism both in the iconographic models and in the illustrative *ductus*" of the cartoons, put forward a date of the middle of the sixth decade, during a time of crisis in which figurative culture in Vercelli was seeking models more aligned with the new Counter-Reformation religiosity and, in our case, it found them not in the "too dangerously true" Gaudenzio of the frescoes of the church of San Cristoforo, but in the more archaic Gaudentian mode of the polyptych of San Gaudenzio in Novara (1514–21). This stiffening is far more evident in the central panel of the aforementioned triptych of Moncrivello, commissioned by the local Confraternity of Corpus Christi, than it is in the work – similarly depicting the Resurrection of Christ – currently in the Galleria Sabauda in Turin, dating from around 1550.

XXXI.
Giuseppe Giovenone the Younger
Saint Eusebius
c. 1555
charcoal, chalk and pencil on paper,
118 × 54 cm
inv. 350

In the list compiled by the Grand Chamberlain C. E. Alfieri di Sostegno at the time of Charles Albert of Savoy's donation, the cartoon was ascribed to Gaudenzio Ferrari as number 50 in the inventory. The attribution to Gaudenzio was accepted by E. Halsey (1904, p. 124) and by N. Gabrielli (1933, pp. 156, 197). Indeed, Gabrielli associated it, alongside cartoon inv. 350 in the Accademia Albertina (depicting Saint Eusebius), with the triptych of the church of Sant'Eusebio in Moncrivello, portraying St Nicholas and St Eusebius in the lateral sections, with the Resurrection of Christ in the central section. The cartoon was also attributed to Gaudenzio by A. Griseri (1958, p. 85), whereas L. Mallé (1971, p. 206) recognised in it the hand of Gerolamo Giovenone. The first attribution to Giuseppe Giovenone the Younger appeared in G. Galante Garrone (*Opere d'arte*, 1976, p. 33), and this view was endorsed by P. Astrua (in *Gaudenzio Ferrari e la sua scuola*, 1982, pp. 198–202). Astrua, underscoring the "refined archaism both in the iconographic models and in the illustrative *ductus*" of the cartoons, put forward a date of the middle of the sixth decade, during a time of crisis in which figurative culture in Vercelli was seeking models more aligned with the new Counter-Reformation religiosity and, in our case, it found them not in the "too dangerously true" Gaudenzio of the frescoes of the church of San Cristoforo, but in the more archaic Gaudentian mode of the polyptych of San Gaudenzio in Novara (1514–21). This stiffening is far more evident in the central panel of the aforementioned triptych of Moncrivello, commissioned by the local Confraternity of Corpus Christi, than it is in the work – similarly depicting the Resurrection of Christ – currently in the Galleria Sabauda in Turin, dating from around 1550.

XXXII.
Giuseppe Giovenone the Younger
Mary Magdalene Carried to Heaven by the Angels
c. 1550–55
charcoal, chalk, watercolour, white lead and pencil on paper, 189 × 129.5 cm
inv. 315

In the list compiled by the Grand Chamberlain C. E. Alfieri di Sostegno at the time of Charles Albert of Savoy's donation, the cartoon was ascribed to Gaudenzio Ferrari as number 15 in the inventory. This attribution was supported by G. Colombo (1881, p. 244), who considered it preparatory for the fresco on the same subject painted by Gaudenzio in the church of San Cristoforo in Vercelli. It was also assigned to Gaudenzio by E. Halsey (1904, p. 123), L. C. Bollea (1932, p. 452) and N. Gabrielli (1933, pp. 154, 197). The latter associated it with the painting depicting Mary Magdalene raised to heaven by the angels in the parish church of Moncrivello, at the time attributed to Giuseppe Giovenone the Elder. A. Griseri discarded the reference to the Gaudentian fresco, linking the cartoon only to the painting in Moncrivello and ascribing it to Giovenone himself (Griseri, 1956, p. 85). Once again attributed to Gaudenzio by V. Viale (1969, pp. 61, 186), the cartoon was ascribed for the first time to Giuseppe Giovenone the Younger by G. Galante Garrone (*Opere d'arte*, 1976, p. 34) – an attribution that, with the exception of G. C. Sciolla (1979, p. 15), was accepted by the subsequent critics. P. Astrua (in *Gaudenzio Ferrari e la sua scuola*, 1982, pp. 202–05) considered the cartoon "one of the most committed tests of the early maturity [of Giuseppe the Younger], revealing the artist to be a skilled illustrator", thus making it possible to propose a date of the beginning of the sixth decade, also postulated by P. Gaglia (in Dalmasso, Gaglia, Poli, 1982, p. 182). The scholar draws attention to the way in which the model of reference imposed by the client – i.e. the aforementioned fresco of Gaudenzio in the church of San Cristoforo in Vercelli – is here interpreted with a "dogmatic compunction" more aligned with the changed political and religious situation, and also underlines the higher quality of the cartoon with respect to the aforecited painting in the sacristy of the parish church of Moncrivello, likely to have been produced with substantial input from the workshop.

XXXIII.
Giuseppe Giovenone the Younger
Annunciation
c. 1559–60
charcoal, chalk and pencil on paper,
108 × 102 cm
inv. 322

In the list compiled by the Grand Chamberlain C. E. Alfieri di Sostegno at the time of Charles Albert of Savoy's donation, the cartoon was ascribed to Gaudenzio Ferrari as number 22 in the inventory. This attribution was endorsed by N. Gabrielli (1933, pp. 155, 197) and by L. Grassi (1941, pp. 186, 204). The first attribution to Giuseppe Giovenone the Younger appeared in G. Galante Garrone (*Opere d'arte*, 1976, p. 33). In the entry included in the 1982 catalogue, the scholar and G. Curto (in *Gaudenzio Ferrari e la sua scuola*, 1982, pp. 206–08) pointed out the influence on the figure of the Virgin exerted by the Saint Dorothy in cartoon inv. 351, attributed to Giovanni Battista Giovenone, as well as the debt owed to the Annunciation frescoed by Bernardino Lanino in Novara Cathedral between 1546 and 1553. The composition of the cartoon was also indebted to the Annunciation, ascribed to Gerolamo Giovenone, previously in the Abrate collection, and to another Annunciation frescoed by Lanino in the church of Sant'Agata, now in the Museo Borgogna in Vercelli. The two experts thus postulated that the work was produced at the end of the sixth decade, when there was a documented collaboration between Giuseppe the Younger and Bernardino Lanino (from 28 August 1559). This dating is supported by the stylistic similarities with cartoons nos. 334 and 353 in the Accademia Albertina, which were preparatory drawings for the Balocco triptych, dating from around 1560.

XXXIV.
Giuseppe Giovenone the Younger
Virgin and Child Enthroned with Two Angels
c. 1560
charcoal, pencil and chalk on paper,
168 × 48 cm
inv. 353

In the list compiled by the Grand Chamberlain C. E. Alfieri di Sostegno at the time of Charles Albert of Savoy's donation, the cartoon (inexplicably cited as "Holy Family") was ascribed to Gaudenzio Ferrari as number 53 in the inventory. This attribution was then supported by E. Halsey (1904, p. 124) and by N. Gabrielli (1933, pp. 156, 198), who associated it with the central section of the scattered polyptych of the parish church of Gattinara, now in the Museo Borgogna in Vercelli. The first attribution to Giuseppe Giovenone the Younger was made by G. Romano (1964, p. 77), who indicated how the cartoon constituted the preparatory model for the central section of the triptych in the parish church of San Michele Arcangelo in Balocco, of which the Accademia Albertina holds the lateral section depicting Saint Michael the Archangel. The cartoon and the triptych were then studied by C. Mossetti and G. Curto (in *Gaudenzio Ferrari e la sua scuola*, 1982, pp. 208–12), who noted the higher quality of the former. The triptych was commissioned by the Confraternity of the Rosary around 1560, during a period in which the documents show how Giuseppe Giovenone the Younger was regularly being commissioned by the confraternities in the Vercelli area, "satisfying their devotional requirements with calibrated exhibitions of religious sentiment". The Balocco triptych features several close similarities in the layout of the frame with the Moncrivello triptych, produced slightly before it. The two scholars highlighted the cartoon's indebtedness towards a number of works by Gaudenzio Ferrari, such as the Virgin and Child with Saints Eligius and Maurice in the Galleria Sabauda in Turin (no. 49) or the Virgin of the Orange Trees in the church of San Cristoforo in Vercelli (for the figure of the angel on the right), and by Gerolamo Giovenone the Elder, such as the Virgin and Child with saints of 1533, previously at the Castello di Rivoli and now in the collections of the Musei Reali in Turin. The references to these two painters from the previous generation are bound up with the influence exerted by Bernardino Lanino, to whom Giuseppe the Younger owed the affectionate sweetness with which the figures of the Virgin and the Child are rendered.

XXXV.
Giuseppe Giovenone the Younger
Saint Michael the Archangel
c. 1560
charcoal, pencil and chalk on paper,
127 × 54 cm
inv. 334

In the list compiled by the Grand Chamberlain C. E. Alfieri di Sostegno at the time of Charles Albert of Savoy's donation, the cartoon was ascribed to Bernardino Lanino as number 34 in the inventory. N. Gabrielli (1933, pp. 157, 197) assigned it to the workshop of Gaudenzio Ferrari, whereas L. Mallé (1971, p. 206) postulated an attribution to Gerolamo Giovenone. The first attribution of the cartoon to Giuseppe Giovenone the Younger was made by G. C. Sciolla (1979, p. 22), who identified it as the model for the left-hand section of the triptych in the parish church of San Michele Arcangelo in Balocco, of which the Accademia Albertina holds also the preparatory cartoon of the central panel. The two cartoons and the triptych were studied by C. Mossetti and G. Curto (in *Gaudenzio Ferrari e la sua scuola*, 1982, pp. 208–212), who noted the higher quality of the cartoons with respect to the painting. The triptych was commissioned by the Confraternity of the Rosary around 1560, during a period in which the documents show how Giuseppe Giovenone the Younger was regularly being commissioned by the confraternities in the Vercelli area, "satisfying their devotional requirements with calibrated exhibitions of religious sentiment". The triptych in Balocco features several close similarities in the layout of the frame with the Moncrivello triptych, produced slightly before it. Mossetti and Curto saw in the cartoon of Saint Michael "an atmosphere of thoughtful tranquillity, borrowed from the latest Laninian models", making clear the influence exerted upon Giuseppe the Younger by a number of "Leonardesque" works of Bernardino Lanino.

XXXVI.
Giuseppe Giovenone the Younger
Virgin and Child
c. 1560
charcoal and pencil on paper,
126 × 64 cm
inv. 352

In the list compiled by the Grand Chamberlain C. E. Alfieri di Sostegno at the time of Charles Albert of Savoy's donation, the cartoon appeared without an attribution, as number 52 in the inventory. In the 1933 inventory it was assigned to Gaudenzio Ferrari's workshop (Gabrielli, 1933, pp. 158, 197). The attribution to Giuseppe Giovenone the Younger was made by P. Astrua (in *Gaudenzio Ferrari e la sua scuola*, 1982, pp. 213–15), who foregrounded the refined archaism of the composition, inspired by youthful prototypes of Gaudenzio Ferrari, such as for example the Virgin and Child in the parish church of Quarona or the painting on the same subject in the Pinacoteca di Brera in Milan. The scholar observed stylistic affinities with cartoons nos. 353 and 334 at the Accademia Albertina, preparatory models for the central and left-hand sections of the triptych of the parish church of Balocco, datable to around 1560, making it possible to posit a similar date for our cartoon. In the same work, Astrua also published the painting corresponding to the cartoon, which is a Virgin and Child that was previously in the Canetti collection in Vercelli though its current location is unknown. For this painting, identified thanks solely to an old photograph that belonged to L. Rovere (Rovere Fund, Musei Civici, Turin), a date of around the eighth decade was put forward. In the painting, the archaic tendencies already evident in the cartoon are further accentuated, deploying decorative motifs from the late-Gothic tradition such as the damasked fabric of the Virgin's dress and the elaborate design of the crown and the hairstyle. The deliberate archaism of the cartoon and the painting is aligned with the tendency to tap the latent sacred and devotional potential of ancient Medieval and early Renaissance images, supported by the Church during the Counter-Reformation. The painting by Giuseppe Giovenone the Younger appeared to his contemporaries very obsequious towards these new demands of the religious culture of the second half of the 16th century (Pagella, Piovano in *Bernardino Lanino e il Cinquecento a Vercelli*, 1986, pp. 195, 200–01).

XXXVII.
Giuseppe Giovenone the Younger
Virgin and Child Surrounded by Saints Anthony Abbot and Francis, the Archangels Raphael and Michael, Two Donors and God the Father Blessing
c. 1560–65
charcoal, chalk, watercolour and bistre on paper, 190 × 136 cm
inv. 316

In the list compiled by the Grand Chamberlain C. E. Alfieri di Sostegno at the time of Charles Albert of Savoy's donation, the cartoon was ascribed to Gaudenzio Ferrari as number 16 in the inventory. This attribution was cast into doubt early on by G. Colombo (1881, p. 244) and, later, by N. Gabrielli (1933, pp. 157, 197), who downgraded it to a work of the studio. Indeed, Gabrielli was the first scholar to associate the cartoon with the panel on the same subject, signed "Iosephus Iuvenonis pinxit", then in the oratory of the church of Sant'Antonio in Vercelli and now in the Museo Borgogna in the same city. P. Astrua (in *Gaudenzio Ferrari e la sua scuola*, 1982, pp. 216–18) reported the information that the oratory of the church of Sant'Antonio was entrusted in 1548 to the Confraternity of the Angels, which had commissioned the painting, and that in 1560 the confraternity had begun the reconstruction of the crumbling building. The painting and the related cartoon date, then, from after 1560. The scholar compared it with cartoon inv. 353 at the Accademia Albertina, noting how in our drawing, presumably later, "the characteristics of the Gaudentian poetics, entirely alien to the new social and religious situation of the time, are now almost lost". Moreover, the higher quality of the cartoon with respect to the painting in the Museo Borgogna was also flagged up, along with a number of differences, concerning above all the Saint Raphael the Archangel on the left (in the cartoon he rests his right hand on Tobias's shoulder, whereas in the painting he points towards the Child; in addition, in the cartoon he looks at the spectator, whereas in the painting he turns his gaze to the client at the lower left).

XXXVIII.
Giuseppe Giovenone the Younger
Saint Eusebius Presenting a Donor, Assisted by Saint Joseph and an Angel
1565–66
charcoal, pencil and chalk on paper, 168 × 58.5 cm
inv. 325

In the list compiled by the Grand Chamberlain C. E. Alfieri di Sostegno at the time of Charles Albert of Savoy's donation, the cartoon was ascribed to Bernardino Lanino as number 25 in the inventory. In the 1933 inventory, N. Gabrielli assigned it to Gaudenzio's workshop, crediting the group of Giovenonians with its production (Gabrielli, 1933, pp. 157, 197). The first attribution to Giuseppe Giovenone the Younger was made by A. Griseri (1956, pp. 85, 140; 1958, p. 85), who saw it corresponding to the right-hand side of the Adoration of the shepherds, saints and donors, sited on the back wall of the presbytery of the parish church of Sant'Eusebio in Moncrivello, signed "Josephus de Juvenonibus fecit". P. Astrua (in *Gaudenzio Ferrari e la sua scuola*, 1982, pp. 219–21) proposed a date for the Moncrivello painting, taking as his starting point a number of aspects concerning the figure of the patron, visible also in the extant fragment of cartoon: Cesare De Majo, Captain General of the Artillery of the *Rex Catholicissimus* in Lombardy and Piedmont who, in his capacity as the Duke of Savoy's Camp-Master General, had distinguished himself through his victorious campaign against French troops from 1537 onwards. For his valour, Duke Charles III of Savoy made him a marquis, enfeoffing him with Moncrivello on 21 February 1538, though it seems that he came effectively into possession of the castle and the associated land only from 1 December 1565, on concession of Emmanuel Philibert. Astrua credits De Majo with a crucial role in the artist's figurative choices, which drew upon the cultured and sophisticated artistic climate of the Milan of Ferrante Gonzaga, in which it was the painter Bernardino Campi who best satisfied the requirements of the ruling class and the neo-feudal aristocracy. De Majo's will, dated 31 December 1566, and the decorations on the armour worn by the patron in the painting (in the cartoon he is portrayed in civilian clothing), which were used in Milan only from the second half of the seventh decade onwards, indicate a date for the painting and the associated cartoon of 1565–66.

XXXIX.
Giuseppe Giovenone the Younger
Virgin and Child Surrounded by Saints Peter and Stephen Who Present Two Prelates
c. 1579–81
charcoal, chalk and watercolour on paper, 190 × 135 cm
inv. 310

In the list compiled by the Grand Chamberlain C. E. Alfieri di Sostegno at the time of Charles Albert of Savoy's donation, the cartoon was ascribed to Bernardino Lanino as number 10 in the inventory, and Saint Peter was confused with Saint Joseph (Bollea, 1936, Appendix 4). This attribution was discarded by N. Gabrielli (1933, pp. 157, 196), who ascribed it to Gaudenzio Ferrari's workshop. The first attribution to Giuseppe Giovenone the Younger was made by A. Griseri (1956, pp. 85, 140; 1958, p. 85) and this was accepted by the subsequent critics (Sciolla, 1979, p. 16; Dalmasso, Gaglia, Poli, 1982, p. 185). P. Astrua (in *Gaudenzio Ferrari e la sua scuola*, 1982, pp. 222–24) cast the spotlight on the quality of the rendering of the two donors, showing how Giuseppe Giovenone the Younger's skill as a portraitist was appreciated both in the contemporary sources and in those from the 18th and 19th centuries. As the scholar demonstrated in a recent essay on the subject (in *Le arti del disegno all'Accademia Albertina*, 1995, pp. 42–43), the cartoon is associated with the painting currently located in the Pinacoteca Arcivescovile in Vercelli, but which was previously on display in the church of San Pietro Apostolo in Crova. The church had been founded by the Benedictines of Santo Stefano in Vercelli (this explains the presence of the two saints in the cartoon), which the Cardinal Archbishop and Commendatory Abbot Bonifacio Ferrero substituted with the Lateran Canons in 1536, in an effort to pull it out of crisis. The attempt proved in vain, but the crisis of the following decades did not stop Ferrero from commissioning Giovenone to produce the painting for the church in Crova, which – according to the hypothesis of Astrua – dates from the very end of the eighth decade or the beginning of the next. The scholar also postulates that Bonifacio Ferrero may be the donor portrayed face-on, accompanied by another cardinal of the same lineage (Pietro Francesco or Guido).

XL.
Giuseppe Giovenone the Younger
Lamentation over the Dead Christ
c. 1574–75
charcoal, chalk, watercolour and bistre on paper, 174 × 142 cm
inv. 324

In the list compiled by the Grand Chamberlain C. E. Alfieri di Sostegno at the time of Charles Albert of Savoy's donation, the cartoon was ascribed to Gaudenzio Ferrari as number 24 in the inventory. This attribution was accepted by G. Colombo (1881, p. 244) and, hesitantly, by E. Halsey (1904, p. 123), whereas N. Gabrielli (1933, pp. 157, 197) cited it as a work produced by Gaudenzio's workshop. The first attribution to Giuseppe Giovenone the Younger was made by G. Galante Garrone (*Opere d'arte*, 1976, p. 33) and was accepted by the subsequent critics (Sciolla, 1979, p. 20). P. Astrua (in *Gaudenzio Ferrari e la sua scuola*, 1982, pp. 224–26) drew attention to the way in which the cartoon constituted the preparatory model for the Lamentation over the dead Christ located on the altar of the right transept of the parish church of Mongrando San Lorenzo. The cartoon is of a higher quality than the painting; in addition, a new iconography of the Lamentation is presented, as an alternative to the Gaudentian model embodied by the Deposition no. 51 in the Galleria Sabauda, often re-cast by the master's collaborators (as evinced by cartoon inv. 327 by Bernardino Lanino in the Accademia Albertina). The male figure holding three nails, who appears at the top right, constitutes a modern meditation on the "loaded" Leonardesque faces, associated with other caricatural solutions deployed by Bernardino Lanino in the church of San Paolo (1565) and in the church of San Giuliano in Vercelli. The Lamentation in the parish church of Mongrando was painted following the instructions arising out of the pastoral visit of 1574, a date that constitutes a sure *terminus post quem* for our cartoon (*Le arti del disegno all'Accademia Albertina*, 1995, p. 43).

XLI.
Giuseppe Giovenone the Younger
Christ's Ascent to Calvary
c. 1580
charcoal, chalk and pencil on paper,
231 × 163 cm
inv. 319

In the list compiled by the Grand Chamberlain C. E. Alfieri di Sostegno at the time of Charles Albert of Savoy's donation, the cartoon was ascribed to Bernardino Lanino as number 19 in the inventory. This attribution was accepted by N. Gabrielli (1933, pp. 163, 197), who associated it with the Christ Going to Calvary of the Archbishopric of Vercelli, a painting (at the time attributed to Pier Francesco Lanino) of which Gabrielli highlighted the lower quality with respect to the cartoon. The cartoon and the painting were ascribed to Raffaele Giovenone by A. Griseri (1956, p. 85), whereas V. Viale (1973, pp. 92–93) made the first attribution to Giuseppe Giovenone the Younger, which was accepted by the subsequent critics (*Opere d'arte*, 1976, pp. 33–34). G. Galante Garrone and G. Curto (in *Gaudenzio Ferrari e la sua scuola*, 1982, pp. 226–28) conducted a stylistic analysis of the cartoon and the painting that, having established a certain *terminus post quem* of 1570 (the date of the Deposition at the parish church of Moncrivello), and an equally certain *terminus ante quem* of 1589 (the date of the altarpiece of the parish church of Casalvolone), led them to propose a date straddling the eighth and ninth decades, subsequently supported by P. Gaglia, who posited a date of around 1580 (Dalmasso, Gaglia, Poli, 1982, pp. 186–87).

XLII.
Giuseppe Giovenone the Younger
Assumption
c. 1580–85
charcoal and chalk on paper,
228 × 160 cm
inv. 320

In the list compiled by the Grand Chamberlain C. E. Alfieri di Sostegno at the time of Charles Albert of Savoy's donation, the cartoon was ascribed to Gaudenzio Ferrari as number 20 in the inventory – an attribution partially accepted by N. Gabrielli, who in the inventory of 1933 ascribed it to Gaudenzio's workshop (Gabrielli, 1933, pp. 157, 197). The cartoon was attributed to Giuseppe Giovenone the Younger by G. Galante Garrone (*Opere d'arte*, 1976, pp. 33–34), who highlighted its use for the Assumption of the parish church of Robbio Lomellina. G. C. Sciolla initially ascribed it to Giuseppe Giovenone the Elder (Sciolla, 1979, p. 19), before accepting the attribution to Giuseppe the Younger (Sciolla, 1980, pp. 157, 169), supported by the subsequent critics (Dalmasso, Gaglia, Poli, 1982, p. 188). S. Ghisotti (in *Gaudenzio Ferrari e la sua scuola*, 1982, pp. 228–32), noting the stylistic affinities with works produced by Giuseppe the Younger in the ninth decade (in particular with cartoon inv. 319 with the Christ Going to Calvary, datable to around 1580), proposed for our cartoon a date of some time between 1580 and 1585. The scholar noted a substantial qualitative drop-off in the painting in Robbio Lomellina, postulating for it a date of a few years after the cartoon and a substantial input on the part of the workshop.

XLIII.
Giuseppe Giovenone the Younger
Virgin and Child Surrounded by Saints Anthony Abbot and Catherine of Alexandria and God the Father Blessing
c. 1590
charcoal, chalk and pencil on paper,
185 × 115 cm
inv. 355

In the list compiled by the Grand Chamberlain C. E. Alfieri di Sostegno at the time of Charles Albert of Savoy's donation, the cartoon was ascribed to Gaudenzio Ferrari as number 55 in the inventory, as can be seen printed in ink at the lower left (Bollea, 1936, Appendix 4). This attribution, accepted by E. Halsey (1904, p. 124), was rejected by N. Gabrielli (1933, pp. 163–64, 198), who ascribed it to the workshop of Bernardino Lanino. The cartoon was attributed to Giuseppe Giovenone the Younger by C. E. Spantigati and by G. Curto (in *Gaudenzio Ferrari e la sua scuola*, 1982, pp. 232–34) who, on the recommendation of G. Romano, associated it with the painting depicting the Virgin and Child with saints and the blessing Eternal Father of the parish of Castelnovetto Lomellina. The scholars noted the higher quality of the cartoon, signed by Giuseppe the Younger, with respect to the painting, produced with substantial input from the workshop, and proposed for both a date of the beginning of the 1590s, based on stylistic comparisons with other works by the painter. The signs left by an 18-century frame along the lower and upper edges indicate a reuse of the cartoon as an overdoor in that period (F. Mazzini in *Gaudenzio Ferrari e la sua scuola*, 1982, p. 54).

XLIV.
Giuseppe Giovenone the Younger
Virgin and Child between Saints John the Baptist and Catherine (?)
c. 1589–90
charcoal, chalk and pencil on paper,
146 × 120 cm
inv. 358

In the list compiled by the Grand Chamberlain C. E. Alfieri di Sostegno at the time of Charles Albert of Savoy's donation, the cartoon was ascribed to Gaudenzio Ferrari as number 58 in the inventory. The attribution to Gaudenzio, accepted by E. Halsey (1904, p. 124), was later rejected by N. Gabrielli (1933, pp. 164, 198) in favour of Bernardino Lanino. The cartoon was attributed for the first time to Giuseppe Giovenone the Younger by C. E. Spantigati and G. Curto (in *Gaudenzio Ferrari e la sua scuola*, 1982, pp. 235–37). The two scholars, noting the stylistic affinities with the last decade of Giuseppe the Younger's output, underlined the close similarity with cartoon inv. 355 in the Accademia Albertina, dating from around 1590, depicting the Virgin and Child amid saints and God the Father blessing, positing for our cartoon a date immediately precedent. It should also be observed how the Virgin faithfully reutilises the solution developed by Gaudenzio Ferrari in cartoon inv. 317 in the Accademia Albertina, portraying the Virgin and Child, datable to between 1539 and 1546.

XLV.
Giuseppe Giovenone the Younger (?)
Saint Margaret before Olybrius
c. 1580
charcoal, chalk and pencil on paper,
65 × 68 cm
inv. 341

In the list compiled by the Grand Chamberlain C. E. Alfieri di Sostegno at the time of Charles Albert of Savoy's donation, the cartoon – identified simply as "drawing with six figures" – was assigned to Andrea del Sarto as number 41 in the inventory (Bollea, 1936, Appendix 4). This attribution was altered to the 16th-century Piedmontese school in the 1933 inventory (Gabrielli, 1933, pp. 181, 197), in which, though, the iconography of the cartoon remained obscure: it was described as a "Jesus before Pilate". The exact iconography and the corresponding painting were identified by G. Galante Garrone and G. Curto (in *Gaudenzio Ferrari e la sua scuola*, 1982, pp. 238–39), who stated how the cartoon may have been the preparatory model for the upper right section of the painting depicting the Martyrdom of Saint Margaret of the Archbishopric of Vercelli, a work bearing close resemblance to the output of the workshop of Giuseppe Giovenone the Younger in the years between 1580 and 1584. The aforementioned scholars thus proposed an attribution to Giuseppe Giovenone the Younger for our cartoon, also highlighting a number of differences between it and the painting in Vercelli: in the latter, the griffin-shaped armrest of the throne is missing, and the figures behind Olybrius are very different (in particular the person shown crying, handkerchief in hand). The cartoon is dated to circa 1580. This date is postulated on the basis of the similarities "in the rapid, spinning style" to the specific sketching in the background of cartoon inv. 319 at the Accademia Albertina, depicting Christ Going to Calvary, which itself is datable to around 1580.

XLVI.
Workshop of Giuseppe Giovenone the Younger
Virgin and Child Surrounded by Saints John, Francis, Sebastian and Roch
c. 1585
charcoal, chalk and pencil on paper,
150 × 134 cm
inv. 354

In the list compiled by the Grand Chamberlain C. E. Alfieri di Sostegno at the time of Charles Albert of Savoy's donation, the cartoon was assigned to Bernardino Lanino as number 54 in the inventory. This attribution, supported by N. Gabrielli (Gabrielli, 1933, pp. 163, 198), was rejected by L. Mallé, who attributed the central section of the cartoon to Gerolamo Giovenone and the four side figures to assistants (Mallé, 1971, pp. 205–06). P. Astrua (in *Gaudenzio Ferrari e la sua scuola*, 1982, pp. 240–43) noted the stylistic similarities with cartoon inv. 303 in the Accademia Albertina, depicting the Adoration of the shepherds, considering them both to be similar to works produced by the studio of Giuseppe Giovenone the Younger around the middle of the ninth decade. The group of the Virgin and Child faithfully recycles the iconography developed by Gaudenzio Ferrari between 1539 and 1546 in cartoon inv. 317 in the Accademia Albertina. The old wooden frame of the cartoon had a mixtilinear shape typical of 18th-century frames – a factor that led to the hypothesis that it had been re-used as an overdoor in that period (F. Mazzini, in *Gaudenzio Ferrari e la sua scuola*, 1982, pp. 54–55).

XLVII.
Workshop of Giuseppe Giovenone the Younger
Adoration of the Shepherds
c. 1585–95
charcoal and pencil on paper, 125 × 123 cm
inv. 303

In the list compiled by the Grand Chamberlain C. E. Alfieri di Sostegno at the time of Charles Albert of Savoy's donation, the cartoon was ascribed to the school of Raphael as number 3 in the inventory. In was subsequently attributed to Gaudenzio Ferrari (Halsey, 1904, p. 123) and, in the 1933 inventory (Gabrielli, 1933, p. 196), to an anonymous master of the Genoese school. P. Astrua (in *Gaudenzio Ferrari e la sua scuola*, 1982, pp. 242–43) focused on the stylistic similarities that link it to cartoon inv. 354 at the Accademia Albertina, depicting the Virgin and Child with saints, associating them both with works of the studio of Giuseppe Giovenone the Younger around the middle of the ninth decade. The influence exerted by the central Italian style on our cartoon is what lay behind the 19th-century attribution to Andrea del Sarto. The attribution to Giuseppe the Younger was based on the iconographic similarities between the painting and the Nativity in the parish church of Moncrivello, produced by the painter around the middle of the seventh decade, although Astrua rightly pointed out that our cartoon does not constitute the preparatory phase of said painting – a phase partially documented by cartoon inv. 325 in the Accademia Albertina (Saints Eusebius and Joseph with donor) – but rather a late return to it on the part of the workshop, carried out, as has been stated, in all likelihood around the middle of the ninth decade.

XLVIII.
Workshop of Giuseppe Giovenone the Younger
Lamentation over the Dead Christ
c. 1570–88
charcoal, chalk and watercolour on paper, 85 × 71 cm
inv. 346

In the list compiled by the Grand Chamberlain C. E. Alfieri di Sostegno at the time of Charles Albert of Savoy's donation, the cartoon was attributed to Gaudenzio Ferrari as number 46 in the inventory. This attribution was endorsed by E. Halsey (1904, p. 124), whereas in the subsequent inventories the cartoon was erroneously associated with the work by Bernardino Lanino in the church of San Giuliano in Vercelli. N. Gabrielli (1933, pp. 157, 197) viewed it as a preparatory sketch for cartoon inv. 324 in the Accademia Albertina, on the same subject, and attributed it to Gaudenzio's studio while recognising Giovenonian characteristics in it. The first reference to Giuseppe Giovenone the Younger was made by G. Galante Garrone (*Opere d'arte*, 1976). P. Astrua (in *Gaudenzio Ferrari e la sua scuola*, 1982, pp. 244–45) reinstated the link established by Gabrielli between our cartoon and inv. 324, produced around 1574–75 by Giuseppe the Younger as a model for the painting in the parish church of Mongrando San Lorenzo, commenting upon the decidedly lower quality of inv. 346. This was deemed to be the work of an unknown collaborator, whom Astrua identified as Amedeo, Giuseppe's brother, who worked with him at least from 1549, and their partnership is documented as lasting until 1588. The reduced dimensions of our cartoon with respect to Giuseppe's prototype indicate that a return was made to it with a view to producing paintings for private use.

XLIX.
Workshop of Giuseppe Giovenone the Younger
Saint Augustine Tramples the Heretics
c. 1590–1600
charcoal and chalk on paper, 184 × 117 cm
inv. 356

In the list compiled by the Grand Chamberlain C. E. Alfieri di Sostegno at the time of Charles Albert of Savoy's donation, the cartoon was ascribed to Gaudenzio Ferrari as number 56 in the inventory. The attribution to Gaudenzio was seconded by N. Gabrielli (1933, pp. 156, 198), whereas A. Griseri (1956, p. 85) associated it with the painting on the same subject in the church of San Sebastiano in Biella, one of the organ doors painted by Raffaele Giovenone in 1579. G. Romano (in *Gaudenzio Ferrari e la sua scuola*, 1982, pp. 246–47) identified the work that matches our cartoon as one of the two facades of the standard in the parish church of San Germano in Casale, a work traditionally attributed to Giorgio Alberini (Negri, 1895, p. 7; Gabrielli, 1935, p. 71; Brizio, 1942, p. 129; Moccagatta, 1962–63, p. 63), who was related to the Giovenone family through his marriage to Barbara, the daughter of Amedeo Giovenone (Romano, 1964, p. 77, no. 3; Romano, 1970, p. 66, no. 2). Romano highlighted the superior stylistic quality of the cartoon, which probably emerged from the workshop of Giuseppe Giovenone the Younger "at a time not after the final decade of the century, under the direct control of the master". Along the upper and lower edges, it is possible to make out colour variations produced by an 18th-century frame: the cartoon was probably used as an overdoor in that period (F. Mazzini, in *Gaudenzio Ferrari e la sua scuola*, 1982, p. 54).

L.
Bernardino Campi
Nativity of Jesus with Saint Bartholomew and Angels Singing
1568–72
charcoal, watercolour, pencil and chalk on paper, 179 × 114 cm
inv. 329

In the list compiled by the Grand Chamberlain C. E. Alfieri di Sostegno at the time of Charles Albert of Savoy's donation, the cartoon was ascribed to Gaudenzio Ferrari as number 29 in the inventory. This attribution was accepted by all of the subsequent critics (Colombo, 1881, p. 244; Halsey, 1904, p. 123; Gabrielli, 1933, pp. 155, 197; Bollea, 1936, pp. 126–27) up until A. Griseri (1956, pp. 84, 138, 143), who ascribed it to Bernardino Lanino's sons. G. Romano (in *Gaudenzio Ferrari e la sua scuola*, 1982, pp. 250–52) posited that our cartoon should be matched with no. 705, described by Antonio della Cornia in the 1635 inventory of the ducal collections in the following terms: "Another large Nativity, with Christ lying before the animals, 4 figures on the ground, 4 angels in the sky, and the annunciation of the angel to shepherds in the distance. Believed to be by Baldessare da Siena. Good" (Baudi Di Vesme, 1897, p. 62). The painter Della Cornia, recognising in the cartoon affinities with the Nativity by Baldassarre Peruzzi, previously seen in Rome at the church of San Rocco, realised that it had no connection to the Gaudentian school, as stressed by the aforecited Romano, to whom we owe the first attribution to Bernardino Campi. The scholar identified in the cartoon the preparatory model for the Nativity with Saint Bartholomew and angels in the church of Sant'Eusebio in Gambolò, signed and dated "Bernardino Campus crem. Fa. 1572" and commissioned by Gian Marco Calvo (Lamo, 1584, p. 92). In addition, he noted how the group with the Virgin adoring the Child, the section with the landscape and the angels up above had already been used by Campi for the Nativity and angels in the church of San Michele in Cremona, signed and dated "1568 Bernardinus Campus Crem.s Fa." (Lamo, 1584, p. 85). The association with this curved painting explains the traces of arching that are visible in the upper part of the cartoon, which would otherwise be mysterious, since the Gambolò canvas is rectangular.

LI.
Giovanni Paolo Lomazzo (?)
Head of Bearded Old Man
1570–71
charcoal, watercolour, chalk and white lead on paper, 56.5 × 43 cm
inv. 347

In the list compiled by the Grand Chamberlain C. E. Alfieri di Sostegno at the time of Charles Albert of Savoy's donation, the cartoon was ascribed to the school of Michelangelo as number 47 in the inventory. We find the same attribution in the inventories of 1856 and 1933 (Gabrielli, 1933, pp. 168, 197). G. Romano (in *Gaudenzio Ferrari e la sua scuola*, 1982, pp. 254–55) proposed a possible match with cartoon no. 707, described as follows in the inventory of the ducal collections compiled by the painter Antonio della Cornia in 1635: "Oversized emperor's head. By Procaccino. Good." This attribution can be explained, according to the scholar, as the recognition in the cartoon of traces of Milanese culture on Della Cornia's part; indeed, aside from the Michelangelesque impressiveness of the image, the cartoon also contains an "evident recourse to an illustrative technique that also connotes a *sfumato* derived from Leonardo, more northern than central Italian". The associating of the cartoon with Giovanni Paolo Lomazzo is based on the comparison with the faces of a number of characters, similarly seen from below and sporting a worried look, painted by Lomazzo on the left wall of the Foppa chapel in the church of San Marco in Milan between 1570 and 1571.

LII.
Lombard-Emilian milieu
Glory of a Saint (?)
c. 1600
charcoal and chalk on paper, 42 × 31 cm
inv. 308

In the list compiled by the Grand Chamberlain C. E. Alfieri di Sostegno at the time of Charles Albert of Savoy's donation, the cartoon was attributed to Guercino as number 8 in the inventory. The subject was identified as "an Evangelist", as it was in the inventory of 1856 and in that of 1933, where the cartoon was attributed to an exponent of the Florentine school of the 16th century (Gabrielli, 1933, pp. 178, 196). A. C. Bertolotto (in *Gaudenzio Ferrari e la sua scuola*, 1982, pp. 258–59) offered a number of significant ideas on the iconography and the style of the cartoon. The character depicted seems to be wearing a habit, and as such could be identified as a young monk saint in glory, associable with the various "glories" of Saint Dominic or Saint Anthony of Padua depicted on ceilings or apsidal domes from the second half of the 16th-century onwards. In relation to the style, the scholar noted how "the airy expansion of the forms, the daring glimpse and the vaguely Correggesque smile would point towards a painter in some sense influenced, albeit indirectly, by the founder of the Emilian school". The cartoon demonstrates a "revisited Correggism which was that of various Lombard and Emilian painters between the end of the 16th century and the start of the 17th". Bertolotto identified the stylistic characteristics closest to those of our cartoon in a drawing depicting a figure recoiling (Bora, 1976), appearing in the Resta Codex, held in the Ambrosiana in Milan, and attributed by Resta to the Crema-born painter Carlo Urbino.

LIII.
Milanese milieu
Virgin and Child with Angels Worshipped by a Devotee Presented by Saint George (?)
c. 1570
charcoal, pencil, watercolour and chalk on paper, 180 × 125 cm
inv. 340

In the list compiled by the Grand Chamberlain C. E. Alfieri di Sostegno at the time of Charles Albert of Savoy's donation, the cartoon was attributed to Bernardino Lanino as number 40 in the inventory. The attribution to Lanino, conditionally endorsed in the 1933 inventory by N. Gabrielli (1933, pp. 163, 197), was rejected by G. Romano (in *Gaudenzio Ferrari e la sua scuola*, 1982, pp. 256–57). On the basis of the heavy drapery of the Virgin and the billowing flag of Saint George, Gabrielli associated the cartoon with the Lombard Mannerism "gravitating around Lomazzo and Aurelio Luini", emphasising at the same time an "authentic human cordiality, of more ancient Lombard tradition", visible in the gestures of the Virgin and of Saint George. The name of the artist remains unknown, but the stylistic characteristics led Romano to posit a date of around 1570.

LIV.
Pier Francesco Mazzucchelli, known as Morazzone
Prophet
c. 1600–10
charcoal and chalk on paper, 195.5 × 85.5 cm
inv. 331

In the list compiled by the Grand Chamberlain C. E. Alfieri di Sostegno at the time of Charles Albert of Savoy's donation, the cartoon was ascribed to Gaudenzio Ferrari as number 31 in the inventory. This attribution, endorsed by the inventory of 1933 (Gabrielli, 1933, pp. 155, 197), was repudiated by A. Griseri (1956, p. 71), who considered our cartoon and its companion on the same subject, also held at the Accademia Albertina with inv. 335, "a 17th-century thing but in the true spirit of Gaudenzio". The first attribution to Morazzone was made by M. Gregori (1962, p. 142) and was discussed in depth by C. E. Spantigati (in *Gaudenzio Ferrari e la sua scuola*, 1982, pp. 262–65), who considered the two cartoons to be studies on Gaudentian works produced by Mazzucchelli in the first decade of the 17th century at the Sacro Monte in Varallo, when he was engaged on decorative works that the clients wished to be as close as possible to the Gaudentian models. The scholar noted strong connections between the prophet in the cartoon and the Zachary (first on the right) frescoed in the chapel of the Annunciation by an anonymous late-Gaudentian painter, in all likelihood inspired by the two prophets frescoed by Gaudenzio on the exterior of the no-longer-extant chapel with the Apparition of Christ to Mary Magdalene (Galloni, 1914, pp. 40–41). It was probably one of these two figures, still visible in 1671, that served as the model of reference for our cartoon.

LV.
Pier Francesco Mazzucchelli known as Morazzone
Prophet
c. 1600–10
charcoal and chalk on paper, 194 × 83 cm
inv. 335

In the list compiled by the Grand Chamberlain C. E. Alfieri di Sostegno at the time of Charles Albert of Savoy's donation, the cartoon was ascribed to Gaudenzio Ferrari as number 35 in the inventory. This attribution, seconded in the inventory of 1933 (Gabrielli, 1933, pp. 155, 197), was rejected by A. Griseri (1956, p. 71), who deemed our cartoon and its companion piece on the same subject, also held at the Accademia Albertina (inv. 331), "a 17th-century thing but in the true spirit of Gaudenzio". The first attribution to Morazzone was made by M. Gregori (1962, p. 142) and was discussed in depth by C. E. Spantigati (in *Gaudenzio Ferrari e la sua scuola*, 1982, pp. 262–65), who considered the two cartoons to be studies on Gaudentian works produced by Mazzucchelli in the first decade of the 17th century at the Sacro Monte in Varallo, when he was engaged on decorative works that the clients wished to be as close as possible to the Gaudentian models. The scholar noted strong connections between the prophet in the cartoon and the Isaiah (on the end wall) frescoed in the chapel of the Annunciation by an anonymous late-Gaudentian painter, in all likelihood inspired by the two prophets frescoed by Gaudenzio on the exterior of the no-longer-extant chapel with the Apparition of Christ to Mary Magdalene (Galloni, 1914, pp. 40–41). It was probably one of these two figures, still visible in 1671, that served as the model of reference for our cartoon.

LVI.
Workshop of the D'Enrico brothers
Saint Catherine of Alexandria
c. 1616–18
charcoal, chalk and pencil on paper, 159.5 × 62.5 cm
inv. 313

In the list compiled by the Grand Chamberlain C. E. Alfieri di Sostegno at the time of Charles Albert of Savoy's donation, the cartoon was ascribed to Gaudenzio Ferrari as number 13 in the inventory. This attribution, accepted by N. Gabrielli (1933, pp. 154, 197), was jettisoned by G. Romano (*Gaudenzio Ferrari e la sua scuola*, 1982, pp. 268–70) who, at the suggestion of G. Testori, attributed our cartoon and its companion piece depicting Saint Lucy, also held at the Accademia Albertina (inv. 318), to the workshop of the D'Enrico brothers. The scholar identified the stylistic affinities that link the cartoon to the four canvases by Tanzio da Varallo in the Museo del Paesaggio in Pallanza, and to the associated preparatory drawings located in the Pinacoteca in Varallo (Baiocco in *Tanzio da Varallo*, 2000, pp. 177–80, nos. 45–48). The grandeur and flowing drapery of the saint in the cartoon are similar to the Saint John, Saint Catherine and Saint Apollonia in Pallanza that, at the time of the 1982 exhibition, were thought to have been produced around 1630. F. Frangi (in *Percorsi caravaggeschi*, 1999, pp. 134–35, 138–39) and, subsequently, S. Colombo (in *Tanzio da Varallo*, 2000, p. 92, no. 10) demonstrated how the production of the four Pallanza canvases can be dated to between November 1616 and January 1618, indirectly providing a new foothold for the dating of our cartoon, once again associated with the canvases in a recent text by S. Baiocco (in *Tanzio da Varallo*, 2000, pp. 172–73).

LVII.
Workshop of the D'Enrico brothers
Saint Lucy
c. 1616–18
charcoal and pencil on paper, 159 × 55.5 cm
inv. 318

In the list compiled by the Grand Chamberlain C. E. Alfieri di Sostegno at the time of Charles Albert of Savoy's donation, the cartoon was ascribed to Gaudenzio Ferrari as number 18 in the inventory. This attribution, accepted by N. Gabrielli (1933, pp. 154, 197), was rejected by G. Romano (in *Gaudenzio Ferrari e la sua scuola*, 1982, pp. 268–70) who, at the suggestion of G. Testori, attributed our cartoon and its companion piece depicting Saint Catherine of Alexandria, also held at the Accademia Albertina (inv. 313), to the workshop of the D'Enrico brothers. The scholar identified the stylistic affinities that, through its grandeur and psychological subtlety, link the cartoon to the four canvases by Tanzio da Varallo in the Museo del Paesaggio in Pallanza, and to the associated preparatory drawings located in the Pinacoteca in Varallo (Baiocco in *Tanzio da Varallo*, 2000, pp. 177–80, nos. 45–48): works that at the time were believed to date from around 1630. F. Frangi (in *Percorsi caravaggeschi*, 1999, pp. 134–35, 138–39) and, subsequently, S. Colombo (in *Tanzio da Varallo*, 2000, p. 92, no. 10) demonstrated how the production of the four canvases in Pallanza can be dated to between November 1616 and January 1618, indirectly providing a new foothold for the dating of our cartoon, once again associated with the canvases in a recent text by S. Baiocco (in *Tanzio da Varallo*, 2000, pp. 172–73).

LVIII.
Giovanni Guerra
Penitent Received by a Pontiff
c. 1590–1600
pen and watercolour on paper,
41 × 29.5 cm
inv. 301

In the list compiled by the Grand Chamberlain C. E. Alfieri di Sostegno at the time of Charles Albert of Savoy's donation, the drawing was ascribed to Paolo Veronese as number 1 in the inventory – an attribution that we find again in the 1856 inventory, whereas in the one drawn in 1933 N. Gabrielli attributed it to the Roman school of the 17th century (Gabrielli, 1933, pp. 182, 196). On the occasion of the 1982 exhibition, the drawing was studied by C. Bertolotto (in *Gaudenzio Ferrari e la sua scuola*, 1982, pp. 272–74), who identified its exact iconography. The scholar highlighted how the figures that populate the drawing are stylistically similar to those drawn by Giovanni Guerra in the Story of Esther in the sketchbook held at the University Library in Genoa, datable to between 1590 and 1600. Recalling that in a letter of 1599 Guerra defined himself a "painter and architect", Bertolotto noted, vis-à-vis the fantastic architecture that can be seen in the drawing, that the "airy backdrop of buildings constantly varying in plan and elevation, animated by niches, exedrae, loggias and balustrades, enriched by flights of steps and gardens, finds innumerable correspondences in the grandiose 16th- and 17th-century villas that popes and cardinals commissioned in Rome and the Lazio region".

LIX.
Giuseppe Cesari known as the Cavalier d'Arpino
Death of a Pontiff
c. 1588
sanguine on paper, 28 × 43 cm
inv. 307

In the list compiled by the Grand Chamberlain C. E. Alfieri di Sostegno at the time of Charles Albert of Savoy's donation, the cartoon was ascribed to Taddeo Zuccari as number 7 in the inventory – an attribution that reappeared in the 1856 inventory, whereas in the one drawn in 1933 N. Gabrielli attributed it to an exponent of the 16th-century Florentine school (Gabrielli, 1933, pp. 178, 196). C. E. Spantigati (in *Gaudenzio Ferrari e la sua scuola*, 1982, pp. 276–77), supporting a hypothesis previously formulated by L. C. Bollea (1932, pp. 457, 461–63), proposed that the drawing could be identified as the "Little drawing in red pencil, by Giuseppino", meaning Giuseppe Cesari known as the Cavalier d'Arpino, cited in the inventory of the paintings at the Castello di Torino of 1 September 1631 (Campori, 1870, p. 93). The scholar emphasised both the reliability of the attributions of that inventory, above all for the contemporary painters, and the fortunes of the Cavalier d'Arpino at the court of Savoy in the early decades of the 17th century, as evinced also by the inventory compiled by Della Cornia in 1635. Spantigati identified Pope Pius V, who died in 1572, as the person lying on his death bed, surrounded by dignitaries and cardinals; the design is thought to be a copy made by the Cavalier d'Arpino in 1588 – the year in which the body of Pius V was transferred from the Vatican to the new tomb in the church of Santa Maria Maggiore with a solemn ceremony – based on a 1572 original probably produced by Federico Zuccari.

Bibliography

Angela Griseri

1584
A. Lamo. *Discorso di Alessandro Lamo intorno alla scoltura, et pittura*. Cremona.

1590
G. P. Lomazzo. *Idea del tempio della pittura*. Milan.

1821
G. Bordiga. *Notizie intorno alle opere di Gaudenzio Ferrari*. Milan.

1830
G. Bordiga. *Storia e Guida del Sacro Monte di Varallo*. Varallo.

1835
G. Bordiga, S. Pianazzi. *Le opere del pittore e plasticatore Gaudenzio Ferrari*. Milan.

1843
A. Perpenti. *Elogio di Gaudenzio Ferrari pittore e plasticatore*. Milan.

1870
G. Campori. *Raccolta di cataloghi ed inventarii inediti*. Modena.

1871
G. Bossetti. *Della vita e delle opere di Bernardino Lanino pittore vercellese*. Vercelli.

1881
G. Colombo. *Vita e opere di Gaudenzio Ferrari pittore con documenti inediti*. Turin.

1883
G. Colombo. *Documenti e notizie intorno agli artisti vercellesi*. Vercelli.

1885
V. Promis. *Disegni della Biblioteca di S.M. attribuiti a Gaudenzio Ferrari riprodotti in XXI tavole da Pietro Carlevaris*. Turin.

1895
F. Negri. "Giorgio Alberini." *Rivista di Storia, Arte, Archeologia della provincia di Alessandria*, January–March, July–September.

1897
A. Baudi di Vesme. "La Regia Pinacoteca di Torino." *Le gallerie nazionali italiane*. Rome.

1904
E. Halsey. *Gaudenzio Ferrari*. London.

1907
B. Berenson. *North Italian Painters of the Renaissance*. London.

1910
G. B. Morandi. "I Giovenone (Notizie e documenti)." *Archivio della Società Vercellese di Storia e Arte* 2, no. 4.

1914
P. Galloni. *Sacro Monte di Varallo. Origine e svolgimento delle opere d'arte*. Varallo.

1920
A. Baudi di Vesme. "I principali discepoli del pittore Martino Spanzotti." In: *Atti della Società Piemontese di Archeologia e Belle Arti*, vol. IX.

1921
S. Weber. "Giovenone" entry. In: U. Thieme, F. Becker, *Allgemeines Künstlerlexikon*, vol. XIV. Leipzig.

1926
A. M. Brizio. "Studi su Gaudenzio Ferrari." *L'Arte* 29.

1927
G. Rodolfo. *Disegni di Gaudenzio Ferrari e di Bernardino Lanino già nella Galleria dei Duchi di Savoia di Torino*. Carmagnola.
S. Weber. *Gaudenzio Ferrari und seine Schule*. Strasbourg.

1928
A. Durio. *Bibliografia di Gaudenzio Ferrari*. Novara.
I. Kunze. "Lanino Bernardino", "Lanino Girolamo", "Lanino Pietro Francesco" entries. In: U. Thieme, F. Becker, *Allgemeines Künstlerlexikon*, vol. XXII. Leipzig.

1932
B. Berenson. *Italian Pictures of the Renaissance, a List of the Principal Artists*. Oxford.
L. Bollea. "Una donazione del re Carlo Alberto alla R. Accademia Albertina." *Bollettino Storico-Bibliografico Subalpino*, no. 5–6.

1933
N. Gabrielli. "Inventario degli oggetti d'arte esistenti nella R. Accademia Albertina di Belle Arti in Torino." *Bollettino Storico-Bibliografico Subalpino*, no. 1–2.
N. Gabrielli. *La Regia Galleria dell'Accademia Albertina di Torino*. Rome.

1935
N. Gabrielli. *L'arte a Casale Monferrato dal XI al XVIII secolo*. Turin.

1936
L. Bollea. *La Galleria dell'Accademia*. Turin.

1939
Mostra di Leonardo da Vinci. Exhibition catalogue. Milan.

1941
L. Grassi. "Gaudenzio Ferrari e i suoi disegni." *L'Arte* 44, no. 4.

1942
A. M. Brizio. *La pittura in Piemonte dall'età romanica al Cinquecento*. Turin.

1954
G. Testori. "Promemoria gaudenziano." *Bollettino della Società Piemontese di Archeologia e Belle Arti*.

1954–57
L. Mallé. "La Mostra di Gaudenzio Ferrari a Vercelli." *Bollettino della Società Piemontese di Archeologia e Belle Arti* 8–11, n.s. (*Studi dedicati a Gaudenzio Ferrari*).

1955
R. Carità. "Ipotesi sul primo Cinquecento piemontese." *Bollettino d'Arte*.

1956
Mostra di Gaudenzio Ferrari. Exhibition catalogue. Vercelli.

1958
A. Griseri. "Una revisione nella Galleria dell'Accademia Albertina." *Bollettino d'Arte*, January–March.
G. Testori. *G. Martino Spanzotti. Gli affreschi di Ivrea*. Ivrea.

1959
G. Testori. *Tanzio da Varallo*. Exhibition catalogue. Turin.

1960
G. Testori. *Gaudenzio alle porte di Varallo*. Varallo.

1962
M. Gregori. *Il Morazzone*. Exhibition catalogue. Varese.

1962–63
V. Maccagatta. "Giorgio Alberini." *Bollettino della Società Piemontese di Archeologia e Belle Arti*.

1963–68
A. Baudi di Vesme. *Schede Vesme. L'arte in Piemonte dal XVI al XVIII secolo*. Turin.

1964
A. Gallino. "Gerolamo Giovenone: precisazioni critiche e nuove attribuzioni." *Bollettino della Società Piemontese di Archeologia e Belle Arti*.
G. Romano. "La tradizione gaudenziana nella seconda metà del Cinquecento." *Bollettino della Società Piemontese di Archeologia e Belle Arti*.

1965
G. Testori. *Il gran teatro montano. Saggi su Gaudenzio Ferrari*. Milan.

1968
C. Debiaggi. *Dizionario degli artisti valsesiani dal secolo XIV al XX*. Varallo.

1969
L. Mallé. *Incontri con Gaudenzio*. Turin.
V. Viale. *Gaudenzio Ferrari*. Turin.

1970
G. Romano. *Casalesi del Cinquecento. L'avvento del manierismo in una città padana*. Turin.

1971
L. Mallé. *Spanzotti, Defendente, Giovenone: nuovi studi*. Turin.

1973
V. Viale. *Il Duomo di Vercelli. La pinacoteca dell'Arcivescovado*. Vercelli.

1974
L. Mallé. *Le arti figurative in Piemonte. Dal secolo XVII al secolo XIX*. Turin (undated).
G. Romano. "Orientamenti della pittura casalese da G.M. Spanzotti alla fine del Cinquecento." In: *Quarto Congresso di Antichità e d'Arte - Casale 1969*. Casale Monferrato.

1975
V. Comoli Mandracci. "Sacri Monti e Territorio in ambito piemontese e Lombardo." *Cronache economiche*, nos. 5–6, 11–12.

1976
G. Bora. "Note cremonesi, II: L'eredità di Camillo e i Campi." *Paragone*. January.
Opere d'arte a Vercelli e nella sua provincia. Recuperi e restauri 1968-1976. Exhibition catalogue. Vercelli.

1977
C. Debiaggi. *Studi gaudenziani*. Biella.

1979
G. C. Sciolla. "I 'Cartoni' gaudenziani dell'Accademia Albertina di Torino." *Cronache economiche*, no. 3-4.

1980
G. C. Sciolla. *Il Biellese dal Medioevo all'Ottocento. Artisti, committenti, cantieri*. Turin.

1982
A. Baudi di Vesme. *Schede Vesme. L'arte in Piemonte*, vol. IV. Turin.
F. Dalmasso, P. Gaglia, F. Poli. *L'Accademia Albertina di Torino*. Turin.
G. Romano (ed.). *Gaudenzio Ferrari e la sua scuola. I cartoni cinquecenteschi dell'Accademia Albertina*. Exhibition catalogue. Turin (with the previous bibliography).

1985
P. Astrua, G. Romano (eds.). *Bernardino Lanino*. Exhibition catalogue. Milan.

1986
G. Romano (ed.). *Bernardino Lanino e il Cinquecento a Vercelli*. Turin.

1993
F. Dalmasso, G. Galante Garrone (eds.). *Accademia Albertina. Opere scelte della Pinacoteca*. Exhibition catalogue. Turin.

1995
F. Dalmasso, G. Galante Garrone, G. Romano (eds.). *Le arti del disegno all'Accademia Albertina*. Exhibition catalogue. Turin.

1996
R. Sacchi. "Gaudenzio Ferrari" entry. In: *Dizionario biografico degli italiani*, vol. LXVI. Rome.

1999
Romano, G. (ed.). *Percorsi caravaggeschi tra Roma e Piemonte*. Turin.

2000
M. Bona Castellotti (ed.). *Tanzio da Varallo. Realismo fervore e contemplazione in un pittore del Seicento*. Exhibition catalogue. Milan.

2001
S. Baiocco. "Giovenone famiglia", "Giovenone Gerolamo", "Giovenone Giuseppe" entries. In: *Dizionario biografico degli italiani*, vol. LVI. Rome.

2003
S. Baiocco. "Gerolamo Giovenone e il trittico di Gattinara". In: D. Sanguineti (ed.), *Gerolamo Giovenone in Santa Maria del Rosario a Gattinara. Il restauro del trittico e il suo contesto*. Genoa.

2004
E. Villata, S. Baiocco. *Gaudenzio Ferrari e Girolamo Giovenone. Un avvio e un percorso*. Turin (with the previous bibliography).

2006
G. Romano. "Pittori in bottega: Gaudenzio Ferrari tra avanguardia e tradizione." In: G. Romano (ed.), *Fermo Stella e Sperindio Cagnoli seguaci di Gaudenzio Ferrari. Una bottega d'arte nel Cinquecento padano*. Exhibition catalogue. Cinisello Balsamo (Milan).

2018
G. Agosti, J. Stoppa (eds.). *Il Rinascimento di Gaudenzio Ferrari*. Exhibition catalogue. Milan.
D. Magnetti (ed.). *Gerolamo Giovenone. Un capolavoro ritrovato*. Exhibition catalogue. Milan.

2019
A. Cottino. *La Pinacoteca dell'Accademia Albertina*. Turin.
E. Pagella, F. P. Di Toedoro, P. Salvi. *Leonardo da Vinci. Disegnare il futuro*. Exhibition catalogue. Cinisello Balsamo (Milan).

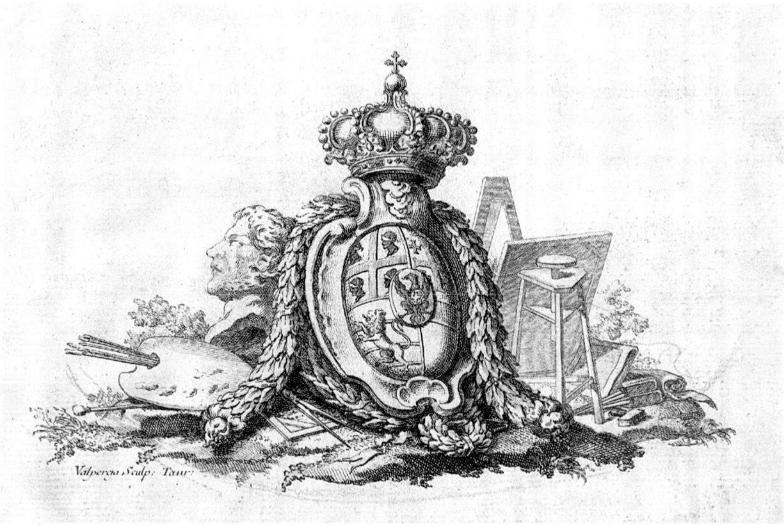
Valperga Sculp: Taur: